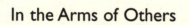

In the Arms of Others

IN THE ARMS OF OTHERS

---

*A Cultural History of
the Right-to-Die in America*

PETER G. FILENE

IVAN R. DEE
Chicago 1998

Illustrations in the text are reproduced with the kind permission of the following sources: page 37, copyright © *New York Daily News*, reprinted with permission; page 43, *France Soir*; page 79 left, *Stanford Daily*; page 79 right, Hugh Haynie, copyright © 1975 *Louisville Courier-Journal*; page 81, Phyllis Battelle, *Karen Ann*, by permission of Doubleday; page 83, Stan Hunter; pages 103, 105, 163, 189, Paul Conrad, Los Angeles Times Syndicate, 1976, reprinted with permission; page 113, Chuck Asay, reprinted by permission of the *Colorado Springs Sun*; page 131, copyright © Marianne Barcellona, *People* Magazine. All efforts have been made to contact the parties who control these permissions.

Library of Congress Cataloging-in-Publication Data:
Filene, Peter G.
    In the arms of others : a cultural history of the right-to-die in America / Peter G. Filene.
      p. cm.
    Includes bibliographical references and index.
    ISBN 1-56663-188-2 (alk. paper)
    1. Death. 2. Euthanasia—History—United States. I. Title.
R726.F45 1998
174'.24—dc21   97-42583

For Erica

and in memory of my parents,

Ursula and Herman Filene

Acknowledgments

WRITING A BOOK is a solitary activity—all those days at a desk—but it is not autonomous. I depended upon generous insights and encouragement from a wide array of people.

First of all, my writing group: Laurel Goldman, Dorrie Casey, Angela Davis-Gardner, Linda Orr, and Peggy Payne. You have put your mark on every idea—literally every word—of this book, clarifying, challenging, and inspiring me through many drafts. You kept me going from one Thursday to the next. I can't imagine writing a book without you.

I had the privilege of talking with three of the people who played central roles in this history. During a delightful afternoon, Paul Armstrong treated me to his witty, incisive perspectives. Julia and the late Joseph Quinlan generously invited me into their home and their memories. To them I offer warm thanks and profound admiration. I also want to thank Barry Keene for sharing his recollections.

Many faculty and graduate students in the Department of History at the University of North Carolina have been true colleagues, offering invaluable suggestions. I'm indebted to Lloyd Kramer, Jack Semonche, Michael McVaugh, Natalie Fousekis, Rachel O'Toole, Michael Trotti, and Scott Perry. I want to single out for special thanks my friend and fellow historian John Kasson. He not only read the manuscript and made his usual probing suggestions for how to improve it. Just as important, his personal support and high intellectual standards helped keep me going when I was tempted to falter.

This project took me far beyond the intellectual territory with which I had been familiar. Fortunately, people in various disciplines were willing to guide me. In Social Medicine, I thank Nancy King, Keith Wailoo, and Larry Churchill. In the Medical School, I'm grateful to George Retsch-Bogart and Kate Veness-Meehan. Don Madison was exceptionally helpful, reading the entire manuscript with his fine-toothed mind and correcting everything from analgesics to Brian Piccolo. My thanks also to Luise Eichenbaum and Ivan Dee for good advice.

As I was writing the last two chapters, I had the good fortune to participate in an interdisciplinary seminar at the University of North Carolina Institute for the Arts and Humanities. What a mind-opening, thought-provoking group!—Ruel Tyson, Lee Greene, Larry Grossberg, Jonathan Hartlyn, William Keech, Tomoko Masuzawa, Carol Mavor, Philip Stadter, Lynda Stone, and Margaret Wiener. They will see traces of their ideas in these pages.

A writer needs time to write. I am indebted for the time provided by the UNC Department of History, the Institute for the Arts and Humanities, and finally the National Endowment for the Humanities. Thanks also to Elaine Tyler May, Linda Orr, Paul Boyer, and John Kasson for writing letters on my behalf.

I'm indebted to William Goodman, my agent, not simply for finding a publisher but for the loyalty and enthusiasm that he gave to my project.

From Erica Rothman I have received many kinds of benefits. Her keen writer's eye helped me discover what I had meant to say. Her training in psychotherapy and gender relations enriched my interpretations. Most of all, we have shared the endlessly interesting journey of our marriage.

P. G. F.

Chapel Hill
March 1998

Contents

Starting Out

ON A COOL, DRIZZLY AFTERNOON in May 1996 I set out from Philadelphia in my rented car to find the house where Karen Ann Quinlan grew up, at 510 Ryerson Road in Landing, New Jersey. After two years of reading about her, I felt an urge to see some actual trace of her. I didn't know what I wanted to do when I arrived there. Maybe walk around the rooms where she had walked. Step back into the past and discover some unexpected meaning. Her parents had moved away, though, so I'd have to explain myself to whomever lived there now.

But first I had to find the house, and that was proving unexpectedly difficult. Landing, New Jersey, didn't appear in the current Rand McNally road atlas, swallowed up by suburbs, perhaps, or Interstate 80. Fortunately the library at the University of North Carolina had a fifteen-year-old atlas that showed where it was, or had been—a few miles east of Netcong, on the southern shore of Lake Hopatcong.

I was twenty-five miles short of there when I stopped in the New York, New York Diner outside Gladstone. "Hopatcong," the waitress said, correcting my pronunciation, as she set down a piece of apple pie. "Haven't been there in twenty years. Used to be a nice place to swim." I pondered that enigmatic "used to be" as I drove north.

At the exit for Hopatcong Park I turned off I-80 and asked directions at a machine shop with a huge American flag hanging down from the roof and a sign on the door, "Italians Only Served Here." That sign made me nervous, given my narrow Jewish face and professorial glasses. But the woman inside readily gave me directions. Up the hill, past two traffic lights and a Dairy Queen, and suddenly I arrived in Landing Township. A few stores, a gas station, a restaurant, nothing fancy: as unpretentious as the Quinlans.

Ryerson Road was more elusive. A couple of teenage boys at an auto repair shop hadn't heard of it, nor had the ranger at Hopatcong Park, but a mail deliverer at the post office knew exactly. I drove along the lake for half a mile, turned right at the IGA grocery store, and looked for the second road on the left. When I saw the street sign, I gripped the steering wheel. In the next minute I would see the house where she lived until a few months before she fell into a coma. Suddenly I thought of the biographer of nineteenth-century Alice James, who went to Mount Auburn Cemetery on Alice's birthday, located the gravesite, and—to her amazement—burst into tears.

Ryerson was a narrow street, the unpretentious clapboard houses on each side almost shouldering one another across aisles of grass or asphalt. Number 510 was on the right. Yellow. Two stories, with narrow white columns. Just like the newspaper photographs twenty-one years ago. A chubby girl, maybe seventeen years old, ambled across the yard and around the corner of the house.

I drove to the end of the street, U-turned, and parked opposite the house to make some notes. There was the second floor that Joe Quinlan had built when Karen was five. There the overhang where Karen used to climb out and perch. On the right a shed, and in front of it a white statue of the Virgin Mary. Was this the same statue the Quinlans had put there, or by some eerie coincidence had the new residents set down their own?

I was beginning to feel disoriented by this confusion of past and present when a man in a T-shirt and jeans, cigarette drooping from his lips, came out the front door. He stood watching me, unsmiling. For a moment I thought of explaining why I was here. *Karen Ann Quinlan used to live in your house. You know, the girl who fell into a vegetative state twenty-one years ago.* No, that would be too intrusive, as if I were telling him a ghost haunted his house. But what should I say? *I'm writing a book about the right to die and . . .* what?

He tossed the cigarette, took a step toward me. I felt a prickle of fear, turned on the motor, drove slowly down the street. No tears. I was disappointed. Life in 510 Ryerson had gone on after Karen's stopped. Strangers had taken over, blocking me. I had wanted to be inside that house, closer to the heart of the Quinlan story. Historians retrieve the past; that's our contribution to public memory.

I came to the stop sign at the IGA. But what would Joseph and Julia Quinlan say? Wasn't I trespassing on their privacy by writing about their anguished decision to let their daughter die? As I turned left along the lake, I felt a chilling sense of estrangement, not only from Landing but from my intended book.

Back at my desk in North Carolina, I brooded upon the journey: imagined what I could have said to that man in the front yard, tried to justify my presence. Finally a friend pointed out: "That man stands in the place of your future readers. They are the ones you're confronting as you figure out what you're trying to accomplish by writing this book." That turned out to be a wonderful insight. It freed me from Ryerson Road and returned me to my manuscript.

This is not a self-help book about living wills or patient rights. Nor is it a therapeutic book about facing death. It's a cultural history of "the right to die" and the complicated issues surrounding it. For understandable reasons, dying is a subject that most people avoid thinking about. I often felt sad, pained, or disquieted while I wrote, but I also felt strengthened. For I was confronting fundamental questions and working out tentative answers, or at least defining the untamable ambiguities. Writing this book has been a meditative journey. I invite readers to accompany me and clarify their own ideas and emotions.

WHEN IS LIFE no longer worth living? Although medical technology can maintain a person in a persistent vegetative state, in what sense is he or she still a "person"? When, if ever, is it right to withdraw life-support? And who should decide? These are the agonizing questions that life-prolonging treatment has posed for patients, families, physicians, and judges. In this book I explore how Americans have struggled to devise satisfactory answers.

To understand "the right to die," I have ventured into a half-dozen fields: medicine, law, religion, bioethics, politics, and mass media. My ultimate purpose is to synthesize this diverse evidence into a cultural history. If I had to distill this book's theme into a single word, I would say it is about *identity*: who we are and want to be, as individuals and as a society.

Culture is the tapestry of shared meanings that a society weaves as it copes with the world.[1] When we study how Americans have dealt with dying, we touch on many different aspects of their experience: technology and the medical profession, for example; political battles about living-will laws; the belief in self-determination; and pain. Everything from the impersonal to the very personal. Outside the Quinlans' house I worried about trespassing on people's privacy, but in a history of dying the boundary between public and private disintegrates. Relatives, doctors, judges, and bioethicists argue, for instance, about whether an unconscious patient is feeling pain, or whether an elderly, demented woman would feel violated by a feeding tube, or whether a severely handicapped infant should be kept alive. At stake in each case is not only a set of medical, legal, and ethical principles but also individuals' inner experiences. We need both perspectives—the abstract and the personal, outsiders' and insiders'—to understand the complexity and ambiguity of modern dying.[2]

Whenever I've mentioned my project to friends, students, and people sitting beside me on airplanes, everyone has recognized the name of Karen Ann Quinlan, even those who were born after she fell into a coma. Public memory matches the historical interpretation in this book. I've cast Quinlan and her parents as central figures in this narrative, not only because their court case in 1976 set the legal landmark for "the right to die," but also because they personify so forcefully the dilemmas of modern dying. Karen became a macabre celebrity upon whom Americans projected their anxieties and confusions. Around her biography I weave three more general plot lines.

The first traces the emergence of the right-to-die movement, starting long before Quinlan entered her vegetative state. As medical technology increasingly prolonged life, patients and their families demanded the right to forgo or withdraw life-support (passive euthanasia) and, more recently, the right to physician-assisted suicide (active euthanasia). I also discuss the ambivalent accommodation by doctors and the adamant resistance by the right-to-life movement.

Woven around this social-political plot line is a bioethical one. Proponents of the right to die based their claims on the principle of *autonomy*, or self-determination: a terminally ill patient has the right to decide how he wants to be treated. In practice this principle proved to have significant limitations. Most Americans have not written living wills, for example. Should they become demented or comatose, doctors or relatives will determine their treatment. Most doctors, meanwhile, avoid discussions of treatment until a patient is within a few days of death, by which time he often is no longer conscious.

I add a social-psychological plot line at this point. Whatever the law or culture may say, no one is altogether self-determining. In sickness and dying we depend upon others. And throughout our lives we shape our sense of self by interactions with others. I close the book, therefore, with an argument for supplementing the ethic of autonomy with the ethic of *relatedness*.

THIS BOOK has two origins. The second took place in the office of my longtime friend and colleague John Kasson, as we were eating lunch in the spring of 1994. I was lamenting that I had become stuck halfway through writing my second novel. The first novel, which I had written and rewritten during much of the 1980s, had been such an exuberant, gratifying experience. But this one, I said, was making me feel frustrated and confused.

"Can I be blunt?" John asked. "I think you're needing to return to historical research and writing."

I held my cup of yogurt in midair. Out in the hallway the bell rang for one o'clock classes. "You're right," I said. "And I know what I want to write about: Karen Ann Quinlan."

The words came of their own volition, out of nowhere. I knew almost nothing about her, was unfamiliar with respirators or informed consent, hadn't read any of the hundreds of books by bioethicists. But within weeks I was excitedly moving in widening circles to the law library, the health sciences library, in conversations with professors of social medicine. Books piled high in my study, ideas in my mind. It was as if I had been unconsciously prepared for this venture into death and dying.

Which brings me to the first origin of this book. As I worked six or eight hours a day through the summer, including most weekends, my wife Erica Rothman—who is a psychotherapist—began asking why was I so driven? "Just excited," I replied.

But in December she and I were seeing the movie *Shadowlands*, about C.S. Lewis—the scene where the boy at his bedroom window watches the ambulance arriving, his fatally ill mother being lifted out on a stretcher and carried toward the front door— and I began to sob uncontrollably. This was what was driving me. I was sobbing for my mother, who had died in 1967 at the age of sixty after a series of strokes had taken away her movement, her speech, her mind. At the time I had been twenty-seven and, too frightened of my feelings, had not cried at all.

My mother had exceptional energy (reading, crocheting, typing letters to friends around the world) and wide-ranging interests (novels, opera, gardening, politics) and generous caring for others (sick friends, Planned Parenthood, a Christmas gift to the butcher). Along with my father, she was the inspiration of my sense of self. Whatever I did or wherever I was, I had sensed her watching over me, and suddenly she was gone. I pushed on into adulthood and didn't look back, until finally, twenty-seven years later, I was able to let loose my grief. At heart, then, this book is about her dying. And once I realized that, I also realized that I had become stuck in my novel at the point where my twenty-year-old protagonist, in 1968, is grieving the sudden, premature death of his father. The unconscious, our shadowland, works in astounding ways.

Why love what you will lose?

There is nothing else to love.

—Louise Glück, "From the Japanese"

In the Arms of Others

Prologue: A Good Death

THE WORDS ONE CHOOSES to describe something will inevitably slant its meaning. Whether the events during 1861–1865, for example, should be called the Civil War, the War between the States, or the War of Northern Aggression is not at all merely semantic. So we begin by taking note of the words people use when they consider how physicians should treat hopelessly ill patients.

Before the twentieth century they talked in terms of *euthanasia*, but they didn't have in mind what we think of today.[1] Euthanasia has come to mean hastening the death of hopelessly suffering patients—"mercy killing"—or, in a more sinister connotation, killing people deemed unfit or defective. To nineteenth-century Americans, on the other hand, euthanasia referred less to the physician's action than to the experience of his patient. "A good death"—that is the literal translation from the Greek term coined by Francis Bacon in the seventeenth century. The question was how best to provide such a death, painless and easy, to someone who was terminally ill.[2]

The newly formed American Medical Association, in its 1847 code of ethics, called upon doctors to comfort but, whenever possible, also to revive. "The physician should be the minister of hope and comfort to the sick, that by such cordials to the drooping spirit, he may soothe the bed of death, revive expiring life, and counteract the depressing influence of those maladies which often disturb the tranquillity of the most resigned in their last moments. . . ."[3]

In practice, however, most nineteenth-century doctors believed that they would best minister and soothe a dying patient by letting nature take its course. " . . . We dismiss all thought of cure, or of the prolongation of life," British Dr. William Munk declared in his influential textbook *Euthanasia* (1887), "and our efforts are limited to the relief of certain urgent conditions, such as pain. . . ."[4] "Where there is no hope . . . ," a Philadelphia surgeon agreed in 1894, "it should be a grateful and sacred duty, nay, it should be the highest triumph of the physician to minister unto the wants of a dying fellow creature by effecting the Euthanasia."[5] In an era when most people died at home rather than in a hospital, physicians were expected to join the family circle around the death-bed and comfort with sympathetic words and gentle touch. As seventy-nine-year-old Eliza Yarnall lay dying in 1870, for example, three sisters, two daughters and a son-in-law, two nieces, and several other relatives hurried to her bedside, along with the doctor. "All the children (sons & daughters) were collected Thursday evening," one sister later wrote to a daughter who couldn't attend. "Friday morning she continued to grow weaker—was catching at imaginary things, & occasionally brushing dust from the bed. . . . The Dr. tho't she would live thro' the day. . . . Between 4 & 5 she stopped breathing—without any seeming suffering."[6]

If the pain grew unbearable, doctors typically administered opium, morphine, alcohol, or some other analgesic, as large a dose as needed for a peaceful passing. Contrary to later medical fears of addicting their patients, Victorian physicians believed that "the risk of the drug habit sinks into insignificance in the presence of approaching death."[7] As a renowned American surgeon said during a public symposium in 1913, "Others have assumed the responsibility which I myself have taken in more than one case, of producing euthanasia."[8]

By the early twentieth century, though, most people no longer argued about producing euthanasia but about committing it. The focus had shifted from the patient's state of mind to the doctor's decision whether or not to hasten death. The paradox of medical progress was beginning to emerge. The more successful physicians became in curing disease and prolonging life, the more they were also held accountable for prolonging suffering. As the president of the American Bar Association, Judge Simeon E. Baldwin, declared in a widely publicized address at the turn of the century: "In civilized nations, and particularly of late years, it has become the pride of many in the medical profession to prolong such life [of terminally ill patients] at any cost of discomfort or pain to the sufferer or of expense and exhaustion to his family." Baldwin called instead for "the natural right to a natural death."[9]

A few years later an Ohio state legislator went a step further, introducing a bill to legalize euthanasia. If a person of sound mind was suffering extreme pain from a fatal injury or terminal illness, and if a physician asked whether he wanted to die and the patient said yes, then (after three other physicians agreed that recovery was hopeless) the physician could administer a fatal dose of anesthetic.[10] Not surprisingly, the bill never got out of committee. More important, though, it defined euthanasia not as a patient's easy death or natural death but as his doctor's action to bring about death. The physician who could not save life was supposed to end it. With the issue framed this way, the public responded in like terms. "Shall we legalize homicide?" the editors of *Outlook* asked in terms that left no doubt as to their answer.[11] *The Independent* berated "the awful frank cruelty and crudity" of this plan for "legalizing the taking of human life. . . ."[12] Leading newspapers in New York, Boston, and Philadelphia, joined by spokespersons of the Catholic church, added their indignant objections. The good death had been turned into murder.

Later efforts to legalize euthanasia imprinted even more deeply this negative connotation. In 1938 various social reformers, physicians, and academics founded the Euthanasia Society of America (ESA). Among the most prominent leaders were Charles Potter, a former minister and now self-styled Humanist; Eleanor Jones, former president of the American Birth Control League; Rabbi Sidney Goldstein; gynecologist Robert Latou Dickinson;

and historian Harry Elmer Barnes. The next year they sponsored a bill in the New York state legislature along the lines of the one in Ohio. No legislator was willing to sponsor it, and what little public response it evoked was hostile.[13] Still, the ESA took heart from an opinion poll reporting that 46 percent of Americans favored "mercy deaths under Government supervision for hopeless invalids."[14] But soon the concept of euthanasia took on more sinister implications. By 1941 news was filtering out of Germany that the Nazi regime had established a program whereby medical personnel put to death mentally retarded children, crippled and ill people, the elderly, and others with "lives not worth living."[15] In other words, euthanasia was being joined with eugenics, the policy of race breeding by weeding out "the unfit."

The ESA frantically tried to explain to the public that its purposes—voluntary euthanasia—had nothing in common with the Nazis' program of involuntary euthanasia. The fact was, however, that most ESA leaders were longtime ardent believers in eugenics. Until now they had kept that side of their ideology discreetly in the background. But their president was candid enough in public statements. "Now my face is set against the legalization of euthanasia for any person, who, having been well, has at last become ill, for however ill they be, many get well and help the world for years after," Dr. Foster Kennedy explained. "But I *am* in favor of euthanasia for those hopeless ones who should never have been born—Nature's mistakes." The feebleminded, idiots and imbeciles, "the completely hopeless defective," said Kennedy, "should be relieved of the burden of living. . . ."[16] Such ideas were already considered cranky and outmoded. When the world learned the horrific facts of the Holocaust, they became unspeakable. The Euthanasia Society nevertheless stubbornly continued trying to organize state chapters, sponsor legislation, and publicize its beliefs, but by 1960 it had virtually ground to a halt.[17] Eugenics, one historian has written, had become "virtually a dirty word," and euthanasia was irremediably sullied along with it.[18]

Advocates of physicians ending the hopeless suffering of terminally ill patients needed to clothe their ideas in a different vocabulary: the language of mercy. If euthanasia were performed as a merciful action, it might be justifiable. Between 1930 and 1960, cases of "mercy killings" made news again and again, arousing widespread fascination and moral debate. John Stephens in Atlanta bashed his sixty-year-old aunt in the head with a flower pot to end her agony from terminal cancer. A coroner's jury exonerated him, saying she had died of natural causes.[19] Louis Greenfield chloroformed the imbecile son he had nursed, washed, and fed for seventeen years. The jury acquitted him of manslaughter.[20] When her policeman father was diagnosed with incurable cancer, twenty-one-year-old Carol Paight shot him to death with his own service revolver. After hearing testimony from psychiatrists, her brother, and her mother, the jury found her not guilty.[21]

But these were the actions of desperate individuals—vigilante euthanasia, one might say. The action of Dr. Hermann Sander, by contrast, evoked Americans' attitudes toward official euthanasia—end-of-life treatment by the medical profession. In December 1949 the 40-year-old New Hampshire doctor was charged with murder after injecting ten cc. of air into the vein of his unconscious patient, Abbie Burroto, and then repeating the process three times until, ten minutes later, she was dead. Mrs. Borroto, 59 years old, had been bedridden for months with terminal cancer, dwindling from 140 to 80 pounds and, Sander later said, clearly within hours of death. Dr. Sander "is a fine man," said the county solicitor, "a good family man, without a malicious bone in his body: he just thought he was performing an act of mercy." Six hundred of the 650 residents in Sander's hometown signed a petition expressing confidence in him. The Congregational minister in nearby Manchester declared: "If this man is felonious then so am I, for I have desired the time of suffering to be short and I have wanted natural and unaided courses to bring relief in death." The Reverend Billy Graham, on the other hand, told an audience of 6,000 people in Boston that Sander should be punished "as an example," a sentiment echoed by various Protestant ministers and even more strongly by Catholic spokesmen.[22]

By the time the Sander trial began, according to *Time* magazine, "the nation's interest in 'mercy killing' [had been] quickened," producing discussions in corner drugstores and church pulpits.[23] Letters to local New Hampshire newspapers were so inflammatory, pro and con, that the editors decided to stop printing them.[24] One hundred and fifty reporters and photographers arrived in Manchester, some from as far as London, including novelists John O'Hara and Fanny Hurst. The trial lasted fourteen days, during which time the press sent out almost as many words per day as during the trial of Bruno Hauptmann, kidnaper of the Lindberghs' baby.[25]

After the prosecutor introduced detailed evidence of murder (including Sander's dictated case notes of the injections), expert witnesses for the defense argued that forty cc. of air was insufficient to cause death and that Mrs. Borroto died from cancer and pneumonia. Sander himself denied he had sought to kill her. "As I looked at her face and all of the thoughts of the past went through my mind, something snapped in me, and I felt impelled or possessed to do something. I couldn't have been thinking the way I ordinarily do or I wouldn't have acted this way."

In the end, the all-male jury deliberated only seventy minutes before deciding that Dr. Sander was not guilty of malice aforethought and deliberation, and that Mrs. Borroto's death had not been caused by the injections. "It was the most heartwarming news I have ever received," said her husband, Reginald Borroto. That night a crowd of five hundred supporters marched in torchlight parade past the Sanders' white farmhouse.[26]

The furor surrounding the trial signaled how strongly Americans cared about treatment of the dying. Even more telling were the words people used. "Euthanasia is *not* the defense," Sander's lawyer insisted.[27] The *New York Times Index* classified its articles under "Mercy Death (Euthanasia)." Most often, whether they opposed or supported what the doctor had done, people called it "mercy killing." The liberal *New Republic* had another suggestion. "If we called these situations 'assisted suicide' rather than 'mercy killing,' the moral context would be considerably changed."[28]

Terminology was in flux because attitudes were in transition.

Although the law and the code of medical ethics forbade a doctor from committing euthanasia, even as an act of mercy, more and more Americans—including some doctors—began insisting that patients deserved to be freed from hopeless suffering. "There has been too little said of a legitimate right, a God-given right, of the dying man," a San Francisco general practitioner stated in 1956. "That is his right to die."[29]

A momentous shift was taking place during the postwar era, but so gradually and invisibly that, like the shift of tectonic plates deep underground, one would realize it only years later when the earthquake happened. Americans began focusing on both sides of the doctor-patient relationship: not only the physician's choice of treatment but his patient's experience. Unlike their nineteenth-century ancestors, however, they did not define "a good death" as a blessing. They defined it as a right. In keeping with the equal-rights movement developing among blacks and the due-process rights being asserted by courts for alleged criminals, Americans increasingly advocated the right to die. Legally speaking, that had no meaning. Nor did it have meaning in common sense. As one commentator has sardonically remarked, "I'd prefer to give up my right to die."[30]

For years Americans were uncertain, unclear, or simply inconsistent about what they were calling for. Not the right to kill oneself. More typically, especially before 1950, they were referring to a doctor hastening death with or without the patient's consent.[31] Sometimes they had in mind suicide with the assistance of a physician. In the fifties and sixties they also focused on what Judge Baldwin in 1899 had prophetically called a "natural death"—namely, the withholding or withdrawal of extraordinary life-prolonging treatment. Americans defined "the right to die" in one or another of these ways, or sometimes left it undefined, but with growing intensity they asserted a claim to a good death.

The voices gradually swelled into a public chorus. "To prolong life uselessly . . . ," a professor of theology wrote in 1954, "is to attack the moral status of a person."[32] "As physicians," wrote an eminent psychiatrist in 1962, "we must recognize the dignity of man and his right to live and die peacefully."[33] "Should a new right—the right to die—be added to the triad of 'inalienable rights' to life, liberty and the pursuit of happiness?" a journalist wondered in 1966.[34] "No one can be against 'dying with dignity,'" declared the editors of an influential Catholic journal.[35] In 1974 ABC television produced an hour-long documentary titled "The Right to Die," a U.S. Senate committee held three days of hearings on "Death with Dignity," and a group of lawyers, doctors, and philosophers gathered at Agnes Scott College for a weekend symposium on death and dying. Even more telling, the Euthanasia Society of America was resurrected by a new set of leaders under a new name, the Society for the Right to Die. Where it had once advocated the active hastening of death, it now argued for the right to forgo or end life-support and promoted the use of living wills.[36]

But the earthquake—the event that reshaped the cultural landscape by giving irrevocable meanings and force to "the right to die"—occurred only in 1975. That was when Joseph and Julia Quinlan went to court in New Jersey, asking that their comatose daughter be taken off a respirator.

1

Death on Trial

For TWENTY-ONE YEARS Karen Ann Quinlan led an ordinary life in suburban New Jersey. But everything changed after she fell into an irreversible coma in April 1975, and her father asked a court to let him disconnect the respirator that was keeping her alive. Suddenly she became the subject of intense public attention. Journalists, physicians, and attorneys as well as her parents and friends searched her past for evidence of what she had done and who she had been.

Their accounts begin clearly enough, but the closer they come to that April night, the more they contradict one another. Her personal identity threatens to dissolve into a frustrating mix of "maybes" and "on the other hands." Then one steps back and recognizes that the ultimate subject is not Quinlan herself but the disagreements among the commentators. Her personal identity was being transformed into an ambiguous cultural identity. She served as the pretext for Americans to work out their beliefs, anxieties, and ambivalence about dying and death. Their process is also ours in the course of this book.

SHE WAS BORN as "Mary Ann" in a Catholic hospital for unwed mothers on March 29, 1954. When Joseph and Julia Quinlan adopted her three weeks later, they renamed her Karen Ann and brought her to their four-room house in Landing, New Jersey. Like so many other young suburbanites, the Quinlans participated enthusiastically in postwar abundance, family "togetherness," and churchgoing. Joe moved up the hierarchy of Warner-Lambert pharmaceutical company. They had two more children (natural born) and added a second storey to the house. Julia attended midweek prayer meetings and worked with the Rosary Society at Our Lady of the Lake Church, where the whole family attended Mass every Sunday. A white statue of the Virgin Mary stood in their front yard.

From the start Karen was in motion, climbing over the sides of her crib, pulling herself up on tables and chairs, walking at seven months, climbing to the tops of trees, clambering along the edge of the roof two stories high. She never walked down the stairs but grabbed the spindles and sailed, landing with a crash. (Over the years Joe had to replace the fourth spindle five times.)

Given such energy, she didn't take well to the demands of school. She wrote poems rather than homework. She chatted with friends when she was supposed to be listening to the teacher. She stopped piano lessons because she could play by ear. When she read books she had a penchant for offbeat topics—extrasensory perception and mysticism—but she spent more time skiing, swimming, and playing softball. "She was a daredevil," her schoolmate Mary Lou McCudden recalled. When they were driving to the mountains to ski, Karen saw a billboard that said "Airplane ride through the Poconos," and "without a second thought she made a U-turn and we took the ride."[1]

She was only five-feet two-inches tall, but she could outdo and outdare anyone. She was the "leader of the pack," two girlfriends recalled, dancing at parties, playing the piano, singing. She sang so well that others hesitated to join in. At Morris Catholic High School she was a member of the Ski Club and Pep Club and worked on the school newspaper. On her sixteenth birthday, Ginny Roche rented the American Legion Hall over at Indian Lake for a surprise party, and more than one hundred people showed up. On her twentieth birthday, thirty friends staged a surprise party, complete with refreshments, presents, and crepe-paper banners.

"There was always a surprise birthday party for Karen," a boyfriend recalled.[2]

In her teenage years she went to church less and less regularly and once complained to her parish priest: "The trouble with religion is—it's dull." Nevertheless Father Trapasso told a reporter, "in her own way I would consider Karen a religious girl."[3] She practiced a private charity. When she read in the newspaper about a family being evicted from their house after the father lost his job, she sent them the twenty-eight dollars she had been saving to buy skis. Karen was "the one who took care of everybody," said Mary Lou McCudden. "Nobody could take care of her."[4]

At sixteen Karen began dating Tommy Flynn, and for the next three years they developed a close relationship—too close for her comfort. One summer she went out with other boys, which provoked Tommy to date another girl, and the romance splintered. "See, she didn't want him to depend on her," Karen's sister explained later. "She always wanted to be free."[5]

Many of her friends went on to college, but that was too straight a path for Karen. After high school she took a series of odd jobs, none for very long, none that anybody later remembered, except pumping gas and repairing cars at a service station. In June 1974 she began working at a ceramics factory as a technician, but an economic downturn caused her to be laid off in August.[6] During these two years she lived at home. As far as Mr. and Mrs. Quinlan understood, their daughter was having trouble becoming "serious" and settling down.[7] Her ex-boyfriend Tommy Flynn, on the other hand, recalled all too much purposiveness. Karen was "obsessed with the idea of challenge. She was looking for a kind of fulfillment and she wasn't finding it."[8]

Eventually she moved away from home—that much everyone agrees on. But they tell drastically different versions of when and where and with whom. In February 1975, according to Julia Quinlan, Karen went to live in "a cute little apartment near here—right down on the lake, on the way to our church," with a friend named Robin Croft, "a nice girl. Very quiet." Two months later, however, Robin had to leave, and Karen decided, over her parents' objections, to rent a room in a bungalow on Cranberry Lake inhabited by two young men. She moved in on April 6, eight days before lapsing into a coma.[9] So goes her family's version.

According to various press stories, however, Karen left home in August or later, 1974, or March 1975 or even April.[10] Some of her former acquaintances said she lived in not one but several houses before moving to Cranberry Lake. And what sort of life was she leading? When she stayed with Robin Croft the two of them "tied one on" every week or so, the housemate recalled, but "Karen was *not* drunk a lot." And she "might have taken a few pills for a high, but she wasn't into drugs."[11] Other former friends said she joined a new crowd, although they didn't know—or didn't choose to give—any details.[12]

One of those two young men in the Cranberry Lake bungalow, by contrast, was very specific. Karen was "self-destructive," Thomas French told the media, "popping whatever pills she could get her hands on," drinking too much and eating too little. "She wasn't what her parents thought she would be."[13] *Time* magazine painted the same portrait, with embellishments. "Several friends [presumably French and others whom *Time* didn't name] describe her as an occasional marijuana user and frequent pill-popper, who took 'uppers' and 'downers' to suit her moods."[14] In a follow-up article, *Time* added a lurid twist: "Indications are that she became involved with a low-level New Jersey underworld figure who supplied her with drugs."[15]

For the story of Karen's activities before April 14, 1975, we must rely on imperfect, self-serving memories. Beginning with the events of that Monday night, we can also turn to police and medical reports—impersonal, antiseptic—but even they contain puzzling inconsistencies.

Karen and her new housemates were planning to celebrate a friend's birthday at Falconer's, a nondescript roadside bar overlooking Lake Lackawanna. Before setting out, Quinlan drank a gin and tonic—more than one, Thomas French says. And sometime that day she certainly took a Valium. At Falconer's she was drinking another gin and tonic when her companions noticed she was "nodding out." They hurriedly got her on her feet, drove her home, helped her upstairs to bed. A few minutes later French looked in on her and found she wasn't breathing.[16] While somebody phoned for an ambulance, French frantically breathed into her mouth. Nothing happened. Her skin was bluish-gray and cold. She had no pulse. He placed her on the floor and performed CPR. At least fifteen minutes passed, perhaps a half-hour, before a policeman and ambulance arrived and began CPR. Gradually her skin turned pink, but she wasn't breathing on her own. At 1:23 a.m., with an oxygen mask over her face, she was taken to the intensive care unit of Newton Memorial Hospital. At 3 a.m. a physician noted: "Pupils unreactive. Patient is unresponsive even to deep pain. Legs: Rigid, curled up. Impression: Overdose, unknown substance, with decorticate brain activity."[17] To prevent pneumonia, the hospital put her on a respirator.

Three days later Dr. Robert Morse, a neurologist, working with Dr. Arshed Javad, a pulmonary internist, tried to figure out the cause of Karen's coma. EEG, X-rays, brain scan, angiogram, lumbar puncture—none of these tests, or any others, produced an answer. Had she suffered lead poisoning at the ceramics factory? Tests were negative. There was a bump on the back of her head. Had she fallen or been the victim of foul play? Negative.[18]

The only plausible explanation came down to the mix of drugs and alcohol in her bloodstream. Yet even the lab reports of the blood tests didn't quite match up. There was quinine, presumably from gin and tonic—no one disputed that. And traces of Valium, everyone agreed. But where Dr. Morse testified that she had ingested no hard drugs and a normal amount of unnamed barbiturates, another neurologist testified that a drug screen disclosed no barbiturates but an amount of Librium.[19]

At the end of this inquiry into her precomatose life, we are left with abundant information but no certainties. Karen's family and friends constructed antithetical stories of what led up to that April night. Her physicians produced a diagnosis that was clearer about what had not happened than about what had. And the person who could have settled these questions lay in a coma, inaccessible.

Among all the available evidence from and about her life, Karen left only two statements in her own voice, two poems. One of them she wrote while living with Robin Croft.

> The sun finally broke through
>   into this gloomy place I
>   call home.
> Time and time again I wonder
>   what the hell am I
>   doing here.
> Silence is my only answer—
> . . . Who am I? Alice or the Pinball Wizard.[20]

NINE DAYS after the accident, Karen was transferred to St. Clare's Hospital, a Catholic facility in Denville, which had a more sophisticated respirator. The MA-1 would pump only as much oxygen as needed: a small dose when she breathed on her own, a larger dose when she didn't. The respirator tube went through a hole in her throat down into her lungs. A pair of tubes poured hydration and nutrition through her nostrils. A tube dripped antibiotics into her kidneys. The girl who had been a member of the Pep Club in the high school across town lay comatose now, kept alive by machines.[21]

Twice a day Mr. and Mrs. Quinlan drove from home or work (often accompanied by nineteen-year-old daughter Mary Ellen) to sit beside Karen's bed. (Seventeen-year-old John couldn't bear to see his sister in this condition.) They talked to her, looked into her open but empty eyes, brushed her hair. "Whenever I thought of a person in a coma," one of Karen's girlfriends recalled a year later, "I'd thought they would just lie there very quietly, almost as though they were sleeping. Karen's head was moving around, as if she was trying to pull away from that tube in her throat, and she made little noises, like moans. I didn't know if she was in pain, but it seemed as though she was. And I thought—if Karen could ever see herself like this, it would be the worst thing in the world for her."[22]

At first the Quinlans rejoiced when her eyes moved away from a bright light or a sound came from her throat or a grimace crossed her face. But soon they recognized these were mechanical reflexes of the body. Her consciousness lay buried somewhere inside. The slow waves flowing across the EEG chart signaled that her brain was alive, barely. Was she hearing their voices, then? Or feeling pain? Or most dreadful of all, as her friend said, was she in any way aware of being in this plight? Dr. Morse assured them that she wasn't feeling pain "as we know it." The Quinlans tried not to imagine what that phrase might mean.

When would she wake up from the coma? they asked. There was no way to predict, Morse said. After she woke, would she be able to talk, eventually to walk, to become the Karen she had been? As each day passed, Morse offered less encouraging responses. Late in May he told them that she had sunk into a deeper kind of coma, one in which she went through cycles of waking and sleeping but remained unconscious. Although Morse didn't use the term, it was what physicians were beginning to call a "persistent vegetative state" (PVS). The Quinlans could only continue their vigil, saying prayers and holding on to hope.[23] (At least they didn't have to worry about expenses. Because Karen was over twenty-one with no income, Medicaid paid her hospital bills—$435 a day.)[24]

It was a bewildering kind of grief. They were watching over a body in which the person they loved had disappeared . . . but had not died. "Maybe I'm going in two directions," Joseph Quinlan remarked in a newspaper interview, "but I've never really stopped to analyze it. In some ways, death is easier because then you accept the fact that she just isn't any more."[25] As long as the respirator pumped air into her lungs, Karen would remain in a twilight zone between life and death.

During the spring and summer of 1975 the Quinlans watched as their daughter's arms folded tighter against her chest, her wrists bent stiffly under her chin, and her knees drew up higher toward her body. Therapists bound her legs and hands to wooden boards, but her limbs kept pulling inward. Week by week her weight dwindled from 115 to 100, 90, 70. She was curling into a fetal position. And all the while the respirator hissed and gurgled. "Sometimes I thought that sound would drive me out of my mind," Julia Quinlan recalled. "While I'd watch Karen pulling her head back and making those agonized faces—that sound was always there."[26]

Julia was the first to give up hoping for a miracle. After asking God to give her daughter back, even with brain damage, she decided to let God's will, not hers, be done. And there were also Karen's wishes to consider. Two years earlier, while a family friend underwent a long, painful death by cancer, Karen had said she would never want to be "kept alive like that." Early in June, Julia decided it was time to detach her daughter from the respirator. But would that be a form of murder, or at least an abdication of moral responsibility? She turned for answers to Father Tom Trapasso at the Our Lady of the Lake Church, where she was working as a secretary.

The young, balding priest explained that the Catholic church did not believe prolongation of human life was an absolute duty. As far back as the sixteenth century, moral theologians had distinguished between ordinary and extraordinary means of sustaining someone's life. Because surgery in the pre-anesthesia era entailed excruciating pain and disfigurement, they said, a patient didn't violate the church's ban on suicide if he refused to undergo such treatment, even though it might save his life. By the twentieth century, anesthesia and modern surgical methods had eliminated most pain and disfigurement, but then resuscitation techniques and the respirator produced a different moral dilemma. Did the physician have the right to discontinue life-support after there was no hope of improving the patient's condition, even if discontinuance meant that the patient would die? In 1957 Pope Pius XII gave a public answer to a conference of anesthesiologists, declaring that a physician was obliged to use only "ordinary means" that didn't impose undue hardship. The respirator and other modern life-support treatment, by contrast, were "extraordinary," interfering with natural process. So, the pope said, a physician was not obligated to initiate extraordinary means, nor need he continue them for an unconscious patient if that substantially burdened the family. For if discontinuance resulted in death, the act was only an indirect cause; the direct cause was the underlying disease.[27]

Joseph held out longer. Whenever his wife or children hinted that Karen's condition was hopeless, he clenched his jaw and walked out of the room. All his life he had achieved his goals by hard work, courage, and prayer, sometimes against terrible odds. While serving in the infantry during World War II, an artillery shell had blown off his left arm. He had built their house on weekends with his artificial hand—the wiring and plumbing and floors, everything but the basic shell. After taking college courses at night, he worked his way up in Warner-Lambert from accountant to section supervisor. Joseph Quinlan wasn't going to give up on his daughter. By July, however, he was beginning to acknowledge that the odds were different this time. Grudgingly he yielded to the facts before his eyes and to the doctors' prognoses. Even if Karen survived, Dr. Morse was saying, she would never come home but would live out her days in an institution.

Now it was Joseph's turn to consult Father Trapasso. Aren't we acting in God's place by unhooking the respirator? he asked. "No," the priest replied, "I don't think it's playing God at all. I can't explain to you, Joe, how God intervenes in the affairs of men, but this certainly is not playing God. We can make decisions, and are expected to." Lying in bed one night, Joseph thought: "Karen is never going to be alive again as I have known her. I have to accept that." The next morning he suggested to Julia that they go to the cemetery and pick out a plot. On July 31 the Quinlans signed a form directing Dr. Morse to "discontinue all extraordinary measures, including the use of a respirator for our daughter Karen Quinlan." They also released Morse and St. Clare's staff from any liability.[28]

To imagine the death of one's child is horrifying enough. Choosing to let one's child die—that stretches imagination to the breaking point. The Quinlans consoled themselves that they were enacting God's will. But there was another emotional complication: Karen was adopted. After enduring three miscarriages and one stillbirth, the Quinlans had applied to Catholic Charities for a baby. In 1954 they were given Karen to bring home from a Pennsylvania hospital. Now, in this New Jersey hospital, they were choosing to let her be taken away.[29]

As the Quinlans concluded their struggle with conscience and emotion, Morse began his. The thirty-six-year-old neurologist faced the kind of situation that even the most experienced physicians dread. His personal sympathies lay with Karen's family (he too was Catholic, and he himself had a daughter named Karen Ann). But his professional obligation was to Karen, and here the moral guidelines seemed to direct him away from what the Quinlans were asking him to do. According to the Hippocratic Oath, "If any shall ask of me a drug to produce death I will not give it. . . ." A physician should adopt treatment "for the benefit of my patients . . . and not for their hurt." In Hippocrates' era—indeed, until the late nineteenth century—physicians' power to heal was limited primarily to techniques that were nontechnological and noninvasive: diet, drugs, bloodletting, and physical therapies such as massage. The only "technology" was the knives, forceps, and saws used in surgery. Given these limitations, physicians had little difficulty deciding when to forgo or discontinue treatment and let nature or God take over. Twentieth-century medical innovations drastically extended their healing power. Insulin coped with diabetes. Sulfonamides, penicillin, and streptomycin in the 1930s and 1940s tamed infectious diseases such as tuberculosis and pneumonia. The "iron lung" in the 1930s kept polio victims alive. The hospital intensive care unit (ICU) in the 1950s saved patients in life-threatening crises. By the 1950s and 1960s, life-prolonging techniques were multiplying even more spectacularly: kidney dialysis, organ transplantation, and the iron lung's descendant, the artificial respirator.[30]

Morse knew that the church deemed the respirator "extraordinary" because it blocked the natural process of dying. And he understood why the Quinlans felt that keeping Karen attached to the machine no longer was for her benefit or theirs. But as her physician, he saw things differently. For him the respirator was one of many marvelous but increasingly ordinary methods of prolonging life. In Karen's case, regrettably, it was vegetative life with no reasonable hope of improvement. Nevertheless it was life. If he were to turn off the machine, she couldn't breathe on her own, and however merciful her death might be, her dying would not. Morse foresaw a gruesome business of thrashing and gasping for who knows how many minutes.

Both medical tradition and professional conscience steered him away from an act with these consequences. And there was the law to consider. Philosophers might argue that, once Karen was detached from the respirator, the cause of death would be the original brain damage, not the act of detaching.[31] According to New Jersey law, though, an intentional act resulting in someone's death, whether an act of commission or omission, was homicide. Karen was irreversibly unconscious but not dead—not even brain-dead. Mercy killing was, after all, killing. To be sure, the Quinlans had released him from liability. But they might change their minds, just as a month earlier they had changed their minds about keeping Karen alive.[32]

On August 2 Morse telephoned them and said he would not comply with their request. They were stunned. What now? Did they themselves have to unplug the machine? That was inconceivable, repugnant. The doctors had put her on the machine and the doctors should take her off.[33] The St. Clare's Hospital lawyer advised them to arrange for Joseph Quinlan to become Karen's legal guardian. But even then, the lawyer said, St. Clare's would not guarantee to turn off the respirator.[34]

Quinlan decided to hire a lawyer of his own. Since Karen was an indigent, he went to the Legal Aid Society in nearby Dover and explained his plight to the first person he came upon. Looking back, he felt God was on his side that afternoon. Paul Armstrong was thirty years old, fresh out of law school, a Catholic, and an idealist. With his wide blue eyes, neatly parted brown hair sweeping across his forehead, elegant tie and vest, and flowery language, Armstrong seemed charismatic as well as reassuring. As he listened to Quinlan's story, he recognized the historic dimensions of the case, but he felt daunted. Give me some time to think about it and talk it over with my wife, he told Quinlan. Two weeks later, after scouring law books by day and lying awake at night, he phoned the Quinlans. He was going to ask the Superior Court to appoint Quinlan legal guardian and thereby empower him to have the respirator disconnected.[35]

For twenty-one years Karen Ann Quinlan had been known to friends, teachers, and a handful of other people in the narrow radius of her life in Landing, New Jersey. Within days after Armstrong filed his complaint "In the Matter of Karen Quinlan, An Alleged Incompetent," she would become familiar to millions of people across the United States and worldwide. By March 1976, when the New Jersey Supreme Court issued its decision *In re Quinlan*, she would symbolize the right to be removed from lifesupport, or as it was commonly called, the right to die.

TURNING THE PAGES of newspapers from September 1975 is a bizarre experience. On September 6 one reads that Lynette "Squeaky" Fromme (a former member of Charles Manson's gang, which had murdered actress Sharon Tate and six others) pointed a pistol at President Ford. A Secret Service agent wrestled the gun away. On September 19 huge headlines proclaim the arrest of twenty-one-year-old Patty Hearst. After being kidnaped nineteen months earlier by the self-styled Symbionese Liberation Army, she had undergone weeks of "brainwashing," then denounced her millionaire parents and joined her captors in robbing banks. On September 24 forty-five-year-old Sarah Jane Moore pointed and fired a handgun at the president. A bystander deflected her aim. The next morning, it so happened, photographs of all three women appeared on the front page of the *New York Times*. Squeaky Fromme, peering out from under a peaked hood as she leaves the courthouse, resembles a soulful pilgrim. Hearst, on her way to a bail hearing, looks mysterious and somewhat sinister behind her sunglasses. Moore looks matronly and weepy.

Among these sensational figures, Karen Ann Quinlan—with her relatively uneventful life—seems an improbable celebrity. In the high school yearbook photograph that the media incessantly reproduced, she has a serene, innocent aura. But "the girl in a coma" embodied a story that proved to be as compelling as theirs. As soon as Armstrong filed his complaint on September 12, the media began shaping the facts into a multilevel narrative. The obvious plot line was a melodrama featuring a pathetic protagonist who hovered helplessly between life and death. The more complex story centered not on the victim but on those surrounding her: the doctors, guardians of the body; the attorney and judge, guardians of the law; a priest, guardian of the soul; and the parents who wished to be appointed legal guardian of their daughter. Each of them was struggling with the decision of whether this young woman should live or die. Fundamentally this was an existential narrative, pitting human will against a superhuman power variously defined as nature, God, the state, or medical technology.

On Friday, September 19, three days before the court hearing, CBS anchorman Walter Cronkite announced in apocalyptic terms: "This could be Karen Quinlan's last weekend of life, such as it is." Viewers were led full-speed through the case. First, with the high school photo on-screen, reporter Steve Young's description of her present condition (in a fetal position, weighing half of what she used to, eyes blinking but seeing nothing). Next, interviews with the Quinlans (whenever she dies, it will be God's will) and Father Trapasso (explaining the church's position on "extraordinary means"). Finally, New Jersey prosecutor Donald Collester (she is not brain-dead, so disconnecting the machine would be homicide).[36]

Cronkite's timing was off. Judge Muir decided to schedule the trial for October 20, five weeks hence. In the interim, newspapers and magazines prepared their readers for what was at stake. "It is, in a terribly literal sense, a life and death decision," stated the *Atlanta Constitution*. "A medical dilemma," said the *New York Times*. More lavishly, the *Chicago Tribune* called it "a human tragedy and bewildering legal riddle."[37]

Moral, medical, legal, and human—the convergence of these perspectives made it a complicated case. But it was a dilemma, a riddle, because the traditional definitions of life and death had dissolved. They had been "made obsolete by medical progress." In their place were three fundamental questions. Should someone like Karen Ann Quinlan, who was in a persistent vegetative state and breathing by machine, be considered legally alive or dead? Where do we draw the line between the state's responsibility to protect life and an incompetent patient's right to end life-prolonging treatment? And who should decide: a parent, a doctor, or a judge?[38] As if to personify these abstract questions, the media printed photographs of Mr. and Mrs. Quinlan staring pensively off into the distance.[39]

It was a dilemma of definitions and means, and also of consequences. "Whatever the decision," a *Washington Post* reporter asserted, "it is one that will haunt us for years to come." If the court favored Mr. Quinlan's plea, that might start us down the slippery slope toward "mercy killing" of ill people, old people, and others deemed unfit. If the court rejected his plea, the hospitals would fill with "medicine-sustained organisms devoid of all human qualities other than their ability to run up huge medical bills."[40]

During the month before the trial, most of the media accounts raised these questions—"cruel questions," *Newsweek* called them—and stopped there. A few also gave answers. There is a difference between ending a life that would otherwise continue, the *Chicago Tribune* argued, and "merely ceasing to prolong a life that would otherwise end." That little adverb "merely" tipped the scales of the dilemma toward the right to die. Syndicated columnist Carl Rowan was more blunt: "What 'sanctity' is there in preserving a mess of flesh which has lost all human capacity?"[41]

Some of the public also had made up their minds. Within a week of the first news reports, the Quinlans were receiving dozens of letters each day, some addressed simply "To Karen Quinlan's Family—U.S.A." We sympathize, the writers said. We're tending our own comatose relatives and share your anguish. We're saying prayers for Karen. Only a few urged the Quinlans to hold out for a miracle. By contrast, those who wrote to St. Clare's Hospital, where mail was arriving by the sackful, found a different meaning in the Quinlan story. Karen should be allowed to live, the majority pleaded. Where there's life, there's hope. The *New York Daily News* produced a slightly more reliable sense of public opinion when it phoned 532 adults in the New York metropolitan area and asked, "Do you agree with Karen Ann Quinlan's parents that she be taken off the respirator and allowed to die in dignity?" Yes, replied 59 percent. No, said 24 percent, while 17 percent had no opinion.[42]

The right to live or the right to die with dignity? Amid this growing public controversy, the lawyers, physicians, and priests, along with the Quinlan family, prepared to discuss the issue in court.

OUTSIDE the white courthouse in Morristown, New Jersey, the crowd began to gather an hour and a half beforehand, standing in a chill drizzle. There were so many reporters, some from as far away as Paris and Tokyo, that the trial had to be moved to a larger courtroom. Of the 137 seats, 100 were taken by the press, the rest by students, nurses, teachers, and others, leaving a score of disappointed people on the steps outside.[43]

Inside, Joseph, Julia, Mary Ellen, and John Quinlan sat behind Paul Armstrong and his partner. Across the aisle sat the group of five lawyers for the defense, each representing a different interest in keeping Karen alive. There was the attorney general of New Jersey, William F. Hyland; the Morris County prosecutor, Donald G. Collester; the attorney representing Karen's doctors, Ralph Porzio; the attorney for St. Clare's Hospital, Theodore Einhorn; and finally, the guardian *ad litem*, Daniel Coburn, whom the court had appointed to be Karen's guardian until the judge ruled on Mr. Quinlan's plea for guardianship. Behind the witness stand was a three-by-five-foot diagram of the human brain, each region labeled: cerebellum, brain stem, pons, medulla.[44]

The presiding judge was Robert Muir, Jr. He was forty-three years old, balding and athletic, born in Newark, father of three children, an elder in the Presbyterian church, a Republican, well known and well liked. Muir had enjoyed a fast-rising success: municipal law, the county bench, and in 1973 the Superior Court.[45]

Now he faced the most important trial of his career, and certainly the most publicized. As if to compensate for the momentousness of the occasion, Muir leaned casually in his chair while taking notes on a yellow pad, spoke in a low-key, amiable tone, and never hammered with his gavel.[46] To control the media frenzy, he barred still cameras, television cameras, and tape recorders from the courtroom. Reporters would have to rely on their words and artists' sketches to convey the scene.

The *New York Daily News* correspondent did more than convey—he wrote a kind of Hollywood screenplay. "The curtain rises on one of the most compelling dramas since the Scopes trial sought to establish the roots of human life," Peter Coutros informed his millions of readers. Paul Armstrong is "young and so all-American wholesome as to make one wonder that his first name is not Jack . . . ," whereas "the adversaries arrayed against Armstrong seem overwhelming."[47]

His prose was purple, but Coutros was on target. The trial would function as a social drama, enacting in microcosm the realignment of power and values that was taking place in postwar America.[48] Fifty years earlier in Tennessee, religious fundamentalists had clashed with civil libertarians over whether John Scopes, contrary to a new state law, had the right to teach Darwinian evolution to his biology students. With William Jennings Bryan and Clarence Darrow playing the leads, the Scopes trial became a sensationalized news story (and would later be turned into a Broadway play and Hollywood film). During the eight days of testimony, the town of Dayton resembled a carnival, crowded by reporters, scientists, tourists, hot-dog vendors, and Bible-hawkers. On a level deeper than entertainment, though, it was a morality play in which old-fashioned, Protestant Americans made their stand against modern, secular Americans. Scopes was found guilty and given a token fine, but that proved to be only a symbolic victory for fundamentalists. During the next fifty years they went into retreat while modernists prevailed.[49]

In the Quinlan trial, science was again pitted against religion: the respirator and Dr. Morse versus the Quinlans. But this time the state of New Jersey sided with scientific authority. In their opening arguments the defense attorneys claimed that Mr. Quinlan in effect was asking to commit homicide, violating the state's obligation to preserve life. "As far as the legal basis for this," said Daniel Coburn, "I've heard 'death with dignity,' 'self-determination,' 'religious freedom,' and I consider that to be a complete shell game that's being played here. This is euthanasia."[50] Quinlan's daughter's condition was certainly pitiable and his religious principles sincere. Nevertheless, the defense reminded Judge Muir, in a similar case only four years ago the New Jersey Supreme Court had ruled against a parent wanting to let her comatose daughter die.

That case was *John F. Kennedy Memorial Hospital v. Heston* (1971). Twenty-two-year-old Delores Heston had suffered a ruptured spleen in a car accident and was in shock. When she arrived at the hospital, physicians said she would die unless they operated immediately. But she was a Jehovah's Witness, so her religion forbade the blood transfusions needed during the operation. Heston's mother (also a Jehovah's Witness) refused consent, whereupon the hospital arranged for a court-appointed guardian to authorize the transfusion. Heston survived and the medical story ended, but the legal story continued as the case went before the New Jersey Supreme Court. Heston's lawyers claimed that the hospital had violated her rights of self-determination and religious freedom. The court unanimously disagreed, saying that these personal rights were outweighed by the state's interest in preserving life. Just as policemen interfered with someone's attempt to commit suicide, courts intervened to let physicians save a patient's life. " . . . There is no constitutional right to choose to die."[51]

Beyond this legal precedent was an ominous historical precedent. "Fresh in our minds are the Nazi atrocities," declared Ralph Porzio, attorney for Drs. Morse and Javed. In the late 1930s Hitler had begun implementing his race-purification philosophy, first by ordering German physicians to weed out the mentally retarded and physically handicapped, then in the early 1940s by building concentration camps to exterminate more than six million Jews, homosexuals, and gypsies. Thirty years later, Porzio said, Karen

Ann Quinlan lay at the brink of a slippery slope. If she were allowed to die, then where would one draw the line against exterminating other Americans who were deemed to be lacking sufficient quality of life? "And so," he said to Judge Muir, "once you make a decision [for the Quinlans], I think it is like turning on the gas chamber."[52]

This was what Paul Armstrong confronted when he stood up to make his opening statement: not only the *Heston* precedent but victims of involuntary euthanasia in the recent past and the hypothetical future. In response he depicted Karen as another kind of victim, constrained by merciless medical technology from proceeding naturally to the end of her life. "The earthly phase of Karen's life has drawn to a close . . . ," Armstrong declared in his lyrical baritone. "The time of life striving is over, and . . . further treatments merely hold her back from the realization and enjoyment of a better, more perfect life." Under the First Amendment right to free exercise of religion, her father should be appointed legal guardian and allowed to disconnect the respirator.

Unlike William Jennings Bryan, though, Armstrong invoked not only religion but a pair of secular rights: Karen's Eighth Amendment right not to suffer cruel and unusual punishment, and her "right of privacy," which the U.S. Supreme Court had recently asserted on behalf of women choosing contraception or abortion (*Griswold v. Connecticut* [1965] and *Roe v. Wade* [1973]).[53] This was not, then, a clear-cut conflict between traditional and progressive values. Modern dying posed more ambiguity than the origin of species. It not only raised a theoretical question about where to locate the source of human life, whether in biology or a supernatural force; it also demanded a practical choice: to continue treatment or to end it. When the patient was PVS, that existential choice became all the more confounding. For then the issue wasn't self-determination, but determination for someone else—"playing God."

Which brings us to the most striking feature of this social drama. As the *Daily News* reporter noted: "All the cast is there," all except one. "The principal character is missing. . . . She is Karen

Ann Quinlan and she is elsewhere. . . ." That might seem too obvious to be mentioned. After all, the trial was being staged precisely because she was "incompetent." Nevertheless her absence exerted an eerie power, somewhat like the vacancy left by a deceased friend, but with the extra poignancy of knowing that she remained alive. Gone but not departed: that paradox was the emotional pivot of the drama.

It was also the crux of the legal issue being argued before Judge Muir. According to long common-law tradition, every individual has the right to determine what shall and shall not be done to his or her body. Bioethicists call this "informed consent": the right to be told the nature and risks of proposed treatment. To perform an operation without the patient's consent would be to commit assault and battery, for which the doctor is criminally liable.[54] Since Quinlan could not say whether she wanted to remain attached to the respirator, however, others had to speak for her (in legal terms, make a "substituted judgment"). Inescapably they also spoke for themselves in accord with the various societal roles they performed. Lawyer, doctor, parent, and priest, each asserted his claim to control of her unconscious body. As various cultural theorists have argued, the body serves as the symbolic object upon which social institutions vie to imprint their values. The modern state has been especially forceful, according to Michel Foucault, with "an anatomo-politics" of regulating bodies not only in schools, prisons, the army, and other public institutions but increasingly also in private life—sexuality, for example, and health.[55] How appropriate, then, that Armstrong sought to free Quinlan's body from a machine by invoking her "right of privacy."

ONCE THE ATTORNEYS completed their opening statements, it was time for another set of authorities to have their say. During the next day and a half (and another day at the end of the week), physicians took the witness stand.

First, Dr. Morse. In his early Beatles haircut, he looked even younger than thirty-six.[56] Calmly, though sometimes disjointedly, he answered questions for the rest of the morning and most of the afternoon. Which tests were administered to Karen and how did they explain her coma? Which parts of her brain were injured, with what effects? What did the respirator do and how did her body react? Ostensibly the lawyers were establishing a factual account of Karen's condition in the ICU since April. But both sides really were more interested in her future than her past. Armstrong hoped to prove that Quinlan's prognosis was hopeless and that prolonging her life would have no benefit. The defense wanted to prove that the treatment was appropriate; however irreversible her condition, she was nonetheless alive. These were the subtexts beneath the question-and-answer exchanges.

> ARMSTRONG: Doctor, do you have an opinion as to how long it would be possible for Karen, her vital processes, to be sustained with the assistance of the respirator?
>
> MORSE: I don't think anybody, Paul, can give an assessment of that. Each individual differs. You don't know the primary lesions. You don't know the extent of the insult. Some people might say one hour; another person, two weeks. . . . I really don't know.
>
> ARMSTRONG: It is possible, though, for Karen to live in this form of existence for a year, is it not?
>
> MORSE: Without the respirator?
>
> ARMSTRONG: With the respirator; I'm sorry.
>
> MORSE: No. Don't forget there are side effects to being on a respirator for a period of time. . . . The movement of air inside the trachea can cause erosion of [the] trachea, and it can erode the vital structure. . . . The basic problem here is that we're fighting infection.

Given that opening, Armstrong tried to pin the physician in a corner.

> ARMSTRONG: Doctor, would it be fair to say that the utilization of the respirator itself, that there are inherent dangers in so doing?

MORSE: There are inherent dangers in everything, even IVs. But beyond the inherent dangers of the respirator, it's outweighed by the benefits it gives to this particular human being, at this particular point in time.[57]

Opportunity lost. Now it was the turn of Daniel Coburn, the thirty-two-year-old lawyer whom the court had appointed Karen's temporary guardian to defend her life. He looked like "a scrapper," one journalist remarked: short and stocky, with wavy black hair and blue eyes. "You'll recognize me," he told a reporter. "I'm the one who looks uncomfortable in a tie and a jacket."[58] Coburn guided Morse in constructing the rationale for the respirator.

COBURN: At some point, the Quinlans' position—Joseph Quinlan's position—changed in this case. Originally their position was to do everything they can to keep her alive.

MORSE: He was very conscientious. . . . He had asked about where we are with the patient; what we should do. . . . Of course, the respirator was considered [by Mr. Quinlan] to be extraordinary means, and [yet] really it is an ordinary means. . . .[59]

Having elicited that crucial point, Coburn made the next move.

COBURN: Is there any chance her condition would improve, off the respirator?

MORSE: Maybe she could go on 24 hours or 72 hours without a respirator. . . . Your guess is as good as mine.

COBURN: We are in the guessing game.[60]

By the end of the first day the defense had constructed an effective narrative. Karen Ann Quinlan lingered in a PVS, brain-damaged but not brain-dead, surviving for months, maybe years, no one could predict. Her physicians were highly trained experts—being addressed as "Doctor" (Morse was only six years older than Armstrong but called him "Paul") and employing sophisticated scientific techniques—who cared about their patient and her family. It was because they cared that they were performing their professional duty of keeping her alive, even if a machine breathed for her.

To develop a counternarrative, Armstrong called on Dr. Julius Korein to testify that the respirator was extraordinary treatment, which should be discontinued. Korein was a decade older than Morse and more self-confident. A New York University professor, chief of the EEG laboratories at Bellevue Hospital, member of a half-dozen neurological associations and author of seventy to eighty scholarly papers, he spoke with a fluent delivery and vivid vocabulary. In short, he was an eminence of the profession and, as it turned out, too professional for his own good. His style overpowered his message. Although he wanted to prove the cruelty of Quinlan's treatment, his clinical, dispassionate approach inadvertently conveyed a cruelty of its own and, by contrast, made Morse seem her protector.

Korein described the patient whom he had examined two weeks earlier.

> She was a young cathetic. . . . Emaciated woman with flexion contractures of the upper extremities, like so (Indicating); and flexion of elbows, wrists, fingers to the chest. The knees . . . were pulled up to the chest also—so she had this position, and I would not call it a fetal position, but it's a flexion and retraction position, with her ankles plantar flexed; that is, down in a ballet-type pose.[61]

By now Julia Quinlan had quietly left the courtroom, tears streaking her cheeks, and Joseph Quinlan was trying to control his emotions, "his head down deep into his shoulders," according to one reporter, "like a wounded turtle withdrawing into its shell."[62] But Korein persisted:

> She had disconjugate movements of the eyes. She would have lip smacking, chewing movements . . . grimacing, grinding movements of the teeth; you could hear the teeth click. . . . When the stimulus was noxious, she would go into this movement more to the right, eyes wide open, random eye movements, with a huge yawning—well, a yawn but not a yawn. Maximal yawning, with the mouth open as far as possible, with tongue protruding and salivating.

The image of the absent young woman had become disturbingly present in the courtroom. Alive, undeniably alive, but not like a human being. "La morte vivante," as *France-Soir* put it.[63]

ARMSTRONG: Continue your narrative, Doctor. . . .

KOREIN: . . . The respirator triggered at approximately 9. It was breathing for the patient at about 9 times per minute. Then . . . , we stimulated very slightly, and she began to trigger, and the rate went up to . . . 20 per minute. It was irregular and disorganized.

ARMSTRONG: What was the nature of the stimulation utilized?

KOREIN: A pin to the shoulder very lightly. . . . Then we stopped and she quieted down. Her eyes closed. . . . [64]

This was a trial about whether Joseph Quinlan should have the power to decide his daughter's treatment. But in terms of public opinion, medical authority was also on trial. Having enjoyed a reputation as paternal caregivers or even miracle workers, doctors were in danger of being considered technicians who treated bodies rather than persons. Although Morse and Korein disagreed as to what was best for Karen, both tended to talk about her as an object of science: tubes thrust into her body, air pumping into her lungs, pins poked into her shoulder.

THE QUINLANS, on the other hand, brought to the witness stand—and to this social drama—the kinds of emotion and uncertainty that the general public could identify with. After a lunch recess the court reconvened (late, Armstrong apologized, because of "a monumental traffic jam"), and the spectators leaned forward to hear Joseph Quinlan. He spoke so softly that Judge Muir asked a clerk to turn on the microphone. Even then, he was often too choked with emotion to be heard.

" . . . It was most difficult," he said, "and it took almost 6 months for me to personally arrive at a decision." There were frequent meetings with Morse and Javed, during which he gradually realized that Karen would never recover. There was also "my own prayer life," in the course of which "I started praying not just that Karen would live, but that the Lord would show His will. Whatever His was, I would accept . . . until I arrived at . . . [the belief] he was going to use Karen and Mr. Armstrong, and possibly even the Judge, and every one of us, for some reason known only to Himself, and I'm convinced of this." Finally there were the conversations with Father Tom, explaining the church's position on withdrawing extraordinary treatment. "This is what I want to do," Quinlan told the court: "Physically take her off the machine, remove all the tubes from her body, since she's going to die anyway, and place her completely in the hands of the Lord."[65]

Neurologists had studded their testimony with arcane terminology—the mask of professionalism. Quinlan talked like an average American. There was, for example, this exchange with Coburn, the lawyer whom he hoped to replace as guardian.

> COBURN: What do you consider extraordinary means to be?
> QUINLAN: What I consider extraordinary means?
> COBURN: Yes.
> QUINLAN: The only one I know of is the machine, but I understand there's a lot of other gadgets.

Karen's father sounded like a layman, but more strikingly he seemed to be a man of feeling. About medical procedure: " . . . I would not take the plug out. . . . I am sorry I used that phrase. I don't like that." About Morse and Javed: "I love them both. I really feel in my heart that they've done everything possible for my daughter. . . ." Ultimately he spoke as an anguished father who was seeking the right path out of this quandary.[66]

When Julia Quinlan testified the next day, she added yet another poignant voice—or really, two voices, hers and Karen's.

> She was very full of life, a very active young girl, and she had always said that if she was dying: "Mommy, please don't ever let them keep me alive with any extraordinary means," or in any way that she could not really enjoy her life to the fullest.

This had been Karen's reaction, Mrs. Quinlan said, when an aunt was dying of breast cancer a few years earlier, and more recently when a girlfriend's father suffered terminal cancer and a family friend was dying at home of a brain tumor. "And that's why, when I see her in this condition, I know in my heart as her mother that it is not the way that Karen would want to be."

The defense lawyers quickly intervened to ask whether those were her daughter's exact words. No, Mrs. Quinlan conceded, but they represented the essential meaning. Had Karen used the phrase "extraordinary means"? the lawyers persisted. Not exactly, Mrs. Quinlan replied, she had said it in her own words.[67]

The Quinlan family was vying with the legal and medical experts to establish their respective interpretations of the evidence. While they spoke inside the courtroom, the media were interpreting their interpretations to the audience outside. Newspapers and television were producing their own narrative, shaped according to the editors' sense of what readers would or should want. In the mediated version, legal issues played virtually no part. This was a personalized dilemma of death or life.

The morning after the trial began, almost all newspapers ignored the attorneys' opening arguments (except for the warning of Nazi atrocities) and skimmed over the bioethical/theological issue of "extraordinary" treatment. What readers learned was that Karen's devoutly Catholic parents wanted to let her die in dignity whereas Dr. Morse explained she was responsive to light, sound, and pain and "I must abide by medical tradition" in continuing the respirator. Reading the headlines in Houston, Chicago, and elsewhere, one couldn't help but sympathize with Morse. "Girl's doctor won't cut off life support." "Doctor fights call for Karen's death." A life-or-death story, but in the editors' judgment, not a sensational story. Most newspapers ran it on page 3 or 4 or, in the *New York Times*, as far back as page 41. The conscientious physician was less newsworthy than the Soviet-American grain deal.[68]

The next day, by contrast, the media's narrative changed utterly. Dr. Julius Korein had given his gruesome description of Karen Ann Quinlan and endorsed disconnecting the respirator because it was extraordinary treatment. But that didn't interest the newspapers; they focused on the Quinlans' tears. "As his weeping family listened," began the Associated Press story, "Joseph T. Quinlan testified Tuesday that 'it's the Lord's will' his daughter Karen Ann be allowed to die."[69] Depending on which paper one read, Joseph was crushed, shocked, saddened, or breaking down frequently as he called for divine guidance. When Korein's testimony was mentioned at all, it was upstaged by Mrs. Quinlan, "this slender, red-haired homemaker," walking "wobbly-legged from the courtroom with tears welling in her eyes."[70] On this second day the story was more often front-page news. In the *Boston Globe*, for example, it moved from page 22 to the bottom of page 1. (Top billing went to Carlton Fisk's twelfth-inning home run, which won the sixth game of the World Series for the Red Sox.) And the headlines, in tones as loud as Mr. Quinlan's had been soft, cast him as the protagonist. "DAD: PUT KAREN IN LORD'S HANDS," said the *New York Daily News*.[71]

This triumph of parental pathos intensified when Julia Quinlan took the stand. Although reporters disagreed about whether she was calm and poised, composed though tense, or frail-looking, they unanimously emphasized one part of her testimony—or rather, Karen's testimony. "'Mommy, don't keep me alive.'" That was the lead paragraph in almost every paper, and it ran in a forty-point banner headline across the *Los Angeles Times*.[72]

Whatever the medical facts or the legal outcome, the media were skewing their narrative in favor of the Quinlans and the right to die. That should come as no surprise. After all, in terms of human interest, the stricken family had an advantage over Dr. Morse or Attorney Collester. Moreover their story drew upon a tried-and-true literary formula. The media were fashioning a twentieth-century version of nineteenth-century melodrama. In that popular Victorian genre, the usual plot featured an innocent girl of modest origins who was being sexually abused by upper-class men while her father stood by helplessly.[73] Quinlan was not being sexually abused, although the penetration of tubes into her body certainly had suggestive overtones. According to her physicians, she

DAILY ☒ NEWS

NEW YORK'S PICTURE NEWSPAPER ®

15¢

Vol. 57. No. 102   New York, N.Y. 10017, Wednesday, October 22, 1975◆   Sunny and mild, 55-78. Details page 103.

DAD: PUT KAREN IN LORD'S HANDS

Scene as Joseph Quinlan (right, on stand) testified at trial in Morristown, N.J., courthouse yesterday.—*Stories on page 3*

State Ends Gyp on Lottery Tix

Front page, *New York Daily News*, October 22, 1975

wasn't being abused at all but being given lifesaving treatment. When they used mechanistic language, however, they sounded less like saviors than victimizers. Likewise, when the defense attorneys deplored the euthanasia of hypothetical patients, their arguments struggled against the image of the real woman lying comatose with ankles flexed in a balletic pose. The combination of Quinlan's absence and her parents' presence exerted a powerful, almost irresistible impact.

ON THE THIRD DAY of the trial, another type of authority—the church—joined the discussion, supplementing the lawyers, doctors, and family. Physicians perform their responsibilities only as long as the body shows signs of life. Priests extend their attention to life after death, the *meta*physical dimension, and obey the supernatural will of God. In this wider context, death is not the end-all, and therefore the quality of dying—"death with dignity"— becomes a stronger consideration. When Father Trapasso took the stand, he not only corroborated the Quinlans' accounts of their conversations during the past summer; for a half-hour or more he discussed the implications of Pope Pius XII's *allocutio* of 1957, which differentiated ordinary and extraordinary means of prolonging life.

Here was a problem for the defense. How could they go about disputing a priest and the papal authority he represented? In his cross-examination, Ralph Porzio, the doctors' attorney, worked assiduously but tactfully to quote the pope against himself. "Now, sir, may I ask you, Father [the *allocutio*] states here" that the church was not competent to decide whether a person should be considered dead who was in a vegetative state and on a respirator. In that light, couldn't the Quinlans continue the respirator and not be committing a sin? The priest agreed—neither a venial nor a mortal sin.

Donald Collester, the county prosecutor, had a more speculative question, "and I'm really out of my league here." According to Catholic doctrine, was Karen's soul still in her body? Yes, Trapasso answered, her soul—"the source of life, . . . the thing that, theo-logically anyway, distinguishes a corpse from a living human being"—remained within her body. "Thank you, Father Trapasso. I don't have any further questions," Collester said, satisfied to have reaffirmed that Quinlan, although PVS, was alive in not only bio-logical but spiritual terms.[74]

It was a remarkable scene. Inside this courthouse in twenti-eth-century New Jersey, not far from traffic jams and the seventh game of the World Series, a group of men were discussing papal doctrine, sin, and the soul. It could have been Paris in 1475. Instead of medieval dispute between church and state, however, it was a dispute between citizens and physicians, with the church as adviser and the state as umpire.[75] This was a secular trial with spiritual im-plications. At stake wasn't simply a young woman's life or doctors' policy. Modern science had reopened age-old issues of life, death, and afterlife.

IN ANOTHER DAY of testimony by physicians, they described in graphic clinical detail Quinlan's vegetative state and gloomy prospects for recovery to a "sapient" condition. Then Judge Muir ordered a three-day recess. On Monday the trial ended as it had begun, with attorneys on each side summoning up their best and basic arguments.

According to the defense, the issue was stark: protecting life against homicide under the guise of "mercy killing." For six months Karen Ann Quinlan had not regained consciousness, breathing only with a machine, but she was alive. True, the prospects for recovery were slim. But "if Karen Ann Quinlan has one chance in a thousand," Ralph Porzio insisted, "if she has one chance in ten thousand, if she has one chance in a million, who are we and by what right do we kill that chance?" And even if one agreed that her condition was irreversible, that did not mean it had no value. "What is 'quality of life'?" the county prosecutor asked. "To see? To hear? To love? To understand? To communicate? The greater peril lies in forgetting the sanctity of life and substituting for it the quality of life. . . ." Everyone sympathized with the Quinlans' anguish and admired their moral devotion to their daughter. But killing with a merciful motive was homicide. If the court overruled her physicians and permitted Quinlan to be disconnected from the respirator and die, other incompetents would be next. Stricken children, paralyzed parents, the mentally retarded. History had taught a horrendous lesson, Porzio declared, about overriding physicians' judgments. " . . . If the medical profession in Nazi Germany had shown more independence—if they had refused to partake in human experimentation, perhaps the Holocaust would not have been so great in terms of human lives and deformities."[76]

The defense had staked out a large sector of ideological ground. In the best meaning of conservatism, they were invoking the rule of law, the responsibility of medicine, and the sanctity of life against social engineering. On a more personalized level, they were defending Karen Ann Quinlan against her father: one claim of paternalism against another.

The Quinlans' lawyer, by contrast, faced a more difficult task. Armstrong needed to justify judicial innovation while citing constitutional and common-law principles—a feat somewhat like running forward while looking over one's shoulder. And specifically he needed to explain why Joseph Quinlan would not be committing murder if he disconnected the life-sustaining machine. He might appeal to compassion for "the poor and tragic creature" who once knew love and promise, peace and joy but now is "no more than 60 or 70 pounds of flesh and bone. . . ." He might also try to appropriate the quality-of-life position. "Can anything be more degrading, than to be offered up as a living sacrifice to the materialistic and misguided belief that death can somehow be cheated, if only we find the right combination of wires and gauges, transistors and tubes?"

But this was a court of law, not a theater, and ultimately Armstrong had to construct his case out of legal rather than emotional reasoning. In the *Heston* case the New Jersey Supreme Court had ruled that "there is no constitutional right to choose to die." But Delores Heston's ailment was curable, Armstrong pointed out, whereas Karen Quinlan's was hopeless. "Medicine must be the servant of man," he said, "and technology must be the servant of medicine." The respirator merely perpetuated her vegetative state. If she could speak for herself, she would exercise her common-law right to refuse treatment. Instead her father, in accord with Catholic doctrine on "extraordinary means," was asking to exercise his First Amendment freedom of religion and make a substituted judgment on his daughter's behalf. More generally, both Karen Quinlan and her father should be granted their wish under their right to privacy, as recently enunciated by the United States Supreme Court. "This right has grown to include individual and familial life-influencing decisions," Armstrong argued, and overrode the state's interest in protecting Karen's life. "Thus it is, Your Honor, that we conclude our review of the sad and weighty issues that have brought us here before you. . . ."[77]

Now it was Judge Muir's turn to review. Promising a verdict within two weeks, he went off to ponder the 745-page transcript, the 12 yellow pads on which he had scribbled notes, and a stack of medical and legal books.

Meanwhile the public remained passionately interested. Six hundred letters poured into the judge's office, two-thirds pleading, "Let Karen live." Two thousand letters arrived at the Quinlans' house, overflowing the cartons that Joe had brought from his office, most of them asking for her to be removed from the respirator. Packages were delivered to the courthouse with vials of "holy water" and crucifixes. Numerous faith healers flocked to St. Clare's Hospital, promising to restore the afflicted girl to health. A few even showed up on the Quinlans' doorstep. (Julia recalled sitting in the living room with a young man and woman from North Carolina, praying together.)[78] In Italy, France, Britain, Switzerland, Sweden, and Denmark, right-to-die movements were under way.[79] In the United States the Quinlan story was no longer front-page news, but columnists voiced their strident opinions for or against. According to a poll of nearly a thousand households nationwide, 59 percent of Americans favored letting a terminally ill patient die. Equally telling only 7 percent said the doctor alone had the right to make that decision; a majority gave that right to relatives with or without the doctor. In West Virginia a high school thanatology class held a mock trial and voted, 26 to 2, that Karen Ann Quinlan be allowed to die.[80]

And people waited for the only opinion that really counted.

"I'M AN ORDINARY human being, with ordinary thoughts, ordinary emotions," Judge Muir remarked during the trial when Armstrong had urged him to visit Karen Quinlan in the hospital. "My position in this case is to decide it on the basis of the evidence presented. . . . Recognizing that emotion is an aspect that I cannot decide a case on, I do not think it's appropriate for me to go see her."[81]

When he finally issued his decision on November 10, the forty-three-year-old judge again spoke of his emotions: "the compassion, empathy, sympathy I feel for Mr. and Mrs. Quinlan and their other two children. . . ." In this life-and-death case, "the onus of the judicial process for me . . . is unparalleled." That weight became even heavier, given the significance of this case for "the raging issues of euthanasia." All the more reason, then, that personal conscience must defer to judicial conscience and objectivity. A judge has the duty to decide each case according to "the high standard of morality and abstract right. . . ."[82]

Given this prologue, one could predict where he was heading. "The single most important temporal quality Karen Ann Quinlan has is life. This court will not authorize that life to be taken from her." The decision whether or not to remove her from the respirator must be a medical, not a judicial one. Every patient places himself in a physician's care expecting that everything possible will be done to protect his life. Likewise a court should defer to medical judgment. Although Quinlan's chances for recovery were remote, none of the doctors had testified there was *no* hope. Consequently, in line with Dr. Morse's judgment, "there *is* a duty to continue the life assisting apparatus. . . ." Indeed, even if she were "on the threshold of death or in a terminal condition," removing her from the respirator would be an act of homicide.

Karen Condamnée à Vivre, *France-Soir*, November 12, 1975

The judge went on to dismiss each of Armstrong's arguments. Quinlan's rights of privacy, religion, and protection against cruel and unusual punishment—none of these outweighed her physicians' authority. It would be a different matter if Quinlan herself could ask to discontinue treatment. But she was incompetent, and her prior statements that Mrs. Quinlan had quoted were "theoretical." Karen had been twenty years old and "full of life," in her mother's words, reacting to someone else's pain rather than her own. "She was not personally involved," Muir said, and was not responding "under the solemn and sobering fact that death is a distinct choice. . . ." Indeed, the doctors' reports indicated that, in her vegetative state, she was feeling no pain.

Finally, the judge said, however sincere and moral Mr. Quinlan was in anguishing over his decision to take his daughter off the respirator, that very anguish disqualified him from being her guardian. In effect, Muir was applying to the plaintiff the distinction between objective and subjective judgment that he had applied to himself. To make the day-to-day decisions about her treatment, a guardian could not be distracted by emotional conflict. Muir thereby came full circle, ending as he had begun on the note of dispassion.[83]

In a small room across the street from the courthouse, two hundred reporters and television cameramen awaited the Quinlans. "What are you going to do now?" a reporter shouted. "We don't know," Joseph Quinlan replied.[84]

Television stations interrupted their regular programs to announce the decision. It was the lead story on the CBS Evening News. It was headlined in newspapers on both sides of the Atlantic. "Karen condamnée à vivre," *France-Soir* declared.[85]

Far from cooling the public controversy, Muir's decision fanned it to new intensity. Spokesmen for the American Medical Association and the American Bar Association applauded the judge for preserving physicians' autonomy. Protestant, Jewish, and Catholic leaders praised him for preventing the first step toward involuntary euthanasia. "Let us not mince words," conservative columnist George F. Will wrote. A decision for the Quinlans "would have authorized a killing." An African-American physician in California breathed relief, because if Quinlan had been allowed to die, that would have encouraged removing other "defectives" and soon "all minorities [would be] in jeopardy."[86]

But dissenters were unappeased. The decision may have been legally correct, the *Los Angeles Times* conceded, but "the iron words of the law" did not resolve the "human tragedy." On the contrary, *Le Figaro* said, the court had spared the life of "an unconscious innocent whose agony is . . . without appeal." Compared to that prolonged "horror," the *Chicago Tribune* agreed, death seems "an unalloyed blessing."[87] Liberal Catholics joined the chorus, reproaching the judge for converting a moral and social dilemma into a "technical" one. As Reverend John Connery put it: "You just can't solve this problem on the basis of medicine alone."[88]

That is exactly what Muir had chosen to do. In a gesture of judicial restraint, he put the life-or-death question back into the hands of the physicians. "This court will not authorize that life to be taken from her." But a pair of basic confusions lurked at the bottom of this decision, leading to woefully ironic consequences.

First, Muir collapsed two distinct issues into one. The issue before the court was not whether Mr. Quinlan had the right to let Karen die. It was whether he had the right on her behalf to discontinue treatment—that is, unplug the respirator. Of course everyone—doctors, journalists, the Quinlans themselves—assumed that without the respirator she would die within hours or days. (Take her off the machine and put her in the hands of the Lord, Mr. Quinlan had testified, "since she's going to die anyway.") So it's easy to understand why the judge equated the question of removing treatment with the question of homicide. The very phrase "right to die" collapses the two. Nevertheless, logically speaking—which also means legally speaking—the right to remove treatment (passive euthanasia) is distinct from the right to have a doctor hasten one's death (active euthanasia). Without treatment, one won't necessarily die. By merging the two rights, Muir could hardly grant Mr. Quinlan's plea to serve as Karen's guardian. That would have been a license to commit murder. The only persons who had the right to decide her treatment, according to Muir, were her physicians.

Here entered the second confusion and the ironic consequences. On the one hand, the judge gave doctors total authority to decide how to treat an incompetent patient. On the other hand, he defined withdrawal of life-prolonging measures as homicide. The second hand thwarted the first. For how could a physician decide, in the face of this reasoning, to disconnect an irrecoverably ill patient from a respirator? Indeed, if withdrawal of life-prolonging treatment was homicide, a doctor would be reluctant to put a patient on life-support in the first place. For once he attached her to the respirator, he would have to keep her attached forever. At the same time, though, how could he in good conscience refrain from trying to prolong, or possibly save, a patient's life? In Muir's zeal to affirm both the state's authority (to protect life) and medical authority (to decide treatment), he had unwittingly put doctors in a double bind.[89]

Consternation spread through the medical profession. With a patient suffering the throes of terminal illness, should one continue "heroic" methods? Until now, doctors had reached their decision behind closed doors, according to their consciences and clinical assessment, sometimes consulting patient and family. After the Quinlan ruling they were fearful.[90]

The decision unsettled more than it settled the existential as well as the pragmatic questions "in the matter of Karen Quinlan, an alleged incompetent." Meanwhile the respirator continued pumping and she remained "condemned to live." On November 17 Armstrong filed an appeal with the New Jersey Supreme Court.

2

Modern Dying

THE QUINLAN case was a landmark in the legal history of the right to die. But when we step back and look more broadly at the post–World War II era, we discover that popular interest in dying was on the rise long before Karen fell into a coma. During the late 1960s and early 1970s one could hardly open a newspaper or magazine, walk through a bookstore, turn on the TV, or go to the movies without confronting some reference to the end of life. Where did this cultural phenomenon come from, and what did it signify? Commentators at the time either shook their heads in bewilderment or, more often, attributed it to "the violent climate."

With hindsight we recognize that the new obsession with dying derived from three unsettling developments in postwar America. It was, first of all, a reaction to medical techniques that kept patients alive while too often prolonging their suffering. It was also shaped by two insurgencies taking place beyond the hospital. Inspired by the 1960s counterculture, a striking number of Americans undertook a spiritual or therapeutic quest to die "with dignity." And in more political fashion, the women's movement spawned a patient rights movement that challenged the power of doctors to dictate end-of-life treatment. By bringing these trends together into a right-to-die movement, the Quinlan trial proved to be not only a legal but a cultural landmark.

IN 1954 Charles Wertenbaker, a fifty-four-year-old journalist and novelist, learned he had fast-spreading, inoperable liver cancer. He decided to take painkillers, live as long as he retained dignity, and then kill himself. In *Death of a Man* (1957) his wife Lael recorded their last three months together. A crucial scene took place after his physician, a Dr. Cartier, recommended a colostomy for temporary relief and Wertenbaker refused.

> Wert was sitting on the sofa, just pulled out of a *crise* [of pain] with his eyes closed. Cartier stood over me and I stood, arms akimbo, fishwife style, at the end of the sofa. . . .
>
> "You cannot let him refuse!" [Cartier] said. "You're responsible. You're the well one. You and I should take him by force if necessary in an ambulance to the hospital. You cannot leave it to him. . . ."
>
> "If he wants it, we'll do it," I said, raising my voice as Cartier had raised his, tried almost beyond my own endurance. "It's his body, his life, his mind! His pain. He's not nuts or weak-minded. He is a man. He can do as he pleases to do."
>
> "I don't understand you." [Cartier said.] "I don't understand either of you. It will make it better for a while."
>
> " . . . And then?"
>
> "Then . . . then. . . ."
>
> "When he wants to die, he can do that, too," I said. " . . . I don't want him to die one day sooner, God knows, but do you understand me, it's up to *him* what he does!"
>
> "You would help him do that!" he said in horrified comprehension. "I believe you would. This is serious. *You must not.*"
>
> I might have said a dangerous thing, then, but Wert interrupted very quietly with such an air of authority that we both obeyed him. "Stop fussing," he said.[1]

The day after Christmas, as the pain and weakness became terrible, the Wertenbakers sat in their upstairs bedroom and he gave himself what he hoped would be a fatal injection of morphine. "I love you and I've had a damned fine life," he said. A minute later: "A gentleman should know when to take his leave."[2]

But he didn't die that night or the next five nights of larger doses, until finally, after administering an injection and slitting his wrists, he succeeded.

Death of a Man appeared in 1957. During the next ten years Americans were constantly being told they were not talking about death. "Death is a taboo subject," social scientists, journalists, and religious evangelists declared again and again until it became a platitude.[3] How often can a taboo be talked about, though, before it's no longer a taboo? The chant became its own refutation. From the late fifties to the mid-sixties there was a steady stream of books and articles about death.[4] Most of them were by professionals—psychologists, sociologists, physicians, and an occasional literary critic—for specialized audiences.[5] The *American Journal of Nursing*, for example, published articles such as "Teaching Students to Work with the Dying" and "Grief and Grieving."[6]

On a more popular level, however, writing about death remained surprisingly sparse, a silence that signaled either denial or at least indifference among ordinary Americans. Then came an equally surprising explosion of interest. During 1968–1973 the number of articles about death in mass-circulation magazines each year doubled, and during 1973–1975 (*before* the Quinlan trial) it redoubled. The trend was the same for books. One bibliographer listed twelve hundred books in English on death and bereavement published during 1935–1968; five years later he issued a supplement for the twelve hundred new books that had appeared.[7] Particularly popular were testimonials by terminally ill patients or their widows: *How Could I Not Be Among You?*; *Stay of Execution*; *A Death of One's Own*; *A Death with Dignity*.[8] There were also cultural critiques like Marya Mannes's *Last Rights* and Elisabeth Kübler-Ross's *On Death and Dying*. "Death is now selling books,"

Publishers' Weekly announced. One Sunday in 1974 eight books on death were reviewed in the *New York Times*.[9]

Beyond the reading public was a larger viewing public. On television an ABC News special discussed "mercy killing." Public television portrayed a young sculptor, paralyzed in a car accident, who wanted to end his life. An episode of "The Bold Ones" explored the struggles of six dying patients. In a made-for-TV movie, a running back for the Chicago Bears died of cancer in *Brian's Song* (1970).[10]

It was also a topic of face-to-face discussion. Behavioral scientists, law professors, ministers, and the lay public flocked to weekend seminars on death.[11] Thanatology courses were under way in seventy colleges and high schools. (University of Cincinnati students visited funeral homes; Minnesota high schoolers tried out a coffin for size.)[12] For individuals who felt isolated, Mrs. Rachel Clark (a graduate of a University of California thanatology course) set up a phone-in information service on death and dying, fielding a dozen calls a day. A group of what would soon be called "bioethicists," led by Daniel Callahan, founded the Hastings Center; two years later another group founded the Kennedy Center for Ethics at Georgetown University. The United States Senate Committee on Aging held hearings in 1972 on "Death with Dignity."[13]

By this time the only thing to be said about the "taboo" of death was that it had gone the way of the taboo of sex.[14] When *Psychology Today* distributed a questionnaire on "You and Death," thirty thousand readers sent replies, half again as many as had responded to a previous questionnaire about sex.[15] In Bible-belt West Virginia, high school officials did not dare offer sex education courses, but on the CBS Morning News they boasted about their course on death.[16] All in all, some commentators wryly pointed out, this public obsession had an almost prurient quality to it, as if death had joined the erotic revolution of the sixties.[17]

Why this vogue? The obvious explanation, one would think, was the fear produced by the unprecedented destruction of human life during the mid-twentieth century. World War II, climaxing in the two atomic bombs dropped on Japan; the Holocaust; the Korean War; and the long war in Vietnam: together they form a grim litany. The primitive "fear of irrational death," wrote editor Norman Cousins a week after the Hiroshima blast, "has become intensified, magnified. It has burst out of the subconscious and into the conscious. . . ."[18] Twenty years later a religion professor at Emory University explained that he had created a course on dying because "the Vietnam War brought death home to us. . . ."[19]

In fact, however, there is only a tenuous linkage between these morbid events and the public's obsession with death. Contrary to the claim by Cousins and many others after him, most Americans—according to opinion polls in the 1940s and 1950s—did not feel afraid of nuclear destruction. Most even welcomed the invention of the A-bomb.[20] "What is your biggest worry?" the pollsters asked. The high cost of living, responded 45 percent of the public. Less than 22 percent cited the threat of war.[21] Only in the late sixties, at the height of the Vietnam War, did the anxiety level rise to notable levels, when 50 percent said they thought "often" about the threat of war.[22]

In any case, public death and personal death are quite different concerns. While 50 percent of Americans thought often about the threat of war, only 32 percent thought often about their own mortality or that of someone close to them. When *Psychology Today*'s readers were asked in 1971 how much the possibility of nuclear destruction had influenced their attitudes toward death, half said "not at all" or "very little."[23]

Even more to the point, public death was unrelated to the dilemma faced by the Wertenbakers or the Quinlans: how to depart life on one's own terms. The controversy over the right to "die with dignity" emerged not from what took place in Hiroshima or Vietnam but from what was happening inside hospital intensive care units. Modern medicine produced modern dying: a prolonged process rather than a distinct event, which thereby made the very definition of death ambiguous and subjective.

AMERICANS in the early nineteenth century were familiar with death in ways that we are not. It came often, struck the young, the middle-aged, and the old, and could not be deterred. As an Alabama schoolboy wrote in his penmanship book in 1852, "Remember this life is not long," and bluntly, "remember you must die."[24] In 1850 in Massachusetts (the only state for which we have mortality data at that time) the average newborn would live to the age of thirty-nine. In the entire country in 1900, men or women could expect to live only to forty-seven.[25] But these averages conceal how indiscriminately death hit. While many Americans lived to a ripe age, as tombstones testify, many others succumbed early along the way.

Periodic epidemics of cholera, yellow fever, and diphtheria were frightening. Consumption, or tuberculosis, was the century's largest single killer. "A family as numerous as ours," the Reverend Lyman Beecher wrote to his son in 1819, "is a broad mark for the arrows of Death." For mothers in childbirth there was puerperal infection, and for infants a host of lethal ailments. "I was not any disappointed when we heard of the death of little Emma," farm woman Anna Pierce wrote to her daughter, who had lost an infant. "I was very sure that I would hear of the death of some one of those dear little ones. . . ."[26] The odds of dying were familiar, and so was the physical actuality. A young Maryland store clerk tended a friend in September 1834, sitting for several nights in a row at the deathbed until the end came at last, shortly before midnight. "I then shaved and washed him, & Marker assisted me in dressing him (*he died hard*)." He performed the same vigil for another friend two months later and yet again the next month for a cousin.[27]

To ease the passage through terminal illness, the best that nineteenth-century Americans could receive from doctors was doses of opium or other painkilling narcotics, along with careful diagnoses and compassionate bedside visits. Patients relied more heavily on care by family members and on their religious faith. Building on the medieval model of the *ars moriendi* (art of dying),

Victorian Protestants hoped for a "good" or "beautiful" death in which the dying person achieved spiritual peace. As Lyman Beecher's first wife was dying of consumption, she recounted to gathered family and friends the blessings of her life and her expectations of heaven. It was "a most moving scene to see eight little children weeping around the bed of a dying mother," wrote a neighbor, but "very cheering to see how God could take away the sting of death, and give such a victory over the grave."[28] To modern ears, such sentiments may sound false—at best a pious cliché—but they expressed a sincere faith among all classes. After their mother died in rural Indiana, for example, John and Rachel Ricketts wrote to a brother: "I feel gratified to inform you that she left the wourld in the triumfs of faith, in her dying moments Jesse and myself Sung a Cupple of favorite humns and She Slapt her hands and shouted give glory to god, and retained her senses while she had breath, which gave us all a great deel of Satisfaction to See her happy."[29] The Victorian deathbed scenes of Little Nell and Little Eva were not simply fiction.

By the twentieth century, however, secular values and medical science were shouldering aside religion. Patients were becoming less concerned with their spiritual state and more anxious to reduce their physical suffering. Physicians, meanwhile, were acquiring the tools to "perform miracles." The identification of the tubercle bacillus enabled them to diagnose (though not cure) consumption. By midcentury, antibiotics cured previously fatal infections. Radiation and chemotherapy attacked cancers. Dialysis prevented death from kidney failure, and cardiopulmonary resuscitation (CPR) overcame cardiac arrest.[30] Whereas the average newborn in 1900 lived forty-seven years, his or her grandchild born in 1970 could expect to live seventy-one years.[31]

But this progress also had unfortunate consequences for patients and their families. With prolonged life came prolonged dying. Instead of succumbing to acute infection or trauma, most people were dying at the end of chronic illness. By the 1980s half of those who died had a disease that had been diagnosed at least twenty-nine months before. As journalist Stewart Alsop ruefully remarked in a posthumous memoir of his two years of treatment for leukemia, "in time one becomes accustomed to living with Uncle Thanatos."[32] The event of death was being transformed into the process of dying.

And as modern medical technology prolonged that process, it often prolonged suffering. Consider kidney and heart transplantation. From one perspective this technique abruptly revised our presumption of mortality by demonstrating that so-called vital organs, however indispensable, were also replaceable. "A surgical miracle," the media exclaimed in 1955 after the first kidney transplant.[33] Even greater excitement—indeed, worldwide awe—greeted South African Dr. Christiaan Barnard in 1967 after he replaced a patient's failing heart with that of a young accident victim. A feat equal to climbing Mount Everest, journalists called it, the "miracle in Cape Town." Barnard's face appeared on the cover of *Time*, and he appeared in person on "Face the Nation" and the "Today" show.[34]

But the miracles cast a shadow. One-third of the first heart-transplant patients survived no longer than three months, and the others often suffered various ailments as their bodies tried to reject the stranger's heart.[35] Thirty-year-old Chuck McCracken—a diabetic gone blind, with thyroid problems and paralyzed legs—chose to end dialysis in order to "spare my family the agony of watching their husband and father deteriorate into a vegetable." Eighty-one days later he died.[36] Chemotherapy and radiation granted extra months or years to cancer patients by attacking their bodies but they also caused hair loss, bouts of nausea, fatigue. While being treated for leukemia, thirty-four-year-old poet Ted Rosenthal wrote:

O people, you are dying! Live while you can.
What can I say?
The blackbirds blow the bush.
Get glass in your feet if you must, but take off the shoes.
O heed me. There is pain all over.
There is continual suffering, puking and coughing.

Don't wait on it. It is stalking you.
Tear ass up the mountainside, duck into the mist.[37]

"Halfway technology" was Lewis Thomas's term for techniques like
these, which treat a disease without knowing how to cure it. To say
it more grimly, they replace one chronic illness with another.[38]

Long before Karen Ann Quinlan lay in St. Clare's ICU, Americans were seeing the ambiguities of medical progress. More
choice but therefore more responsibility and doubt. As they placed
their faith in the power of science, they forfeited the consolation
of accepting God's will. Longer life but not necessarily more gratification. Instead of dying at home surrounded by loved ones,
three-fourths of Americans spent, on the average, eighty days of
their last year of life in a hospital or nursing home, often tethered
to bottles and machines. Death no longer was beautiful or good. It
had become the process of dying, fraught with the confusions of
modern culture.[39]

THE AMBIGUITY multiplied as people pondered not only when
life was no longer worth living but when exactly a patient ceased to
be alive. How much of a person needed to have stopped functioning before he or she was dead? Traditionally doctors had used the
criterion of heart and lungs, feeling for a pulse and holding a mirror to the mouth. Cardiopulmonary resuscitation and the respirator jeopardized this age-old standard, however, because doctors
could keep someone's heart and lungs pumping long after his or
her brain had ceased to function. Unresponsive, in a vegetative
state, showing no signs of the personality that used to inhabit this
body: in what sense was this patient alive? No matter which "vital
signs" were being reported by the dials and beeps of the ICU machines, hadn't she slid beyond the boundary of what we call "life"
into some zone of suspension with no meaning for her, her family
and friends, her doctors . . . for anyone but the machines? These
were the questions that Father Trapasso and other theologians discussed in terms of "the soul," and philosophers as "the mind-body

problem," and bioethicists as "the quality of life." For physicians, on the other hand, these approaches were all too metaphysical and subjective. Doctors did not wish to "play God" on these terms. To mark the point of death along the continuum of dying, they needed behavioral, objective categories.

In 1968 an ad hoc committee of ten Harvard physicians (plus one law professor, one theologian, and one historian of science) responded by formulating a criterion of "brain death." To put it simply, their criterion shifted the locus of death from heart and lungs upward to the brain. If a patient exhibited (1) unreceptivity and unresponsivity, (2) no movements or breathing, and (3) no reflexes, and if there were two flat EEG readings over a twenty-four-hour period, then a physician was justified, medically and morally, in considering the patient dead and discontinuing the respirator.

The Harvard committee hoped to anchor the definition of death in physical rather than metaphysical criteria—holding a mirror to the brain, one might say. It also sought to preserve doctors' exclusive authority, recommending that a physician consult his colleagues before taking final action, but merely "inform" the patient's family. "It is unsound and undesirable to force the family to make the decision."[40] As it turned out, the committee failed in both its aims. The standards for determining death had consequences that reverberated beyond the hospital to the society around it. Ironically the same technological progress that had expanded doctors' power to fend off death also increased their vulnerability to intervention from outsiders. Judges, legislators, bioethicists, and ultimately the patients themselves wanted a voice.

When death had been a matter of heart-and-lungs failure there had been little need for rulings by judges. When the definition of death became ambiguous, relatives of deceased patients began taking doctors to court for homicide. The "trigger" for lawsuits was heart transplantation, or to put it more brazenly, "organ snatching." There was the case of a fifty-six-year-old black laborer in Richmond, Virginia, for example, which stirred national consternation. Bruce Tucker had been working for an egg-packing plant for some twenty-five years. Late on a Friday afternoon in May

1968 he was sitting at a local gas station, talking and drinking with a friend. When he tried to get to his feet, he fell and struck his head on the concrete. An ambulance took him to the Medical College of Virginia where doctors operated to relieve brain hemorrhaging and swelling. The next morning they put him on a respirator. By then Tucker's prognosis was so grim that the deputy state medical examiner told Dr. David Hume (chief of surgery and head of a world-renowned heart transplant team) to locate Tucker's family for permission to use his organs for transplantation. Shortly before noon a neurologist ran an EEG and after twenty-five minutes declared that, although heartbeat and blood pressure were strong, Tucker's brain was dead. Dr. Hume telephoned the police, but as of 2:30 they still hadn't reached any next of kin. An hour later Tucker was taken to the operating room, the respirator was turned off, and within five minutes he was pronounced dead. Hume immediately removed the heart and prepared to implant it into Joseph Klett, Jr., a retired white purchasing agent who was being treated in the hospital.

It had all been done with unseemly, not to say suspicious, haste. After all, Tucker's wallet contained the business card and phone number of his brother William, who was working in a shoe-repair shop fifteen blocks away. In addition, Virginia law required that an unclaimed body be held for twenty-four hours, to permit location of kin, before being donated to a hospital or medical school. These ugly features were overshadowed, though, by a more ominous question. If Tucker's heart was beating, his lungs breathing (with mechanical assistance), and his blood pressure and body temperature holding, wasn't he still alive when the doctors turned off the respirator? His brother filed a suit for "wrongful death" and was represented in court by State Senator Douglas Wilder (later the first black governor of Virginia).

At the trial, physicians and a professor of medical ethics claimed that when cerebral function has ceased, a patient should be considered dead even though other bodily functions continue. In response, Wilder cited Virginia law, which defined death in traditional terms: the cessation of pulse and breathing. In his turn, the judge instructed the jury that they could use either the medical or the legal definition. It took them only seventy-seven minutes to render a verdict in favor of the transplant surgeons. "It was clearly proved," one juror explained, "a man . . . cannot live without a functioning brain." But the decision didn't satisfy Bruce Tucker's brother. "There's nothing they can say to make me believe they didn't kill him."[41]

Nor did it prevent surgeons in Georgia, California, and elsewhere from being taken to court on murder charges after transplanting organs. When is a person dead? Physicians insisted that the definition of death was a professional question, one that they alone could answer, but they faced a growing number of challengers. Not only patients' next of kin. Also bioethicists, who argued that modern dying had more than physiological implications. They said it raised moral questions (who should decide: doctor, court, or patient?) and metaphysical questions (when has a patient lost his identity?). The uncertainty "has scared hell out of doctors and coroners," said a California medical administrator.[42]

Judicial rulings were piecemeal, inconsistent, and unpredictable, varying according to particular judges or juries. In an effort to create consistency, state legislatures stepped in and devised statutory definitions of death. But they too produced confusion. The Kansas law in 1970, for example, which was the first in the nation, contained not one definition but two: brain and also heart/lung function. Physicians were to use the brain-death criterion when taking organs for transplantation, and otherwise use the traditional criterion. But these options muddled the meaning of death. Depending on what was to be done with the body, a patient would be treated as either dead or alive.[43] Subsequent laws in other states were somewhat better, but not much. Individually they contained vague or contradictory language; collectively they were a patchwork.[44]

The American Medical Association (AMA) continued to demand that physicians, not legislatures, determine death, but that idea seemed increasingly obsolete. Finally the medical leaders decided that if they couldn't be autonomous, at least they could have a coherent criterion of death. In 1980 the AMA joined the American Bar Association and the National Conference of Commissioners on Uniform State Laws in advising a commission appointed by President Carter—a kind of summit conference of professional and public authorities. After a year of deliberations, the president's commission drafted the Uniform Determination of Death Act, which stated that a person was dead when his heart and lungs *or* his brain—his *whole* brain—had irreversibly ceased functioning.[45]

The genie could not be put back into the bottle, though. The meaning of modern death was inescapably subjective, therefore debatable. Just as the Harvard ad hoc committee could not confine the definition to purely medical terms, other authorities couldn't confine it to their terms. Adding brain death to the traditional definition did not close the debate but joined one that bioethicists had been waging since the early 1970s. At issue was the same question: how much of an individual has to die before he or she is dead? Now, though, the locus of dispute had moved from heart/lung versus brain to *within* the brain: whole versus higher brain. When a patient had suffered irreversible damage to the neocortex but remained able to breathe and integrate bodily functions, should he or she be considered alive? In that case, death would be declared only after the brain stem—that is, the whole brain—ceased to function. Or was *consciousness* the crucial criterion of life? That is, when the patient had lost the capacity to remember, feel, reason, and interact with others, we would consider him or her essentially dead.

As soon as consciousness became an issue, in the late 1960s, the terms of the discussion were radically transformed. Biological criteria competed with psychological ones: body versus mind. The subjectivity that physicians and legislators had been trying to exclude now surged back in doubled form. Authorities were now making subjective (rather than objective) judgments of death, and they were doing so according to what the patient was experiencing: the patient as mental subject rather than physical object. Death was a loss not simply of bodily functions but of personal identity.

The Quinlan case dramatized the controversy with disturbing clarity. Even though she lay in a persistent vegetative state, her doctors worked to preserve her life. Her parents, on the other hand, believed she had lost the qualities that had constituted the daughter they loved. They wanted to release her, the metaphysical Karen, from the body. Patient was redefined as person.[46]

This redefinition held radical implications not only for how a patient was to be treated but who was to choose the treatment. For if the criteria of death included consciousness, or the patient's subjectivity, then the subject herself should be heard from—either firsthand or, if incompetent, via directives written beforehand or reported by family members. Decision-making would thus expand beyond doctors. Authority would be redistributed. In political terms, the patient would become a citizen of the medical republic, claiming the right to die.

AS THE SUBJECTIVITY of death brought the patient more fully into the treatment process, it did the same for the physician. He—and almost always it was a he—was being asked to confer with the patient, to consider not simply the etiology but the experience . . . to join the process of dying with all its ambiguities. For most doctors, that was a disquieting prospect.

In 1972 JoAnn Kelley Smith's longtime internist (and fellow Christian) sat beside her bed to report the test results. "Tears were freely running down his face," she recalled. "They rolled down the cheeks and off the end of his nose—like a little boy who can't admit to emotion so just lets the tears flow unchecked. He told me that the scan revealed a liver studded with cancer tumors. Then he told me, 'We're in the fourth quarter of the game, and there is no way we can win.'"[47]

Smith's physician was acting untypically, not only by weeping but by informing her of her condition. According to various surveys during the 1950s and 1960s, the vast majority of doctors never or at best "sometimes" informed patients with incurable cancer. Silence was for the patients' own good, they claimed. Why add dread and hopelessness to the pain? Moreover, the moment of death could never be exactly predicted: a month, a year, who knew? All in all, doctors argued, patients and their families would rather not hear a death sentence.[48]

On the contrary, surveys made clear that most patients did want to be informed if they were dying. And a few medical spokesmen urged their colleagues to give dying patients the chance to come to terms with their lives.[49] But surveys and admonishments didn't change doctors' behavior, because silence also suited their own needs. Bad news is harder to deliver. Professors avoid telling a graduate student he is in academic jeopardy until it's too late. Bosses delegate someone to fire an employee or they send a pink slip. Physicians have all the more reason to dread telling a patient he is dying. For one thing, they thereby acknowledge their own impotence, healers unable to heal. "Every death corresponds to a failure" was the adage they remember from medical school. When one of Dr. Michael DeBakey's patients died on his operating table, he would cancel the rest of the day's schedule, lock himself inside his office, and brood.[50]

A physician wanted to avoid delivering a message of failure ("the fourth quarter and no way we can win") for fear of the feelings it would arouse in the patient but also inside himself ("like a little boy who can't admit to emotion so just lets the tears flow unchecked"). "I must admit," said a family physician from Michigan, "that when the anxiety, the fear provoked within me as the physician becomes too great, it's very, very comfortable to deal with the dying process on a technical level. Because then there is no real involvement. There have been times when I haven't been able to cope with an individual patient in a terminal situation, and in a cowardly way, I have run to the stereotyped role of myself as a scientist and technical expert, who doesn't concern himself with people's feelings."[51] He was not alone. A poignantly telling pattern occurred midway during a survey of Detroit doctors in 1972. When they discovered the survey was about death, sixty of seventy-three broke off the interview.[52] Indeed, according to at least one study, physicians were *more* fearful of death than either healthy persons or patients.[53] Medical school taught them how to treat ills of the body, not the psyche. The intangible realm—wounds of the spirit, intimations of mortality—belonged to chaplains, psychiatrists, social workers, and maybe nurses.[54]

If few doctors told patients they were dying, fewer still discussed the possibility of hastening death. Euthanasia was not only a touchy subject, it was a crime. Privately, however, they faced the issue every time they treated a terminally ill patient. If we measure their interest in "the right to die with dignity" by the annual number of medical articles on the topic, it's clear that concern rose dramatically during the 1960s.[55] "[Your] editorial has struck a responsive chord," Dr. Ronald Andree wrote to *Science* in 1970. "As anesthesiologists intimately concerned with the preservation of life in a hospital intensive care milieu, my colleagues and I are frequently plagued by uncomfortable introspections concerning the quality of life we preserve."[56]

A more direct measure emerged in various opinion surveys. As a result of those "uncomfortable introspections," between 60 and 80 percent of physicians during the 1960s performed passive euthanasia—that is, let patients die by withholding or withdrawing treatment.[57] Nurses advocated passive euthanasia even more strongly. They were the ones, after all, who spent more time with terminal patients and witnessed the indignities of those last days and nights.[58]

And there was the most overt sign: the "DNR" written on charts of certain patients, which all hospital staff understood to mean "Do Not Resuscitate."[59]

Nevertheless a unilateral decision to let a patient die is not the same as granting "the right to die." In fact, it is the antithesis. Unless physicians conferred with patients and families about treatment, or recognized patients' prior wishes (so-called "living wills"), they were denying the right to participate in decisions. Earlier in the century, this had not been an issue because Americans gratefully deferred to medical authority. The tireless, compassionate family doctor—Will Kennicott in Sinclair Lewis's *Main Street*, or Marcus Welby on television—knew best and did good. Even though he couldn't cure many diseases—perhaps *because* he couldn't, he had a personal relationship with his patients. An elderly physician recalled in the 1980s that he had been trained "to cure now and then, to help often, to comfort always."[60]

But as technology grew, the family doctor and house calls gave way to specialists and hospital treatment. By the 1950s only one of ten contacts with doctors took place in patients' homes. All but 4 percent of births occurred in hospitals. And when patients did visit one of the dwindling number of family doctors, the consultation was brisk—in 1984 lasting an average of eleven minutes. Still, public esteem remained high. According to a common metaphor, the modern physician was "playing God" in the best sense, by performing miracles.[61] As late as 1972, 70 percent of the forty thousand *Life* readers who answered a questionnaire rated their medical treatment good or excellent and said their doctor cared about them personally.[62]

But like *Life* itself, which had fossilized into a monthly magazine, those attitudes were quaint. During the late sixties popular feelings toward doctors turned more and more sour, suspicious, adversarial. The phrase "playing God" acquired a hostile meaning: technicians appropriating the power to prolong or end people's lives.[63] A diffuse rebellion against medical dictatorship was under way. Partly spiritual and partly secular, this rebellion would change what Americans thought and did about dying.

JOHN CARMODY, a professor of comparative religion and a former priest, was deeply upset as he tended his dying father in a Catholic hospital. The condescending nurses, the smug and businesslike doctors, the Muzak, the visitors and aides who babbled on and on about flowers, food, humidity. . . . "No one seems able to shut up, let alone contemplate, let alone pray. No, in that hospital death is a physiological problem and a cultural embarrassment. The modern hospital is the greatest enemy of meaningful death."[64] Carmody was "radicalized" by this experience, he told readers of the *Christian Century* in 1974. In the spirit of antiwar and civil rights activists, he wanted to overhaul the atmosphere surrounding terminal patients.

In fact that challenge was already well under way, led by a young Swiss-born psychiatrist named Elisabeth Kübler-Ross. She began her rebellion unwittingly. In 1965, shortly after starting work at a Chicago hospital, Kübler-Ross agreed to help four theology students do research on the experience of dying. Their plan was to interview terminally ill patients, although they wondered whether such patients would be willing to talk. The first surprise was that it was physicians and nurses who were unwilling. "Let me think about this," they said politely. Or in hostile tones: "Why would you inflict such a trauma upon someone!" When Kübler-Ross and her students finally circumvented these obstacles and reached the patients' bedsides, they had their second surprise. The patients were eager to express their feelings, desperately grateful to break through the doctors' and relatives' conspiracy of euphemisms. They needed empathy as much as painkillers (and more than false cheer) to help them make their way out of life. As Kübler-Ross discovered after interviewing two hundred patients, they typically went through a series of five attitudes: initial denial (not me) followed by anger (why me?), then bargaining (not now), depression (it's no use), and, finally, acceptance.[65] The dying were teaching her. And in the seminar she established at the hospital, they taught physicians, nurses, orderlies, and chaplains.

When *Life* magazine featured her in 1969, she began to attract nationwide attention. Her book *On Death and Dying* was issued in paperback and each year it sold more copies than the year before— by 1976 a total of a million-plus. She was traveling hundreds of thousands of miles a year as a star on the lecture circuit and received 3,000 letters a month. By 1973, 70 hospitals had established seminars on dying. When 150,000 nurses were asked to discuss their attitudes toward death, they named Kübler-Ross as their greatest influence. Readers of *Ladies' Home Journal* chose her as "woman of the year" in 1977 and, three years later, as one of 11 "women of the decade." "[N]o other single person," exclaimed a journalist, "has so dramatically turned around a whole generation of opinion-makers on a single subject."[66]

Kübler-Ross's abrupt celebrity had to do with more than what was happening inside hospitals. She was benefiting from developments in the culture at large. A quest for personal fulfillment was under way. The sixties counterculture of hippies, be-ins, and drug trips had bloomed quickly and withered just as quickly. It had left a legacy, though, of an alternative culture that was less flamboyant but more widespread and effective, touching not only the young but the middle-aged, radical as well as mainstream. During the seventies a remarkable number of Americans sought salvation in various guises. Fifty million found it in evangelical or charismatic Christianity, creating a new Great Awakening. By 1978 two of five adults claimed to be "born again" (as compared with 24 percent in 1963).

Others, meanwhile, adopted secular doctrines. Psychotherapy was booming, not in the traditional one-on-one analytic style but in encounter groups, T-groups, weekend marathons. This "human potential movement" located grace in the self rather than in a higher Being. At heart, though, it shared the same goal as the evangelical movements: to replace anxiety, guilt, and alienation with a sense of being "together" . . . with others and inside one's self.[67] The same motivations were at work in innumerable self-help groups, which followed the model of Alcoholics Anonymous in enabling people to overcome adversity. Parents Without Partners, for example, Gay Fathers, Overeaters Anonymous, Synanon (for drug addicts), to name a few. Some of these groups had a Christian rubric, most did not, but they all believed in what one might call social sacredness: namely, looking inward as well as outward, and valuing people as ends rather than means.[68]

In worldly form these were the motivations propelling the quest for bodily fulfillment. More Americans were hiking, biking, jogging, running marathons. They were "working out" and playing racquetball. Millions stopped smoking, swallowed vitamins, drank wine instead of liquor, ate soyburgers instead of hamburgers, and shopped at organic-food stores. In a private version of the ecology movement, they tried to restore the natural equilibrium of their bodies.

At this point one might be wondering how Kübler-Ross fits in with these efforts at well-being. Death and health certainly seem at odds. But on deeper analysis we see that her therapeutics of dying contained the same two principles as those other therapies: experiential process and self-help. The runners' bodies were rejuvenating whereas the patients' bodies were degenerating, but all were part of a natural process. They simply occupied different points along the route to the finish line. For people who suffered handicaps, whether alcoholism or abusive parents or terminal cancer, these therapies offered ways to help them help themselves: the twelve-step program of AA and OA (Overeaters Anonymous), the five-stage program of Kübler-Ross.[69] Regardless of differences in detail, all encouraged individual expression, a grassroots rather than a top-down approach.

And then there was the shared sense of spirituality. "We admitted we were powerless over alcohol": so reads the first step of AA. "Let me not pray to be sheltered from dangers but to be fearless in facing them." So reads the first of the epigraphs from Rabindranath Tagore with which Kübler-Ross opened each chapter of her book. They suggest the spiritual quality permeating all these self-help approaches, even the most apparently worldly. "Our running begins to keep our bodies fit . . . ," Joel Henning explained in his thoughtful book on *Holistic Running*, "but it also progresses through stages of deeper meaning, to expand our self-awareness, to become a holistic aspect of our lives. It is indeed a form of worship, an attempt to find God, a means to the transcendent."[70] (Henning prescribed a six-step program.) For people lying on their deathbeds, Kübler-Ross's therapy offered a means to reach the state of acceptance, beyond the struggle with "fate," where they peacefully awaited whatever death would bring. Like a priest, she performed last rites. No wonder one journalist characterized her as "a certain kind of saint—in this case a thoroughly secular saint, let it be said."[71]

Success was treacherous, though. In the same way that the

counterculture was all too easily corrupted by feel-good consumerism, "dying with dignity" proved susceptible to being translated into self-indulgence. On the dust jacket of Stanley Keleman's *Living Your Dying* (1974), for example, one reads: "Is there a person alive who wouldn't like to go to their dying full of excitement, without fear and without morbidity. This book tells you how."[72] In the "Tempo" section of the *Chicago Tribune*, an article on "Facing Death's Reality Can Make Life Easier" was wedged between articles on pet insurance and sexual impotence. Marjorie McClay's book explained how *To Die with Style!*[73] These authors echoed the kind of cheeriness that Carmody had found so repugnant in the hospital where his father lay dying. While ostensibly confronting death, they performed a smiling version of denial. Kübler-Ross herself contributed to this process when she began lecturing and writing about life after death and about her encounters with materialized spirits.[74]

In the nineteenth century a "good death" meant one in which the person endured suffering or even welcomed it as a test of fitness for heaven. In twentieth-century consumer capitalism it meant painlessness or gratification, a quick fix. How does one distinguish self-actualization from narcissism? That ambiguity of modern American life also extended to modern dying.[75]

PICTURE THE right-to-die movement as a river emerging at midcentury from the site of medical technology, then surging in the late sixties as it is fed by two powerful social forces, the therapeutic human-potential movement and the equal-rights movements for blacks and women. The first of these forces—"death with dignity"—emphasized the personal, while the second—"the right to die"—emphasized the political. But we can't draw a firm line between the two, any more than we can draw a line on water. To borrow the feminists' slogan, the personal is the political. As death evolved from event to process, its definition became increasingly personalized. First, physicians shifted the site from heart and lungs to brain, opening the way for consciousness or personhood as the criterion of having died. Then Kübler-Ross focused on the dying patient's state of mind instead of body. At the same time a growing majority of the public were claiming the power to decide for themselves when life was no longer worth living. In the early 1970s (before the *Quinlan* case), 62 percent of Americans (and 82 percent of Californians) agreed that an incurably ill patient should have the right to refuse life-prolonging treatment.[76] "The right to choose death . . . ," one journalist announced, "is not only the next liberation, but the last human right."[77] With amazing speed, a medical civil rights movement was cutting across the cultural landscape.

The civil rights movement of the fifties and sixties had moved at the grass roots as well as in the courts, in streets and colleges and churches, mobilizing ordinary men and women to defy racism. The New Left had organized poor people in Northern cities and students on college campuses to achieve social justice. And the antiwar movement had taken direct action against the most powerful institution of all, the federal government. Needless to say, the vast majority of Americans were not radicals. But as a consequence of these protest movements, and even more as a consequence of the Kennedy assassination and the seemingly futile war in Vietnam and the Watergate scandals, Americans steadily lost confidence in their institutions. The presidency, Congress, the military, higher education, big business: between 1965 and 1973 each slid precipitously in opinion poll ratings, earning confidence from no more than 44 percent of respondents. The church fared better, but in 1977 only 64 percent expressed a "great deal" or "quite a lot" of confidence in organized religion.

This tide of disaffection reached the medical realm as well. To be sure, medicine outranked all other institutions, but it too was losing public esteem (from 72 to 57 percent during 1965–1973).[78] Fifty-six percent of Americans in 1976 thought doctors had "high" or "very high" ethical standards (more than any other occupation), but that meant 44 percent did not think so.[79] This suspicion had been growing for a long time, bred by the depersonalization of health care. In the medical historian David Rothman's apt phrase, doctors became "strangers at the bedside" and hospitals became alienating institutions. Whereas critics before World War II had complained about health care being too expensive, in the 1960s and 1970s they complained about physicians being mercenary and callous. One symptom of the new iconoclasm was the so-called "malpractice crisis." According to one estimate, 90 percent of all malpractice suits in American history were filed between 1965 and 1977.[80] Taking the gods to court!

Then came the women's movement. All at once this demystification gathered speed and acquired a political analysis. During the summer of 1969 eleven women in Boston met to discuss their discontents with their doctors. Out of this consciousness-raising they decided to do research on women's bodies, which in turn became a course they taught to other women in the area, which in turn became a book. *Our Bodies, Ourselves* quickly found its way into the hands of hundreds of thousands of women eager to learn more about nutrition, birth control, menopause, vaginal infections, and other topics. It served as a self-help manual, but more significantly it delivered a message about power and gender. Physicians were men who had been trained to act omnisciently, the authors argued, while women had been socialized to defer to physicians' judgments. The fact was, doctors often misdiagnosed female maladies, prescribed needless or dangerous treatments, and deprecated women's problems as psychosomatic. As for questions of sexuality, the ob/gyn couldn't help bringing a masculine prejudice. "Doctors are not gods but human beings. . . ." Once women recognized this fact, they should resist the "imperialism of knowledge" and claim their rights in the doctor-patient relationship.[81]

You shall know the truth and the truth shall set you free. When applied to women's health the familiar adage acquired a novel dimension, because the authors were promoting body knowledge. Originally they had titled their book *Women and Their Bodies*, then more personally *Women and Our Bodies*, and finally *Our Bodies, Ourselves*. The strategy against medical paternalism was for women to take ownership of their bodies.[82] Quite literally, that is what Carol Downer and Lorraine Rothman did when they began meeting with feminists around Los Angeles and, with flashlight, speculum, and mirror in hand, viewed one another's cervixes. For the first time they were seeing—knowing—the most intimate part of themselves. That little opening is the os, they explained. Do you notice the different color of this cervix? Red, because she's pregnant. If you see a milky white area, that's a yeast infection. "I hesitate to use the word 'revolutionary,'" Ellen Frankfort declared in an influential *Village Voice* article, "but no other word seems accurate. . . . It was a little like having a blind person see for the first time. . . ."[83] This kind of introspection was the physical equivalent of the emotional introspection that Kübler-Ross encouraged in patients. By no coincidence, both approaches were initiated by women and, not surprisingly, both aroused hostility among doctors. Self-help threatened the medical patriarchy. As one woman recalled, "Telling [her ob/gyn] that I had been examining myself for some time with a plastic speculum, I explained that that was why I wanted to watch. Incredulous, he then looked at me as if I were a rare species of caterpillar. Like a little boy whose toy had been taken away, he said, 'You have no business doing that!'"[84]

Downer and Rothman went on to demonstrate cervical self-examination in Wichita, Kansas; New Haven, Connecticut; and twenty-five other communities. "Vaginal politics" was Ellen Frankfort's label for what health feminists were doing. Returning home, Downer and Rothman created the Los Angeles Feminist Women's Health Center, which spawned all-female gynecological clinics in cities and towns from Alaska to Florida, along with rape-crisis centers, gay/lesbian centers, abortion counseling services, and, simply, "women's resource centers."[85]

The feminists were performing collectively what other Americans had been expressing individually in opinion polls and malpractice suits. Soon patient rights groups and publications were proliferating almost everywhere one looked. The Health-Activation Network at Georgetown University provided a clearinghouse for people seeking self-care classes, and by 1978 had developed a network in 37 states. A center in New York City created a free phone number for listening to any of 120 tapes on various diseases and procedures. Books appeared with titles such as *Talk Back to Your Doctor* and *The Active Patient's Guide to Better Medical Care*. Harvard Medical School published a Health Letter for nonspecialist readers. *Better Homes and Gardens* ran a health column.[86] A populist rebellion against medical patriarchy was under way.

Doctors may have hoped to ignore it or repress it, but the tide was too powerful. So they chose, as they had in the struggle over Medicare, to concede details while preserving the essential, which was professional autonomy. The American Hospital Association in 1973 adopted a Patient Bill of Rights. First among the twelve points was the right to "considerate and respectful care." Other points promised confidentiality of a patient's medical records, pledged to disclose if therapies were experimental, and required doctors to provide information in terms that a reasonable patient could understand. These were essentially matters of etiquette, which hospitals should have been doing all along. As one doctor caustically remarked, this was an instance of "the thief lecturing his victim on self-protection." [87]

The choice of treatment, by contrast, was a matter of power. The Patient Bill of Rights also said that a patient has the right to refuse treatment "to the extent permitted by law." Did that right extend to the ultimate form of treatment, namely life-prolonging treatment? For years most physicians had opposed advance directives, or "living wills," as an infringement on their professional authority. They had let hopelessly ill patients die, but that decision had been theirs alone. Now they performed a strategic retreat. The AMA resolved that when death was inevitable, a patient and/or family could decide, with the approval of family physicians, to withdraw extraordinary treatment.[88]

Why this enormous concession? The health rights movements were one reason, but at least as compelling a reason was the fear that legislatures and courts would step in. Twenty-six states already had enacted statutes defining death, for example, and the American Bar Association was proposing a model statute.[89] As of 1975 no state had passed laws endorsing living wills, but bills had been introduced (and defeated) in Florida and California.[90] And Senator Frank Church had turned a favorable spotlight on "death with dignity" in two days of subcommittee hearings.[91] Better to share some authority with patients, medical leaders decided, than be governed by statutes or judicial edicts. As of 1974, according to a (rather unreliable) survey by *Medical Opinion*, 79 percent of physicians agreed that, before illness struck, "people have a right to choose how they die."[92]

There is an interesting paradox here. Treatment was more than ever a matter of arcane technology and evidence, but at the same time medical experts were having to cope with laypersons trespassing on their jurisdiction. Psychologists, bioethicists, and legislators were trying to reshape health care. Closer at hand, patients were claiming a voice in deciding their own treatment—including the final say-so about dying.

"You and I should take him by force if necessary in an ambulance to the hospital," Dr. Cartier had shouted in 1954 to the wife of cancer-weakened Charles Wertenbaker.

"It's his body, his life, his mind! His pain," she shouted back. "He is a man."

"Stop fussing," Wert said finally.

In the 1950s it was rare for patients to defy their doctors. The Wertenbakers were making their dreadful choices in a social and ideological vacuum. During the late sixties and early seventies the patient rights movement developed, emulating the equal-rights movements for blacks, the poor, and women. More important, death was redefined from an event into a process, from a conclusion into a quandary of choices.

Even though the Wertenbakers were on their own, at least Lael had the reassurance that her husband could speak his intentions and act on them. But what if the patient were unconscious or otherwise incompetent? Then the "right to die" became a deeper quandary. When, if ever, could someone decide that another person's life was no longer worth living? That was the question that Karen Ann Quinlan's parents brought before the New Jersey Superior Court and then appealed to the New Jersey Supreme Court. *In re Quinlan* was the *Brown v. Board of Education* of the right-to-die movement.

3

The Subjectivity of Dying

ONE MORNING in 1973, fifteen-year-old Karen Vikinstad—an A student who swam and ran track—began choking, her tongue hanging out, eyes rolling in their sockets. Before her parents could get her to the hospital, her brain suffered irreparable loss of oxygen. Two years later she was still alive, in a vegetative state. "If I had known two years ago what I know now," her mother said, "I would have pulled every one of those plugs that kept my daughter alive. I wish I had [had] the courage, but I didn't, and what can I do now?"

This is all the *New York Times* reported on September 25, 1975, on page 91 of the suburban edition.[1] Why did this Karen emerge into public view for no longer than a day and then recede, while the other Karen became a celebrity with security guards to shield her from photographers and faith healers?

The obvious answer is that Mrs. Vikinstad did not go to court asking to remove her daughter from the respirator. Similarly, no one beyond Karen Ann Quinlan's family, friends, and hospital staff paid attention during the first six months that she lay comatose. Only when her father filed for guardianship on September 12, 1975, did the media discover her . . . and quickly discover others like her.

Karen Vikinstad, for example. And ten-year-old David Meir, in a coma since being hit by a truck, whose mother disconnected him from a respirator in 1973.[2] And sixteen-year-old Randy Larsen, brain-dead, whose father told the doctors to "go ahead and pull the

74

plug, which wasn't easy. . . ." But Ohio law forbade that, so for three weeks until Randy died, his mother wiped the fluid draining out of his mouth ("the odor was tremendous, you know," she told CBS News. "I would not want any other mother to have to experience that. . . .").[3] There was also a story with a happier outcome. After a car wreck in 1966, homecoming queen Carol Dusold had been comatose, with limbs contorted, her weight dropping to only sixty-five pounds. Terminate life support, the doctors advised, but her devoutly Lutheran mother refused. Four months after the accident, Carol revived. During the next eight years she became rehabilitated, married, and had a son, with only a limp and mildly slurred speech to show for her ordeal.[4]

Until 1975 these and other victims had been surviving for weeks or years without publicity. At the same time popular interest in death and dying was rising. Thus far it had focused on how to define death and on how terminally ill persons might die with dignity. Sooner or later, though, the discussion would move on to the issue of who should decide to remove life support from an incompetent patient. All that was lacking was the appropriate subject. When Joseph Quinlan went to court, he unwittingly stepped into history's spotlight.

But legal controversy wasn't the only factor. If it had been, newly married Judith Ann Debro would have earned more public attention. For three weeks after an automobile accident in October 1975 she lay brain-dead while her husband Gary filed suit in both Missouri and federal courts to have her life-support machine turned off. All this took place at the same time as Judge Muir was pondering how to rule on Quinlan. In legal terms the Debro case was better qualified for a right-to-die decision, because she was brain-dead. But except for one article in the *New York Times*, only St. Louis and Kansas City newspapers covered the story.[5] Why this obscurity? Timing was one reason. Not only had the Quinlans come first, monopolizing media attention, but Mrs. Debro didn't live long enough for interest to build around her. When she died on November 9 (ironically, the same day as Muir's verdict), her husband dropped his appeal.

Even if the Debro case had reached the Missouri Supreme Court, however, it would have lacked another kind of ingredient for celebrity. Thirty-three-year-old Judith could not be cast as "the girl in a coma," cruelly stricken on the verge of womanhood, nor did the childless Debros constitute a family in the traditional sense. They did not fit the conventions of a melodramatic narrative.

The Quinlans, by contrast, had the kinds of qualities the media could use in constructing a sympathetic story of "the right to die." Given the medical and social developments of the preceding decade, the American public was predisposed to welcome that story. *In re Quinlan* was more than a court case; it was a cultural phenomenon.

JOSEPH AND JULIA QUINLAN were ordinary Americans who had extraordinary virtues. Thrust into the limelight, they displayed a modest courage and moral sincerity, which the media translated into almost saintly terms. Although they had given up hope for their daughter's recovery, they visited her at least once a day. "I don't believe I could go to bed without saying anything to her," Julia Quinlan told readers of *Time*. "Just like saying good night, you know, to your other children." [6] At the same time, however, they were seeking to let her die—or rather, as Joseph put it, to place her in the hands of the Lord. He was asking to be his daughter's guardian in order to lose her. That was the agonizing responsibility that modern medicine had imposed on him and on innumerable parents reading about him. As a syndicated columnist wrote after attending the trial: "The poor man, with his obvious sincerity and basic decency, may well go down as one of our modern folk heroes." [7]

Karen herself was no saint but, in her mediated identity, neither was she a sinner. Although she had long ago stopped attending Mass, her parish priest attested that "in her own way I would consider Karen a religious girl." Although she had moved into a bungalow with two young men, no reporter ever suggested any sexual liaison. She may have mixed gin and tonics with a tranquilizer or other drugs, but she did so "mistakenly." A few reports alleged she had been a "pill-popper" and marijuana-user who had become involved with "a counterculture lifestyle" or even with underworld hoodlums. But these allegations receded as abruptly as they appeared.[8] In December the New Jersey attorney general asked a grand jury to investigate whether an "egg-shaped lump" on the back of her head and bruises on her lower body were the result of a beating. But in February he denied any foul play.[9] In other words, her lapses were not sins or crimes; they were mistakes committed out of innocence.

Ultimately readers and viewers of this coming-of-age story were left with the impression of a virtuous young woman who was a little too adventurous for her own good. Twenty-one years old, she was called a girl as often as a woman, sometimes both in the course of a single article. The Associated Press and the *New York Times* referred to Miss Quinlan, but in *Newsweek*, *Time*, and most other publications she was Karen. In headlines as far away as France, the public knew her on a first-name basis. She was a celebrity but not exotic or larger than life. On the contrary, she seemed familiar, a member of everyone's family, in need of rescue.

One has to wonder why the media were so forgiving, especially considering how they treated another young woman in the news at this time, Patty Hearst. Before she was kidnaped in 1974 by left-wing revolutionaries, Hearst had led a life as unremarkable as Quinlan's—except for being the granddaughter of a famous press tycoon and daughter of a millionaire. Unlike Quinlan, there was not the slightest reason to blame her for her plight and every reason to sympathize with her, at least in the beginning of this melodrama. After two months in the hands of the Symbionese Liberation Army, however, she issued a taped message proclaiming a new identity. "I have been given the name Tania after a comrade who fought alongside Che in Bolivia. . . . I know Tania dedicated her life to the people, fighting with total dedication . . . , which I will continue in the oppressed American people's revolution."[10] The innocent girl sounded like an outlaw, a subversive—but then again she might be talking under duress. Captive or convert? A noisy public debate began.

Two weeks later the answer seemed to have been provided by a piece of visual evidence. A surveillance camera in the Hibernia State Bank in San Francisco showed Tania holding a semiautomatic carbine while the SLA performed a robbery. Her arrest in September 1975 (the same month as the Quinlan trial) led to yet more damning evidence. Outside the San Mateo jail, Hearst smiled into the cameras and raised one shackled fist for revolution.

At the trial four months later the defense developed a scenario that, in its essential structure, resembled the one on behalf of the Quinlans: an innocent young woman held captive and violated, in this case by political rather than medical captors. Hearst testified that the kidnapers had kept her blindfolded for two weeks in a closet, sexually molested her, and then threatened her with death unless she joined them. Defense psychiatrists argued that she had been the victim of "coercive persuasion," brainwashed like captive American soldiers in the Korean War. But that theory never displaced the prosecution's version of what happened. Shortly after being kidnaped, they said, Hearst voluntarily took up terrorism because she lacked a clear sense of values. As the hollow daughter of wealth, she consumed SLA propaganda, converted to "Tania," and acted out her resentment toward overbearing parents.

Long before the jury found her guilty of bank robbery and possession of a firearm, the press had already slanted its analysis against her.[11] As happens so often in rape trials, the alleged victim was transformed into an accomplice. Above an article recounting "Travels with Tania," for example, *Newsweek* published a photograph in which Hearst seems plaintive, perhaps scared, in any case sobered as she's being led by the elbow by an unseen attendant. If this image permits a sympathetic response, though, the drawing beside it demands scorn. One half of the face shows a pretty, smiling, coiffed Patty; the Tania half, with its sneer, dangling cigarette, dark eyeglass over a narrowed eye, man's shirt, and uncombed black hair, portrays a girl-gone-bad.[12] Tania personified the social disintegration that a growing portion of Americans were decrying

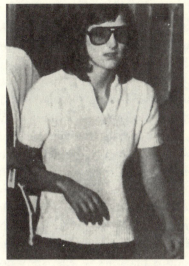

'You must believe that I'm a sweet, innocent, brain-washed victim . . . or else Tania will be forced to . . .'

Patty Hearst and Tania

in the early 1970s: left-wing protest, unmarried sexuality, and feminism.

Quinlan didn't rob a bank and issue revolutionary manifestos. Equally important, the damage to her brain was not psychological and metaphorical—"brainwashing"—but a physiological fact that rendered her incompetent. Unable to take the witness stand, she escaped cross-examination. If Hearst had died in the fire that killed most of the other Symbionese Liberation members, she might have received more sympathy from the media and public. If she had fallen into a coma, gone in mind but not body, she would have received more sympathy yet. That was Quinlan's advantage (if one may be permitted, for a moment, to speak of her disability in such terms). She was an absence, onto whom people could project what they wanted to believe.

A good girl, felled by tragedy. This narrative was promoted not only by the words written and said about Quinlan but even more effectively by the photographs of her. In these visual images she was a presence. A photograph offers what seems to be objective evidence, "the true picture," unmediated except by a camera. But it's a limited truth, because the camera's eye excerpts only a split-second of reality and only from a particular angle. The viewer has to supply the context.[13] Who had Quinlan "really" been? What did she look like now? Available photographs furnished vivid but tantalizingly fragmentary clues. In devising answers, the public inevitably projected their own feelings onto her image.

All in all, only four different black-and-white photographs of Quinlan appeared in the press and on television: as a smiling baby; as a smiling young teenager with a girlfriend; as an older teenager, laughing with another girlfriend; and as a senior in the high school yearbook. At least 90 percent of the time, however, the media reprinted only the last one. Twenty years later it's the one people still recall. She is facing slightly toward her right, unsmiling, looking out into the distance. Her straight dark hair, neatly parted in the center, falls alongside her pale, wide face down to her shoulders. A pretty young woman. A serious person—at least she's not giving the standard yearbook smile. Rather, she wears a serene or composed expression. Perhaps someone with dreams of what she wanted to make of herself—although now we're reading meanings into her lack of expression. It's equally plausible to infer that she was vacuous. But young—that's undeniable—which prompts us to follow her gaze toward an adulthood full of possibility.

This is the photograph that illustrated most news articles. In fact, however, it was three years out of date, Quinlan as she used to look. All photographs, by definition, start becoming historical objects the moment after the shutter closes. The more time passes, the more quaint they seem and the more nostalgia they evoke.[14] In this case the discrepancy between *then* and *now* was more obvious and painful than usual, because the viewer couldn't help juxtaposing this image of a pretty eighteen-year-old woman with the twenty-one-year-old who lay in a vegetative state, folded stiffly upon herself, shrunk to seventy pounds, responding to sound and light but "not feeling pain as we know it." Instead of growing up during those three years, she had regressed into a fetal position and into a pre-infantile mentality. Her life was interrupted at age twenty-one and fixed in a vegetative present-time. And how did she look now? The audience was given one or two sketches derived

Karen at her high
school graduation, 1972

from artists' imaginations, but otherwise they had to fill in the blank on their own. By mentally revising that serene high school image, they became that much more involved in shaping this poignant narrative.[15]

The public would have been more distressed if they had seen the gruesome details that Quinlan's parents and nurses witnessed every day. She was not Sleeping Beauty. When awake, her mouth opened and closed in a series of grimaces, her head swiveled back and forth, and she seemed to be fighting against the respirator tube. During the winter of 1975–1976 her lower jaw began to recede, so that she was biting with her upper teeth into her lower lip, sometimes to the point of bleeding. Dr. Morse brought in an orthodontist who fitted a clear plastic palate into the roof of her mouth to prevent the biting. "Oh God, how Karen fights that," Julia exclaimed. "She hates it, gags on it, tries to spit the thing out."[16] Whatever the doctors claimed, these seemed to be reactions of someone who was feeling pain.

Even without knowing these graphic details, the public expressed an astounding degree of empathy. "Karen is being tortured by medical technology," someone wrote to the *New York Daily News*. "It is her parents' request that the sadism be ended. . . ." [17] Five thousand people wrote directly to the Quinlans during the months after the trial. Many of them said they too had lost loved ones or, worse, were tending relatives on respirators and wished that years ago they had decided to let them die. [18] But those who hadn't gone through the Quinlans' experience were just as likely to identify with them. As the *Milwaukee Journal* declared, "Few people can avoid asking what they would do if she were their daughter, or what they would want if they were she." [19] One amateur poet even felt able to read Karen's mind and speak for her.

> They hold me here
> between two worlds
>> The flesh leaves my hollow bones
>> Even my breath does not belong to me
>
>> I curl into a shape
>> which I remember from another time
>> but here
>> my mother does not nourish me
>> I am sheltered
>> in that secret room
>> Mother?
>> My eyes open and close
>> but they look
>> on another place
>> where something
>> waits for me
>
> Why won't they
> let me go? [20]

The media's narrative of the Quinlan family had personalized modern dying, and that high school yearbook photograph played a large part in the process. "The pretty, solemn face," a bioethicist remarked, "has been staring out from magazine covers, newspapers

The girl in a coma: Stan Hunter's sketch of Karen Ann Quinlan being kept alive on a respirator at St. Clare's Hospital, Denville, New Jersey

and television sets . . . , forcing each American, as no public event ever has before, to see not just the consequences of today's technology, but his own inevitable end."[21]

One can partly explain the Quinlan story's power by thinking of it as a perverse version of *Sleeping Beauty*. In the fairy tale a beautiful princess is cursed by a vengeful fairy. On her sixteenth birthday she pricks her finger on a spindle and, along with everyone in the palace, falls asleep for a hundred years. An impenetrable hedge of briars grows around the palace. When the century ends, a prince penetrates the hedge, awakens the princess with a kiss, and they live happily ever after. By contrast, the real-life, modern version was bleak. After being struck by her mysterious curse, Quinlan's body grew ugly during her long sleep. Even more perversely, every possible outcome would be unhappy. Whether she died soon or remained unconscious for months or awoke into a brain-damaged state, there would be no happy ending. These were not the kinds of outcomes that twentieth-century Americans had grown up expecting. They had triumphed over the Great Depression and then over the Axis powers. But just as most of them by 1975 had grudgingly conceded that the best resolution to the Vietnam War was withdrawal, so the best resolution to modern medicine's battle with illness was, sometimes, to withdraw.[22] The media, following social, political, and medical trends, had disposed most Americans to support Quinlan's "right to die." Now they awaited what the judiciary would say.

IN TRENTON on January 26, 1976, two and a half months after Judge Muir's decision, the New Jersey Supreme Court convened to hear Paul Armstrong's appeal. Seven black-robed justices sat in a line along the dais at the front of the hushed chamber, flanked by the United States flag at one end and the New Jersey flag at the other. From large oil portraits on the wall behind them, a pair of august predecessors gazed down upon the rows of benches occupied by lawyers and visitors.

This time there was little for the media to depict and the public to become excited about. No parents in tears or doctors offering graphic testimony, only the same set of attorneys responding to questions by the justices. And instead of lasting a week, the hearing was finished shortly after lunch. The drama in this courtroom was more like a chess game. With each of their questions the justices pushed the discussion in this direction or that, and the attorneys devised answers to defend their positions. It was an abstract, lawyerly, often zigzagging Socratic dialogue. (It is rendered yet more abstract for the historian, because the transcript rarely attributes statements to justices by name, merely "Justice.") But this was not a law school classroom. A young woman's life—and her family's anguish—hung in the balance. As Justice Morris Pashman exclaimed at one point: " . . . Really doesn't the horror of continued pseudo-life cry out for some type of handling, some type of treatment by a court . . . ?"[23] Somehow or other, these seven men needed to find a way through the impasse of doctors and parents. As they focused on certain issues and ignored others, they hinted at their eventual solution.

Quinlan herself earned remarkably little attention. In the lower court trial she had been physically absent but, via the testimony (and symbolically via the diagram of a human brain), she had exerted a constant presence. In the Supreme Court, by contrast, she receded into the background. To be sure, the justices and attorneys conducted several discussions about whether, medically and legally speaking, she could be considered dead. Eventually they acknowledged that she was alive, though irreversibly unconscious. They also had some exchanges about how long the doctors predicted she would survive if taken off the respirator. A year at most, everyone concurred, and more likely a few months.

Otherwise the justices strangely ignored two crucial questions concerning Quinlan. What had been her precomatose preferences about medical treatment? In the lower court the attorneys had debated heatedly whether to credit the previous statements quoted by Julia Quinlan ("Mommy, don't let them keep me alive by extraordinary means"). And what was she experiencing now? If she were feeling no pain, as the doctors claimed, then her "pseudo-life" would be "a horror" to others but not necessarily to her. Both issues were keys to the case, but the justices said nothing about either. One could read the silence in two ways: either the court was going to ignore what Karen Quinlan wanted, or the court so fully agreed with her preferences that it saw no need to discuss them.

The justices were very much concerned, on the other hand, with a third question: who should decide on her behalf? Judge Muir had come down on the side of exclusive medical authority. The Supreme Court reopened the question and seemed to be looking for a more complicated arrangement by which authority would be shared between doctors and family. That was on their minds, for example, when they quizzed Paul Armstrong as to what exactly he wanted for his client. "You're not asking the Court to order the doctors to terminate the apparatus?"

"Absolutely not," Armstrong replied.

"Aren't you really asking us to overrule the doctors' decision?"

"No," Armstrong reiterated. "What essentially we are asking for is that, if the physicians don't feel that they are capable of doing this . . . , that they not interfere with a physician who would be wont to grant the request of the family."

What about vesting decision-making in a group of representatives from several professions, medical as well as others, who would proceed according to judicial guidelines?

Armstrong shook his head. "It just [doesn't] apply in the instant circumstances, Mr. Justice."[24]

Regardless of whether one, two, or several parties decided treatment, however, the problem of criminal liability remained. Muir had flatly declared that disconnecting Quinlan would be an act of homicide. Here too, some members of the Supreme Court seemed open to more nuanced approaches. Chief Justice Richard Hughes, for example, got the county prosecutor to concede a difference between active and passive euthanasia. "Supposing that Dr. Morse, on the night Karen Quinlan was received in that hospital, knew then all that he knows now about her condition and prognosis, and he decided, with the consent let's say of her father and mother, not to apply the life-sustaining apparatus. Would you think of prosecuting him in that case?"

"I don't think so, no," Collester replied.[25]

If letting someone die was not the same as committing homicide, why was Dr. Morse adamantly resisting the Quinlans' wishes? In his trial testimony, Morse had explained he was upholding his Hippocratic oath. The justices, on the other hand, translated moral duty into pragmatic fear. "If the doctor has to worry about the personal consequences to himself, civil or criminal," Hughes remarked, "how can his opinion be considered on that lofty plane of the best interest to his patient? That's what bothers me."[26] Conceivably this legalistic emphasis signaled how the chief justice was intending to decide. Liability, unlike conscience, was something a court could remedy. If they ruled that disconnecting the respirator was passive euthanasia, not homicide or negligence, the way would be cleared for family and physicians to act without penalty.

In an exchange with Ralph Porzio, the attorney for Karen's doctors, other justices pressed the issue. "Mr. Porzio, I was wondering why your clients are resisting the order that the Plaintiffs seek here? It's an order which, if granted, . . . would not force them to participate in life discontinuance. It would simply say that if they decided to do so, in consultation with the parents, they would have no liability. Why should they object to that?"

"Simply because there is a duty on their part," Porzio replied.

Judge Milton Conford wasn't satisfied. "The relief the Plaintiff seeks would not compel them to do anything they didn't want to do. It would simply say that . . . they would have no liability." And Hughes chimed in: " . . . A doctor ought not to have to carry this burden of wondering what a distant relative, or a prosecutor will do to him if he sees a case which is so plainly and tragically desperate . . . as this one is."[27]

The court could have taken the safe course of action and let Muir's decision stand. By the end of the morning, though, it was clear that, despite the legal obstacles and pitfalls, the justices were contemplating a different solution to the predicament. As one justice remarked, the case "should never have been started, but it was started, and it's here. Now . . . usually we try to contribute something towards a solution. I guess that's our primary and ultimate function here."[28]

But a solution of which aspects? And with how much applicability beyond Karen Ann Quinlan to the principles of "the right to die with dignity"?

TWO MONTHS went by. As the Quinlans waited for the court's answer, they continued the daily ritual of visiting St. Clare's Hospital, talking to their daughter, combing her hair, sitting by her bed, and watching her empty eyes.

Her twenty-second birthday arrived on March 29. A year ago there had been a big family party, with various cousins and friends, after which Karen had driven to New York City to see a Broadway musical. This year it was hard to know how to commemorate the occasion. Doing nothing at all would have been understandable, but that wasn't the Quinlans' way. They performed their obligations, however painful. "The answer finally came to me," Julia recalled. "We'd have a Mass for Karen" at home. They invited relatives, a few friends, five of the nurses tending Karen in the

ICU, the hospital chaplain, Paul Armstrong and his wife, and Father Tom Trapasso. They ordered enough flowers to fill the family room. It was a bitterly cold evening when everyone gathered in the house on Ryerson Road. "We are waiting for a human being who is dying," Father Trapasso said. "Waiting is the best way to show our faith. God never gives us things immediately. Why doesn't God take Karen? I don't know. I only know that twenty-two years ago a child was born who will probably in some way change the world. Her name will go down in history." [29]

The next day Chief Justice Hughes announced that the court would issue its ruling on March 31.

IN PREDAWN DARKNESS the Quinlans and their two pastors drove to the Nassau Inn at Princeton, where they could wait without being pestered by reporters. At 10 a.m. Armstrong walked into the Supreme Court building in Trenton, joining the other attorneys in the case. Minutes later the clerk of the court arrived with an armful of copies of the fifty-nine-page decision—a unanimous decision. [30]

"The central figure in this tragic case is Karen Ann Quinlan, a New Jersey resident. At the age of 22, she lies in a debilitated and allegedly moribund state at Saint Clare's Hospital. . . ." So began the decision, but almost immediately the justices pointed toward the momentous issues surrounding her plight: the definition of death; the prolongation of life by artificial means; and the rights of an incompetent and her family. "The matter is of transcendent importance," the court declared, and proceeded to devise solutions that were breathtakingly radical. They not only affirmed Karen's constitutional "right of privacy" against intrusion by doctors and the state. They also embraced the principle of subjectivity, claiming that the wishes of an incompetent patient, her family, doctors, and others necessarily entered into the course of modern dying. [31] Father Trapasso had been right. *In re Quinlan* would be historic.

Judge Muir had ruled out Karen's precomatose statements about withdrawing life-support and had read into her vegetative condition the belief that her "single most important temporal quality . . . is life." [32] For the New Jersey Supreme Court the choice was not simply death or life. Rather it lay in the ambiguous twilight zone between them—in dying as a process—and also in the still more ambiguous meaning of the dying person's experience. Who should decide whether or not to prolong that process? On the one hand, the court affirmed that the decision belonged to Karen herself, as her "right of privacy." On the other hand, "the sad truth . . . is that she is grossly incompetent," and her prior statements were too "remote and impersonal" to bear significant weight. What then? Granting her a right that she couldn't exercise would seem to leave her exactly where Muir's ruling had. To escape this bind, the judges made two bold leaps into subjectivity. First, they substituted their judgment for hers as to how she would experience her situation. "We have no doubt . . . that if Karen were herself miraculously lucid for an interval . . . and perceptive of her irreversible condition, she could effectively decide upon discontinuance of the life-support apparatus, even if it meant the prospect of natural death." [33]

So Paul Armstrong had won the most fundamental and innovative part of his case. Nevertheless, since Karen was unable to exercise her right of privacy, in practice her "right to die" depended upon how the court resolved the conflict of authority: Joseph and Julia Quinlan versus Dr. Morse and the State of New Jersey. Here the ruling was brief but also radical. However greatly Mr. Quinlan was affected by grief, "his strength of purpose and character far outweighs these sentiments and qualifies him eminently for guardianship. . . ." [34] So much for Muir's argument against allowing subjective judgment into the process. And if Mr. Quinlan chose to detach her from the respirator, what about the legal consequences for him and her doctors? In that case, said the court, they would not be committing homicide. Rather than unlawfully taking another person's life, they would be ending "artificial life-support systems as a matter of [her] self-determination." [35]

Regardless of how one read Karen's mind, though, and even if her family and doctors were exempt from prosecution, what about the state's interest in preserving life? In *John F. Kennedy Hospital v. Heston* this very court, five years earlier, had upheld doctors who gave a blood transfusion to Delores Heston, a Jehovah's Witness in extreme shock, even though she would likely have refused—and her mother did refuse—the treatment on religious grounds. The parallel to Quinlan seemed inescapable. But if one looked more closely, the high court explained, the two young women's situations were diametrically opposite. Heston was being saved for a long and healthy life, which scarcely was the prospect for Quinlan. "We have no hesitancy in deciding . . . that no external compelling interest of the State could compel Karen to endure the unendurable, only to vegetate a few measurable months with no realistic possibility of returning to any semblance of cognitive or sapient life." Just as a conscious patient, "terminally ill, riddled by cancer and suffering great pain, . . . would not be kept *against his will* on a respirator," so Karen should not be.[36]

By now we can recognize how far the justices had accepted the subjectivity of dying and, what's more, how radically they were defining it. According to all physicians, Quinlan felt no pain—indeed, was unaware of her condition. Nevertheless the justices decided that someone in her condition would not want to continue living. A persistent vegetative state was an unendurable kind of existence. Dignity, not pain or suffering, was their measure.

Leaping squarely into the ambiguity of modern dying, they reached the crux of their ruling. "We think that the State's interest *contra* weakens and the individual's right to privacy grows as the degree of bodily invasion increases and the prognosis dims. Ultimately, there comes a point at which the individual's rights overcome the state interest."[37] This was truly historic. In keeping with the egalitarian revolution that courts and legislatures had been waging on behalf of blacks, women, and the poor, the New Jersey Supreme Court was proclaiming the principle of equal rights in the arena of health. Medical paternalism was converted into a democratic process whereby family members could speak for incompetent patients.

Physicians also played a part in decisions to forgo treatment, said the court. When faced with terminally ill patients, many doctors frequently chose not to prolong the process of dying. The trouble was, the court went on, doctors couldn't practice this humane nontreatment openly—by consulting with patients' families—because they were in danger of being sued or prosecuted. If they decided to let a patient die, they had to make that decision furtively, self-protectively, and, to that extent, nonobjectively.

To solve this dilemma, the court proposed a remedy that divided decision-making even further than among patient, family, and physician. Hospitals should set up ethics committees, consisting of doctors, social workers, attorneys, and theologians, which would review ethical dilemmas in cases like the Quinlans' and would offer guidance to attending physicians and patients' families. Much like an appellate court of several judges, these committees would protect a doctor by diffusing responsibility. Equally important, they would help him to decide whether a patient had a reasonable chance of regaining "cognitive and sapient life" or, on the other hand, had no hope beyond "the forced continuance of that biological vegetative existence to which Karen is doomed."[38]

By now the court had not simply reversed Muir's conclusions on homicide and on Quinlan's right of privacy. It had turned his epistemological premise of "objectivity" inside out. Muir had decided according to "abstract right" instead of Karen's wishes, and he had disqualified Mr. Quinlan as guardian because Karen's father couldn't make disinterested decisions about her treatment. By contrast, the Supreme Court made empathic judgments about her "enduring an unendurable" vegetative state and appointed Mr. Quinlan guardian precisely because he was sufficiently involved with his daughter to represent her wishes. More subtly, with even farther-reaching consequences, the court said that doctors could not make disinterested decisions about life-support treatment as long as they feared criminal prosecution. Only by legalizing passive euthanasia and by diffusing decision-making authority could one approximate "objectivity." In other words, modern dying was so ambiguous that one needed to combine various subjectivities in order to reach an answer.

Finally, the decision was notable for what it excluded: religion. The defense had built much of its case around the pope's *allocutio* condoning the withdrawal of "extraordinary means" to prolong life. Correspondingly, Joseph Quinlan had based his appeal for guardianship on the First Amendment right to exercise his religious beliefs. He was not seeking to kill their daughter or even simply to let her die, but to allow the Lord's will to take effect. In three swift paragraphs the New Jersey high court dismissed this argument, citing a dozen cases in which patients' religious beliefs had been outweighed by the state's interest in preserving life.[39] As the justices themselves had done, Mr. Quinlan could substitute his judgment for his daughter's and, in the name of her right of privacy, disconnect the respirator. Whether the constitutional premise was religious or secular, in practice the effect was the same. In ethical terms, though, the implications were markedly different. The Quinlans believed they were deciding their daughter's fate in harmony with her wishes and ultimately in deference to God's will. They were not "playing God." On the other hand, when the court used the principle of substituted judgment on behalf of Karen's self-determination, it was intervening in at least a radical, if not a Godlike, way.[40]

At the time no one paid any attention to this ethical discrepancy. The court had given the Quinlans a secular victory of "privacy," and the Quinlans received it as a victory of Catholic faith. That was what mattered. To be sure, it was ironic that the U.S. Supreme Court had first asserted the right of privacy (in its *Griswold* and *Roe v. Wade* decisions) on behalf of women who wanted to use contraception and to have an abortion—practices that the Quinlans' church forbade. But no one commented on that, either. Only later would these inconsistencies emerge with stark practical consequences. In a ferocious irony, evangelical Protestants and conservative Catholics would mobilize against the consequences of *In re Quinlan* in the name of "the right to life." As modern Americans constructed new meanings of death, they couldn't help mirroring the fault lines of their culture.

PAUL ARMSTRONG wept as he read through the decision. Then he phoned the Nassau Inn and said to Julia Quinlan: "Our prayers have been answered." Late that afternoon the Quinlans sat alongside Armstrong and three priests on the stage of a grammar school auditorium, facing a hundred reporters and television cameras. "We are grateful to the Supreme Court," Julia said. "We can't use the words 'glad' or 'happy' to describe our reaction, because we may be losing our daughter." Later Father Trapasso added: "I think we would be more comfortable now if nature would take its course first, before the court decision has to be implemented."[41]

It appeared to be the beginning of the last act of the melodrama that the media had started writing six months earlier. Opening the CBS Evening News, Walter Cronkite announced in somber tones: "The Supreme Court of New Jersey ruled today on an issue that has tormented the consciences of the legal and medical professions."[42] Now the responsibility shifted from these public authorities to her father, who held his daughter's fate in his hands. In the media's view, this was as it should be. "Millions of us," said the *Chicago Tribune*, "supported the Quinlans' courageous determination to give their daughter the right to die when the right to life had lost all meaning." Newspapers on both sides of the Atlantic agreed. It was a "merciful" decision. "Une délivrance."[43] The press spent little if any time analyzing the court's assumptions about Quinlan's vegetative state or the ramifications of ethics committees deciding whether a patient could regain "cognitive and sapient life." Overwhelming these abstractions was a sense of relief, emotional and moral, after the long ordeal. Unless the defense appealed to the U.S. Supreme Court—and they quickly declined to do so—the end of the story seemed imminent. "KAREN CAN DIE," said the *Newark Star-Ledger* headline. "Karen Quinlan will die [mourra]," predicted *France-Soir*. It was only a matter of how soon.[44]

For the professionals who were directly involved in the "social drama," on the other hand, the story was far from over. As clergymen, doctors, and lawyers saw it, the decision didn't resolve the dilemma of "the right to die" but added new confusions and (some said) dangers.

Catholic, Protestant, and Jewish spokesmen generally favored the ruling, although with wariness. The right of privacy could be spread too wide, they said, obscuring the responsibility of public authorities to protect life.[45] Some physicians were more vehement. Dr. McCarthy DeMere, chairman of the American Bar Association committee that had defined brain death, denounced "one of the worst decisions the country has seen in the last fifty years. [It rules on] the quality of life and when you do that you're going back to Nazi Germany." Many physicians, by contrast, glad to be relieved of the fear of malpractice suits, hailed "the kind of wisdom that should come from justices."[46] Polarized, predictable responses like these served journalists' desire to "hear from both sides," but they didn't promote thoughtful understanding. For the right to die had more than two sides; now, more than ever, it was kaleidoscopic.

Legal scholars, for example, supported the court's intention but found flaws in the reasoning. William F. Smith could not understand the logic of authorizing a third party to exercise Karen Ann Quinlan's right of privacy. By definition it belonged to her alone, and therefore the court should have relied on her prior oral statements. Harvard law professor Laurence Tribe considered it "perplexing" and "problematic" that the court attributed rights to Karen in a vegetative state when she couldn't exercise them. And he found "most troubling" that parents' and doctors' interests were given constitutional status. The decision would have been more effective, he said, if it had come later, after state legislators had decided whether or how to sanction "living wills."[47]

Two bioethicists, George Annas at the Boston University School of Law and Paul Ramsey in Princeton's Department of Religion, devised the most illuminating critiques. Both were strong advocates of granting terminally ill patients the right to forgo or withdraw treatment. They didn't object to the court's conclusion but to the reasoning that led there. The decision confused a dying patient with an incurable patient. Quinlan would never become cognitive and sapient, but she was not dying. By merging these two conditions the court departed from medical criteria and was instead using "quality of life" as the criterion. As a result, Ramsey warned, "the *Quinlan* case has gone a long way toward obliterating the distinction between voluntary and involuntary euthanasia. . . ."

In these bioethicists' views, the court made the right decision for the wrong reasons. It should have permitted Mr. Quinlan to withdraw his daughter's respirator as a way of resuming the natural process of dying. In fact, Ramsey also advocated withdrawing the feeding tube. This wasn't simply a matter of constitutional right. It was a way to permit her family to care for Karen during what was left of her life. Ramsey even offered to accompany the Quinlans and their priest to her room and pray while her parents disconnected the life-support apparatus and held her in their arms until she died.[48]

It may have been a sincere gesture, but it was intrusive. The Quinlans wanted to be left alone now. They had become the focus of nationwide—even worldwide—controversy about the "right to die," but that was for others to settle: bioethicists, judges, legislators, citizens' action groups. Joseph and Julia never sought celebrity; they accepted it as the price of resolving the ordeal that God had given them. In a poignant irony, to obtain their constitutional right of privacy they had forfeited their privacy. Even more poignantly, they had won the right to let die the daughter they had adopted. The best they could hope for now was to carry out their grievous victory without delay.

4

The Politics of Dying

O N MONDAY, November 29, 1976, as seventeen-year-old Karen Pomeroy was walking home from school in Long Island, a man attacked her with an iron railroad spike and robbed her. She was found unconscious in a wooded field, taken to a hospital, and placed on a respirator. After two days with no sign of improvement, her parents agreed that, if she didn't survive, they wanted her eyes and kidneys transplanted. By Thursday, after administering three EEGs, doctors declared her "neurologically" and "clinically" dead. The Pomeroys gave their consent, and Karen was disconnected from the machine while her heart was still beating. The case, said a spokesman for the Suffolk County district attorney, was fraught with "Karen Anne [sic] Quinlan overtones."[1]

That same month in Georgia, yet another young Karen— Karen Keatley—had a car accident and fell into a coma. Three months later, still comatose, the former Miss West Virginia Teenager was brought home to be tended by her parents. "Well, when you have a child that you love," her mother told CBS Morning News, "you just—you don't give up." To which Mr. Keatley added: "Where there's life, there's hope." Their daughter would have said much the same—did say, in fact, back in 1975 when she had participated in a high school debate on whether Karen Ann Quinlan should be allowed to die. CBS had covered that event and now, while she lay comatose, it replayed the tape of Karen Keatley saying: "I want to go ahead and live . . . , because . . . you don't never know. . . . Something could happen [and] you just, you know, [might] real quickly come back."[2]

Which choice should a parent make: to let go or hold on? There is no objective answer. Doctors may offer diagnoses and probabilities, but members of each family must still make up their own minds, decipher right from wrong, sort out frantic hopes and numbing hopelessness. And whatever decision they extract from this disorderly process, it will carry shreds of ambivalence: *if only . . . ; but just suppose. . . .*

During the late 1970s and early 1980s these issues moved beyond hospital rooms and courtrooms into the political arena. State legislators argued and bargained with interest groups as they drafted statutes authorizing the withdrawal of life-support. Power was at stake—doctors defending their autonomy, patients and families demanding theirs. But religion gave the disputes a special intensity. When conservative Christians mobilized against what they interpreted as disguised eugenics, the debate turned vehement, positions polarized. The right to life versus the right to die. The quiet, personalized choices by the Pomeroys and Keatleys were translated into the ideologies of warring social movements. The dilemma of dying became political, absorbing the passions and anxieties of modern America.

EVEN BEFORE the Quinlan case dramatized the need to redefine the legality of treating (and especially not treating) irreversibly comatose and terminally ill patients, state legislators had begun to take action. On the one hand, they dealt with the situation of patients like Karen Pomeroy, whose brain had ceased to function but whose lungs and heart were kept pumping by machine. Between 1970 and 1981 twenty-seven states enacted laws permitting physicians to declare a person dead (using the Harvard ad hoc committee's criteria) and to end life-support without fear of prosecution. These measures passed with no public controversy and with almost no attention from the legislators themselves.[3] If opponents of the right to die took notice, they welcomed brain-death legislation for drawing a clearer line between life and death and, they thought, relieving the pressure to legalize euthanasia.[4] "Living will" laws, on the other hand, stirred up enormous tumult.

The first such law—the California Natural Death Act of 1976—originated from one man's personal frustrations. In the early 1970s Barry Keene, a thirty-three-year-old state assemblyman from Eureka, was called upon by his neighbor for help. The neighbor's wife had terminal cancer and had vowed not to be hooked up to machines that would prolong her suffering. On his latest visit to the hospital, however, her husband found her tied by the wrists so that she wouldn't pull out the nasogastric and ventilator tubes. Didn't they have some legal power, the husband asked Keene, to prohibit such treatment? The assemblyman promised to find a remedy, but after searching the statute books he came up empty-handed. Soon Keene went through the same experience again, this time closer to home and more galling to his professional principles. His mother-in-law developed cancer and signed a statement directing her physicians not to use certain aggressive treatments. But after she entered the hospital the doctors disregarded her wishes, and she had no legal power to override them. As Keene later remarked bitterly, a living will without legislative backing was "a well-intentioned but feeble exercise that raises more questions than it solves."[5] So in 1974 he drafted a bill declaring: "Every person has the right to die without prolongation of life by medical means."[6]

Given public attitudes at the time, one would expect the bill to have won easy passage. "Death with dignity" had become a familiar concept, almost a "vogue," while the patient rights movement had acquired remarkable influence. More specifically, advance directives, or living wills, were attracting public interest as a method to counteract the dictates of doctors and life-prolonging technology. When a "Dear Abby" column described the model document drafted by the Euthanasia Educational Council, 50,000 people sent in requests for a copy. During 1970–1975 the Council mailed out a total of 750,000 copies (and in the nine months after the Quinlan trial, another 600,000).[7]

Keene was hoping to ride this wave of public enthusiasm when he introduced his bill in California, but all too soon he collided with hostile interest groups. The California Medical Association, first of all. CMA officials heartily supported more communication between physicians and patients but thought legalization of living wills would be a mistake. How could a layman choose appropriate end-of-life treatment, they argued? Moreover, living wills were unenforceable, because the ICU staff wouldn't consult them during life-or-death emergencies. And finally, regardless of what the right-to-die advocates claimed, there was not a desperate need for living wills. As an oncologist testified during public hearings on Keene's bill: "I think that this great bugaboo of a bunch of evil doctors keeping a huge number of comatose patients alive is really much less of a problem [than people believe]."[8]

The medical profession mounted less vehement opposition than the California Catholic Conference and the California Pro-Life Council. These two organizations represented the new but already significant national movement that was fighting against abortion in the name of "the right to life." Ever since the Supreme Court in *Roe v. Wade* (1973) had held that "the right of privacy" (implicit in the Fourteenth Amendment) allowed a woman to have an abortion during her first trimester of pregnancy, Catholics had divided into two increasingly polarized camps, liberal and conservative. According to Gallup polls, 48 percent favored a woman's right to abortion, 40 percent objected (with the others undecided).[9] For many conservative Catholics, it was not a disagreement about the right of privacy; it was a question of "infanticide." Taking the Bible as their guide, they followed an absolutist line of reasoning. Life was sacred and should be preserved from the moment of conception, no matter what the woman's wishes or circumstances. To save the lives of fetuses, they organized a crusade.[10] By the mid-seventies the National Right to Life Committee was coordinating chapters in almost every state, issuing a torrent of publicity (heavily financed by the United States Catholic Conference), testifying before congressional committees, and publishing the biweekly *National Right to Life News*.[11]

It was a short step of logic from fetuses to terminally ill adults. What Keene defined as the right to die, the California Catholic Conference and the California Pro-Life Council denounced as a wedge for involuntary euthanasia. These organizations did not speak for most Californians. Quite the contrary. According to a statewide opinion poll, 87 percent of adults (and 77 percent of Catholics) believed that "an incurably ill patient should have the right to refuse medication that would prolong his or her life." Indeed, two-thirds (including half the Catholics) also endorsed voluntary euthanasia ("an incurably ill patient should have the right to ask for and get medication that would painlessly end his or her life").[12] But interest groups exert more influence than "the person on the street." Even with support from the speaker of the Assembly, Keene's bill went down to quick defeat.

The young legislator had learned his lesson. During the next two years Keene crafted a strategy that would appeal to the self-interests of key constituencies and "embrace [their] objections."[13] To begin with, he retitled the bill "the Natural Death Act"—death neither as the taking of life ("mercy killing") nor as the outcome of medical heroics but as part of a natural (God-given) process, a human ecology. The bill authorized persons over the age of eighteen to write a living will specifying which end-of-life treatment they wished to receive—and, equally important, not to receive—when they were terminally ill.

As critics quickly pointed out, many questions remained unanswered. Who determines that a patient is "terminally ill"? What if someone on his deathbed changes his mind? And what about people who haven't written a living will? Have they tacitly forfeited their common-law right to refuse treatment?

Despite these ambiguities, certain groups readily gave support: the California Nurses Association, various senior citizens' organizations, hospice associations, the Episcopal Diocese of Northern California, plus one hundred other Protestant and Jewish organizations. After years of public agitation for patients' rights and "death with dignity," they welcomed this legislative approach. But three other groups needed to be won over by amendments. First of all, physicians. Amid the so-called malpractice crisis and sharply rising malpractice premiums, the California Medical Association was pleased that the bill would grant doctors immunity from liability when they agreed to take a patient off life-support. But the CMA wanted more. If patients had the right to refuse treatment, so should doctors. Keene agreed to exempt from liability any physician who wouldn't comply with a living will.

Satisfying the second major opponent, the California Catholic Conference (CCC), required a wider "embrace of objections." The bishops were squeezed between the liberals in the church, who agreed with the papal *allocutio* rejecting "extraordinary means" to prolong life, and conservatives who warned against starting down the slippery slope toward involuntary euthanasia. Ideally the Catholic leadership would have preferred to stay out of the battle. Pragmatically, since the Medical Association's support had improved the bill's chance of passage, the Catholics had better jump in and take what they could. So the Reverend John Cummins, the CCC's executive director, sat down with Keene to negotiate adding various safeguards. To ensure that a patient hadn't changed his mind, for example, Cummins proposed that a living will be valid for only five years, after which it must be renewed before two witnesses. As a yet more stringent safeguard against mistakes, he said a living will shouldn't take effect until fourteen days after two doctors had certified that the patient was "terminally ill" (meaning "an incurable condition which, regardless of life-sustaining procedures, would produce death"). This provision would disqualify large categories of patients: those receiving kidney dialysis, for example (who would be terminal only after dialysis was removed), and those in a persistent vegetative state.[14] Altogether, these and other amendments sought to keep both doctors and patients from ending life-support except in the most unarguable circumstances.

After earnest negotiations, Keene acquiesced. In response, Reverend Cummins wrote a "Dear Barry" letter announcing that the CCC would take a neutral stance toward the bill. "Too many of our people still have problems" with legislation, he explained, for the CCC to be more than neutral. But "on my own behalf, I wish to express appreciation for your sensitivity to the questions we had."[15] This was not the outright endorsement Keene would have wanted, but also not the opposition that had helped defeat his effort last time.

By the end of this bargaining, the Natural Death Act barely resembled the sweeping right-to-die bill that Keene had proposed two years earlier. Had he in fact lost the essential principle amid the thicket of pragmatic qualifications? Marc Lappe, the state's officer of law, health, and values, thought so. Along with the state health director, Lappe openly lobbied against Keene's bill, arguing that it impaired patients' rights to refuse treatment and thus strengthened medical paternalism. Better to have no law than this one.[16]

At the other end of the ideological spectrum, meanwhile, the Pro-Life Council saw the bill as a step toward "mercy killing" (involuntary euthanasia). Its members tried to alert the public by picketing and shouting outside Keene's office, hanging him in effigy, and distributing handbills comparing him to Hitler. At one committee hearing, a pro-life spokesperson placed a copy of William L. Shirer's *Rise and Fall of the Third Reich* on the witness table.[17] In more temperate style, the Senate majority floor leader spelled out the same fearful logic. "The so-called 'living will,'" he warned, "like 'mercy' killing, is yet another euphemism for the intentional killing of a human being."[18] And the *Los Angeles Times* cartoonist attacked twice with his pen—once portraying a man in hell plaintively asking the devil, "Who do I see about canceling my natural death release?" and a month later, over the caption "Womb to Tomb," portraying the Grim Reaper carrying a physician's bag labeled "Abortion on Demand and 'Right to Die.'"[19]

Most Californians, however, welcomed the Natural Death Act or at least, like the Catholic leadership, kept a neutral silence. According to an admittedly "unscientific" poll by the *San Francisco Examiner*, 96 percent of its Bay Area readers supported the right to die. Newspapers as well as television and radio not only devoted a lot of attention to the issue but issued editorial endorsements. Reminding readers that Karen Ann Quinlan was "a hopeless heap devoid of human spirit," the *Examiner* said that Keene's bill would

Womb to Tomb (Paul Conrad, *Los Angeles Times*)

save people from such an ordeal.[20] Stirred by this publicity, a large number of people wrote to their legislators and newspapers, some against but most of them for the right to die.[21] "I think people have a right to say they don't want to be kept alive by some machine," wrote nine-year-old Susan Longworth. "My father explained about that stuff." One woman cited a higher authority: "God gave man free will and he should be allowed to use it freely."[22]

Keene's previous bill had been soundly defeated. This time his pragmatic strategy promised more success. "Thank God a compromise was reached with the Pro-Life people," one legislator told a newsman. "Their organization may not be that big, but they have long memories—and a lot of people here don't want to cross them." But even with compromises, the bill offended some conservatives. "God created us all and God should make the decision about when we die," Assemblyman Vincent Thomas said. The next bill, he warned, will be "to get rid of all the people in Pacific State

[Mental] Hospital." Other legislators remained uneasy. "God, this is a rough one," one assemblyman moaned to another shortly before the vote, "a really personal decision we have to make." After an hour of emotional debate, including repeated references to Karen Quinlan, the bill passed the Assembly by twenty votes. Two months later the Senate went through similar anguish. James Wadsworth, a Democrat from Torrance, recalled how his father "died a little every day. But he didn't want to die. . . . He wanted to live." Senator Peter Behr responded in a cracking voice: "[My brother] shrunk to 89 pounds and was in such bad shape that morphine didn't help any longer. I wish he had a living will. I would have been proud as hell to pull the plug." In the end, the Senate approved by eight votes.[23]

It was a narrow victory but a momentous one. Amid nationwide media attention, on September 30 Governor Jerry Brown (himself a former Jesuit seminarian) signed the first living-will law in the nation. The dilemma of modern dying had moved beyond the hospital intensive care unit and the courtroom to the statehouse and out into the public domain.

On the day of triumph in the Assembly, Keene remarked: "The image of Karen Quinlan haunts our dreams."[24] On the one hand, the *Quinlan* ruling had opened the way for his achievement, while her plight—her image—had worked its way deep into public consciousness. On the other hand, in October 1976, six months after her father won the right to take her off the respirator, she hovered in her twilight, neither dead nor meaningfully alive. Despite what her parents said she would have wished, her body went its own way.

There was something else Keene could have said, but understandably he didn't, because it was too bitter an irony. Even if Karen had been living in California, had written an advance directive telling physicians not to use a respirator, and had then fallen into a persistent vegetative state, the new law would not have benefited her. For she was in a vegetative (not "terminally ill") condition. Keene invoked her as an inspiration for a Natural Death Law that wouldn't have let her die.

"Who Do I See About Canceling My Natural Death Release?" (Paul Conrad, *Los Angeles Times*)

BEFORE Keene's victory, fifteen legislatures had rejected living-will bills. Within a year afterward, seven states enacted them, followed by eight more states in the next five years.[25] But there was another side to this progress of the right to die: success galvanized the opposition. Right-to-life activists were deploying most of their resources against abortion, but wherever possible they also fought against living-will legislation. The more states enlarged the realm of choice, the harder conservatives fought to confine it. "Sanctity" versus "quality" of life. Where Catholics were most numerous, living-will legislation came late and with difficulty, or sometimes not at all. In Connecticut, even the testimony by a professor of religion at the College of Holy Cross and printed statements from the Catholic Hospital Association couldn't sway hostile legislators until 1985. In the Quinlans' own state, New Jersey, living wills weren't legalized until 1991. And in Massachusetts, New York, and

Michigan, the church (bolstered in New York by Orthodox Jews) blocked legislation altogether.[26]

For the most part, though, conservatives lost the battle against living wills. By 1986 all but eleven states had joined the ranks. Most of them went beyond California's model, setting more liberal terms. They didn't require, for example, that the document be renewed every few years. And patients could end life-support on the basis of previous *oral* statements. Only a handful of states, however, included persons in a persistent vegetative state.[27]

But on the issue that formed the heart of their movement— abortion—the pro-life activists made a significant impact. In Virginia, for example, the Richmond Catholic diocese collaborated with a committee of the House of Delegates to draft an exceptionally comprehensive and flexible living-will bill. As a quid pro quo, the diocese insisted on exempting pregnant women. A woman could choose not to prolong her own life by extraordinary treatment, but she could not choose to end her unborn baby's life. That would be incidental abortion. The bill was moving smoothly ahead until committee member Mary Marshall proposed an amendment to include pregnant women through their first trimester. The lawyer for the diocese, Nicholas Spinella, became angry. "What the bill advocates now is an unnatural death, not a natural one," he declared. "We will not compromise." To which Warren Stambaugh, an Arlington Democrat (and Catholic), retorted: "This is not an abortion bill." In the end the Virginia legislature approved the bill *with* the amendment, although by a razor-thin margin of three votes in the Senate.[28] Thirty-five other states, by contrast, refused to grant pregnant women the right to forgo life-support.[29]

Until the late 1970s the Catholic pro-life movement was a marginal force, but then it acquired two sets of powerful allies. The first was a group of secular conservatives, led by Richard Viguerie among others, who were working to take control of the Republican party on behalf of what they called the New Right. Small government, free enterprise, and anticommunism were their major themes. As Viguerie recognized, abortion aroused more grassroots passion than any of these, so he established ties with the

National Right to Life Committee.[30] Then in 1980 the pro-life movement acquired an even more significant ally: evangelical Protestants.

As the heirs of early-twentieth-century fundamentalism, evangelicals had stayed aloof from political activity, confining their energies to the private religious realm. But the cumulative pressure of post-1960 developments incited them to erase this boundary between public and private. Most alarming to them were the Supreme Court's prohibition of prayer in public schools and its endorsement of abortion. More generally they deplored Americans' growing tolerance of homosexuality and pornography. Finally they claimed that feminism, symbolized particularly by the campaign for the Equal Rights Amendment, was subverting the traditional family. "It is time that we come together and rise up against the tide of permissiveness and moral decay that is crushing in on our society from every side," declared the Reverend Jerry Falwell. "America is desperately in need of a divine healing. . . ." To salvage the collective moral order these religious conservatives in the mid-1970s entered the political arena. They founded a multitude of organizations such as the Christian Voice, Concerned Women of America, and, best known, Falwell's Moral Majority. Via direct-mail campaigns, rallies, and television, they courted followers with growing success, especially in the South and West. Meanwhile evangelists such as Jimmy Swaggart, Pat Robertson, Tammy and Jim Bakker, and Falwell reached an even larger audience with their weekly television programs. (Swaggart was broadcast on a thousand stations; the Bakkers' "PTL" reached thirteen million homes.)[31] What had begun as a predominantly Catholic crusade was now a Christian one, riding the momentum behind Ronald Reagan's campaign for the White House, dedicated above all to saving fetal lives.

And what about the right to life after birth? During the decade following *Roe v. Wade*, pro-life spokespersons had fought against living wills but otherwise ignored that question. Their concern was primarily for the "preborn."[32] Then, in response to the death of an anonymous infant, they also took up the rights of the born.

"INFANT DOE" was born on April 9, 1982, in Bloomington, Indiana, with Down's syndrome and esophogeal atresia (an obstructed esophagus). When his parents asked about surgery, physicians gave very different opinions. Some predicted a 90 percent chance of success and recommended the boy be operated on immediately; others offered only fifty-fifty odds and recommended nothing but oxygen and antibiotics. Given these alternatives, the parents decided against surgery and also against intravenous feeding—decided, in short, to let their son die. Hospital administrators quickly went to court demanding treatment, but the judge upheld the parents' right to decide. Three days later county prosecutors filed an emergency petition to have the court take custody of the child, but the judge refused. They appealed to the Indiana Supreme Court to order feeding and surgery, but the justices voted not to intervene. Early on the morning of the sixth day, the deputy prosecutor flew to Washington, D.C., hoping to convince Supreme Court Justice John Paul Stevens that Infant Doe had been denied equal protection under the law. But the baby died before the plane landed.[33]

"Down's Syndrome Baby, Barred from Food, Dies." There seemed to be no ambiguities here, no room for the fine distinctions and second-guessing of previous right-to-die cases. Unlike Karen Ann Quinlan, a *Washington Post* editorial pointed out, Infant Doe was neither comatose nor without brain function. "The Indiana baby died not because he couldn't sustain life without a million dollars worth of medical machinery, but because no one fed him." Linda McCabe, an RN in the special-care nursery of Bloomington Hospital, recalled that the nurses refused to be "part of the killing," forcing the parents to hire private nurses. "Who did they think they were—asking me to do something like that?"[34] Quinlan may have haunted people's dreams but, writing to the *Washington Post*, a man in Virginia protested: "the cries of a starving infant are apt to haunt my nightmares."[35]

It's hard to put that sound aside, even temporarily, in order to hear how Infant Doe's parents and physicians justified their decision. It's equally hard to step out of our own medical frame of reference and understand why, according to the expertise of their time, they believed themselves to be acting in the baby's best interest. Between 40 and 60 percent of Down's children are born with heart disease, and 12 percent with various gastrointestinal anomalies. In the era before 1968 they tended to die young—one-third by age six. Since then, new surgical techniques have raised their average life expectancy from sixteen years to fifty-five. Nevertheless, at the time Infant Doe was born a large majority of surgeons were still recommending that parents not treat the physical defects of Down's infants.[36] At best, they said, surgery would make death come a little less early; at worst it would cause useless pain and expense.

And meanwhile there were the mental consequences of Down's syndrome. We now know that only a small percentage of children born with this chromosomal abnormality are severely retarded. As recently as the late 1960s, however, everyone called them Mongoloids (because their flat facial features resembled Mongolians') and believed (to quote the authors of a 1965 psychology textbook) "most mongoloid children rank at an imbecile level. . . ." By the time of Infant Doe's birth the label had changed and so had the mental assessment. Those same textbook authors, in their updated 1979 edition, wrote that "the intellectual development of the individual with Down's syndrome is quite variable. . . ."[37] But if that individual was only a few days old, it was impossible to measure how retarded he was.

When they asked the experts, then, Infant Doe's parents were given ambiguous answers. If his esophagus were repaired, their child would probably have physical problems that would be solved only by laborious, painful surgery, and certainly he would be retarded to some degree. Infant Doe was a semiblank slate. To assess his "best interest," his parents had to figure out whether these handicaps would be outweighed by the satisfactions of living. Julia and Joseph Quinlan could at least reassure themselves by quoting Karen's previous statements that she didn't want to be kept alive. Infant Doe was too young to state his preferences. In deciding his fate, his parents necessarily projected their own values, feelings, and needs about whether extending his life would be worthwhile.

If he was a virtual blank to them, they were also a virtual blank to the public. By insisting on anonymity, they preserved their privacy at the price of forfeiting public sympathy. Unlike the Quinlans, the parents of Infant Doe gave no interviews to the media and no testimony in court explaining why they let their child die. All the public knew of them was sociological silhouettes. The mother was a twenty-nine-year-old housewife with two healthy children, the father was a management executive, and both had once taught handicapped and retarded children. All the public heard from them came through the voice of their lawyer on the sixth day. "It wasn't a case of abandonment," he said. "It was a case of love."[38] The Quinlans had prayed to God, argued with doctors, recalled their daughter's wishes, and only then, after six agonizing months, decided to let the Lord's will take effect. Mr. and Mrs. Doe had decided within a single day to let their anonymous son die. In this case the public knew facts, not human motives, and not even all the facts. Although newspapers and television consistently referred to his Down's syndrome, they mentioned the infant's blocked esophagus only several paragraphs later and sometimes not at all.[39]

Conceivably Mr. and Mrs. Doe might have earned more sympathy if they had explained in anguished detail how they reached their decision. In 1982, six years after the *Quinlan* decision, most Americans endorsed the right of a terminally ill patient to have his doctors "withdraw artificial life support" or "forgo extraordinary treatment." But Infant Doe was not terminally ill or even, like Quinlan, in a permanent vegetative state. He had a conscious life awaiting him, albeit handicapped and foreshortened. Moreover he was not being deprived of what people readily understood to be "extraordinary treatment." He was being deprived of nutrition. Nontreatment appeared to be mistreatment. (In reality the two situations were analogous: Infant Doe would have been connected to an IV feeding tube whereas Quinlan was connected to a ventilator tube. For doctors, both devices were "ordinary." But the technical facts couldn't displace the connotations of "starving him to death.") Above all, shadowing everything, was a gruesome difference: Quinlan may not have "felt pain as we know it," but surely Infant Doe did. (Here again reality diverged from perception. His doctor later said the baby was given morphine, but the media didn't report that at the time.)[40]

Public sympathy had flowed toward the Quinlans, embracing their anguish if not always endorsing their decision. In the Infant Doe case, commentators mustered at best a perfunctory support. These "sensible parents" had been right to avoid "prolongation in pain," said several readers of the *Washington Post*. They were "a family that had kindness in its heart."[41] It sounds like the eulogy by a minister who hadn't known the deceased. Whereas the Quinlans became the protagonists of a melodrama, Infant Doe's parents were impersonal figures in a medical case, so their defenders had to resort to abstractions and qualifications. "This particular set of circumstances," said bioethicist Robert Veatch, "is in my view the most difficult and we'll be struggling with it for a while."[42] According to the *Louisville Courier-Journal*, "If there is one overriding moral in the case of Infant Doe, it's that there are no simple answers." We all wish "things neat and simple," *Washington Post* columnist Richard Cohen wrote, "the way we think it once was before man started to play God, talking in trimesters, knowing gender before birth, creating life in test tubes and, worse yet, being able to sustain something less than life—unfortunate creatures like Karen Quinlan. [We don't] want to hear the words, 'it depends.' But what else is there to say?"[43]

Conservative Americans had much else to say, and it was defiantly "simple." Janet Rebone, president of the Monroe County, Indiana, Right to Life Committee, said "I think it's really disgusting." Shirley Wright, the mother of a retarded child, offered to adopt Infant Doe. "I've got lots of love," she said, "and [retarded children have] got a lot of love." Nationally syndicated columnist George F. Will condemned the "homicide" in Bloomington. "The baby was killed because it was retarded," he asserted flatly. But the memorable portion of his article came toward the end, when he disclosed his personal relationship to the case.

> Jonathan Will, 10, fourth-grader and Orioles fan (and the best wiffle-ball hitter in southern Maryland), has Down's syndrome. He does not 'suffer from' (as newspapers are wont to say) Down's syndrome. He suffers from nothing except anxiety about the Orioles' lousy start.[44]

Even the liberal bioethicist John D. Arras, who argued for an "ethic of ambiguity" toward handicapped newborns, had to admit that Infant Doe's death belonged among "a few miscarriages of justice."[45]

For proponents of the right to life, this was no miscarriage. "Infanticide." A "court-ordered execution." Death by "a rationale that has terrifying similarities to the Nazi Reich's brand of eugenics."[46] That's how they deplored the death of "the Bloomington martyr" who was born on Good Friday.[47] And then there was the cartoon in the *National Right to Life News*.[48] A garbageman is casually dumping trash that contains "the constitutional right to life" and (we abruptly notice) the body of an infant. But we shouldn't blame him; he's just doing his job. The trash cans are property of the Indiana Supreme Court, which looms in marbled aloofness behind the fence. It's a crude scenario, brutally crude, but it also forms a deft parody of pro-choice propaganda. Feminists deplored "back-alley abortions" that maimed or killed women, but in this back alley they have chosen to discard a living baby. Legalized abortion has led to legalized infanticide. And worse was to come, pro-life conservatives warned. Ostensibly the "right to die" enhanced personal autonomy, but it masked a policy of weeding out the handicapped, the old, the mentally retarded, whoever didn't fit "secular humanist" notions of the "quality of life."[49]

"What we are involved in is a war for the soul of America," said a Tufts University medical professor and anti-abortion activist. "It is the first rule of war to know the enemy."[50] And who was the enemy? Pro-life advocates accused the "elite." It was a vague label

(Chuck Asay, *Colorado Springs Sun*)

but all the more effective because it was vague. Depending on your prejudices, it could mean *judges* who put handicapped infants in the garbage. Or *bioethicists* who twisted clear-cut right and wrong into an ethic of ambiguity. "There is a clear 'simple' answer. This is not something so esoteric one needs a medical degree to understand. In a humane society, you don't starve defenseless babies to death because they won't all be Albert Einsteins."[51] Or vaguest of all, *arrogant snobs.* "Parents who conjugate French verbs for their superbabies," wrote George Will, "are unnerved by what they think is the meaninglessness of a life that will not include New York Times editorials."[52] Or with the specificity of a murder indictment, the elitists were *doctors* who played God with infants' lives.

Years have gone by since the death of Infant Doe, but as one reads the grainy microfilmed newspaper stories, even an advocate of the right to die must feel appalled. Infant Doe—too short-lived to have a name. He was a person identified by his "defects": Down's syndrome, esophageal atresia, heart and gastrointestinal ailments. He was measured by subtraction from the yardstick of what his parents thought he should be or thought they could endure. They visited him frequently, said the doctor, and held him during his six days of life while they let him die.

On the other hand, the righteous fury of the right-to-life advocates is also repellent. They warned of evil in the extreme: infanticide, Nazis. They left no room for complexities or doubts. Dying deserves a more humble approach—more respect for its mystery and for our confusion.

THE FUROR did not subside in the wake of Infant Doe's death. On the contrary, when conservatives learned in 1982 that his case was not unique, not even unusual, they joined forces with the Reagan administration to defend the sanctity of infant life. More than ever, the right to die became politicized.

The instigation was a *New England Journal of Medicine* article by two doctors back in 1973. Raymond S. Duff and A. G. M. Campbell had reported that they and their staff withheld treatment from 43 of 299 infants in the Yale–New Haven special-care nursery. These were infants suffering from total or nearly total absence of cerebral hemispheres, who deserved to escape a "wrongful life," the doctors said, and whose parents were spared the "chronic sorrow" of caring for them. So, with parents' consent and "as physicians have done for generations," Duff and Campbell let the infants die. Or to use their peculiar phraseology: "these children eventually acquired the right to die." [53]

In the mid-1970s the article aroused furious debate within pediatric circles but only fleeting attention among laymen . . . until the death of Infant Doe. [54] Suddenly in 1982 U.S. Senator Jeremiah Denton was reprinting Duff and Campbell's article in the *Congressional Record* as he introduced a resolution (cosponsored by Jesse Helms, Orrin Hatch, and three other conservatives) on handicapped children's right to life. [55] One can't help wondering how the Alabama senator happened to be reading back issues of the *New England Journal of Medicine*; more likely he was guided there by C. Everett Koop, whose address on "The Silent Domino: Infanticide" the senator also inserted in the *Congressional Record*. In 1982 Koop no longer was a pediatric surgeon in Philadelphia but the surgeon general of the United States, chosen by the Reagan administration because of his fervent hostility to abortion. In his speeches and writings Koop had frequently cited the Duff-Campbell article as an omen of what the Nazis had practiced in Auschwitz. "If the mongoloid is chosen as the first category whose life is not worthy to be lived[,] what about the blind and deaf?"[56] Beware of "the silent domino," he said, metaphorically equating the "quality of life" philosophy not only to Nazism but to international communism.

One infant murdered in Bloomington. Forty-nine in New Haven. One hundred in twenty states around the country, according to a television series on "Death in the Nursery." In the war for the soul of America, the time had come for pro-life forces to launch a counterattack.[57]

On April 30, 1982, two weeks after Infant Doe died, President Reagan ordered the secretary of health and human services (HHS) to notify doctors, nurses, and administrators in the nation's 6,800 hospitals that the Rehabilitation Act of 1973 forbade them to discriminate against handicapped newborns. In subsequent regulations HHS spelled out the meaning of "nondiscrimination." Hospitals could not deny treatment on the grounds that "a particular infant is potentially mentally impaired, or blind, or deaf, or paralyzed, or lacking limbs." They could do so only if the infant's death was imminent and if treatment would merely prolong his dying. But physicians must base their judgment entirely on *medical* criteria. Any qualitative considerations—such as the infant's pain or future impairment—were ruled out.[58]

No more ethic of ambiguity, no more subjective judgments. Strict adherence to the sanctity of life. The Reagan administration was translating the pro-life philosophy into political policy—policy that it was determined to turn into practice. Early in 1983 HHS ordered hospitals to post seventeen-by-fourteen-inch signs in delivery rooms, pediatric wards, nurseries, and neonatal ICUs: "Any person having knowledge that a handicapped infant is being discriminatorily denied food or customary medical care should immediately contact . . ." The signs listed an around-the-clock toll-free telephone number (the "Baby Doe hotline") that would summon HHS personnel and pediatrician consultants ("Baby Doe squads") to investigate.[59]

The pro-life movement seemed to be on the eve of victory. HHS received more than sixteen thousand letters, 97 percent in support, many with identical wording suggested by the Christian Action Council. " . . . In years to come," the editor of the *National Right to Life News* declared, "we will look back at the tragic death of Infant Doe and see his martyrdom as the turning point in what had up until that point seemed to be an unstoppable campaign to legalize infanticide. . . . Even the hardest core quality-of-life types [have] temporarily scurried for cover."[60] Pro-life advocates prepared to roll back the tide of the preceding ten or twenty years, only to discover they had miscalculated their strategy and misjudged public opinion.

Their strategic error was to be so aggressive that they united four major interest groups against them. Until now physicians had been defending their professional autonomy against patients. Patients and ethicists, in turn, had challenged physicians' power to "play God." With the *Quinlan* case, judges had stepped into the tug-of-war as umpires. In the face of the Baby Doe regulations, however, these rival authorities coalesced in an alliance against right-to-life absolutism, asserting the legitimacy—and the necessity—of considering the quality of life. Four days before the regulations were to go into effect, the American Academy of Pediatrics and several other medical groups filed suit in U.S. District Court against HHS, protesting governmental intrusion into the neonatal ICU. While treating the sick, they said, doctors should not be looking over their shoulders to bureaucrats and hot-line zealots. They should be able to do what they and the family decided was best for the patient. That was necessarily a subjective decision, varying from case to case—something that no doctrinaire regulation could anticipate. "The issue in neonatal intensive-care units is *not* one of [a patient's] 'worthiness,' but one of future suffering," an editor of the *New England Journal of Medicine* protested. "Do we have the right to inflict a life of suffering on a helpless newborn just because we have the technology to do so. . . ?"[61]

Ethicists joined in, protesting the government's simplistic notion of "discrimination." Unequal treatment was not necessarily unjust, they argued. Often, in fact, people were treated unequally in order to make legitimate distinctions. Law schools, for example, discriminated between applicants on the basis of grades. Doctors discriminated between patients on the basis of medical prognoses. The crucial point was not the differential treatment but the relevance of the criteria being used. If a law school rejected an applicant solely because of gender or religion, that would be discrimination of a morally invidious sort. Gender and religion, unlike intellect, were irrelevant to the business of studying law. Likewise, a patient's physical condition, not his intellect or gender, should be the criterion for treatment.

Even when using relevant criteria, however, physicians necessarily made reasoned distinctions—that is, discriminated—in deciding whether to perform treatment. Consider, for example, an infant born with Trisomy 13 (undeveloped forebrain, major eye abnormalities, and heart disease) and also with a blocked esophagus. Such a child would not live long—six months or a year, regardless of whether the esophagus was repaired. Should that surgery be performed? The federal regulations required treatment of "life-threatening conditions," which would call for immediate surgery even though the infant would die some months later. He would be given longer life but also more pain. In such a case, an absolute injunction against "quality of life" judgments didn't clarify what was best for the baby. To operate or not to operate: whichever choice one made, one had to weigh conflicting factors and values—that is, to make reasoned discriminations.[62]

Doctors, patients, and ethicists were soon joined by the courts. In April 1983 Federal District Judge Gerhard Gesell voided the regulations on procedural grounds: HHS had not granted the required length of advance time for comment by affected parties. But Gesell also had harsh words about the regulations' substance. The rules did not define "customary medical care"; the hotline was "ill-considered"; all in all, the rules were "arbitrary and capricious" and "virtually without meaning beyond [their] intrinsic *in terrorem* effect."[63] (Terrorism. Even cloaked in Latin, it was an extraordinary accusation for a judge to levy against the government.) Parents,

Gesell concluded, are in the best position to evaluate babies' best interest.

In response, HHS reduced the size of the "hotline" poster and required hospitals to hang it only in neonatal nurses' stations rather than in waiting rooms. More important, HHS exempted therapies that would only prolong an infant's dying. Still, at heart the regulations remained unchanged. If physicians and parents took into account "non-medical considerations, such as subjective judgments that an unrelated handicap makes a person's life not worth living," they would be guilty of discrimination. And to ensure that the rules were being obeyed, HHS investigators could look into confidential hospital records.[64]

As they fought against a united front of doctors, ethicists, and judges, right-to-life leaders were confident that they were persuading the American people. Certainly the circumstances of the early 1980s seemed to favor them. In the glow of Reagan's popularity, these conservatives were defending handicapped children's lives against "the elite." Surprising though it may seem, however, they won media attention far out of proportion to their public support. Consider the anticlimactic sequel to the HHS regulations. The Baby Doe signs hung on the walls of nurses' stations, but they did not elicit the barrage that conservatives hoped for and liberals feared. During the first nine months, fifteen hundred phone calls were made on the "hotline"—an average of one call per five hospitals. Most were comments, requests for information, or wrong numbers. Of the rest, the government found only three cases of inappropriate care.[65]

Beyond this issue, religious conservative activists also made a surprisingly feeble impact on public opinion. In 1980, the year Reagan was elected, half of Americans hadn't heard of the Moral Majority; and of those who had, only one-fifth were favorable toward it. Two years later these proportions were almost unchanged. Still more telling, religious conservatives were evenly divided for and against the Moral Majority. Indeed, 58 percent of evangelicals and 64 percent of Catholics opposed a ban on all abortions.[66] In sum, right-to-life activists constituted a fringe group rather than a vanguard, who could not halt the cultural trend toward the right to die. While Koop captured headlines, most Americans in the 1980s continued struggling to come to terms with modern dying. For the parents of Karen Pomeroy, Karen Quinlan, Infant Doe, and countless others, the answers were far from simple.

"There have been cases where a patient is terminally ill, in a coma and not conscious, with no cure in sight. Do you think that the family of such a patient ought to be able to tell doctors to remove all life-support services and let the patient die. . . ?" When pollsters posed this question in 1977, shortly after the Quinlan case, 66 percent of Americans said yes. By 1985, 80 percent said yes.[67] If the question described a terminally ill (but not comatose) patient who himself asked for removal of life-support, public approval rose even higher. Catholics, Jews, Protestants—including fundamentalists and "born again" Protestants—all gave equally strong endorsement.[68] Most Americans across almost the entire ideological spectrum were rejecting the absolute principle of prolonging life.

Even more significantly, they made distinctions about when life-support should be withdrawn. Like the bioethicists, they advocated "discrimination." If the mother's life was endangered, 94 percent of the public in 1988 endorsed a legal abortion. If the mother was not in danger but the baby would be deformed, approval dropped to 60 percent.[69] As the *Washington Post* columnist Richard Cohen had insisted, *it depends*.

And after that deformed baby was born, what then? Almost no one spoke out in defense of letting Infant Doe die. But more handicaps evoked more uncertainty. When pollsters asked Americans whether they would tell doctors not to perform surgery on "a badly deformed baby . . . born in a Midwestern city who would live only a few years," the public was evenly divided.[70] Five months later this baby became all too real.

"BABY JANE DOE" was born on Long Island, New York, in October 1983, with spina bifida (an opening in the spinal cord), microcephaly (abnormally small head), hydrocephalus (excess fluid in the brain), inability to close her eyes or to use her thumb to suck, and a prolapsed rectum. During the pregnancy, her parents—a thirty-year-old building contractor and his twenty-three-year-old wife, married one year, both of them Catholic—had added two rooms to their brick-and-shingle ranch house. A crib and cradle were waiting in their bedroom, baby clothes in the drawers. But now they had only gruesome futures to choose between. Surgery could extend the baby's life—perhaps to the age of twenty, a neurologist said—but she would be severely retarded, paraplegic, epileptic, and constantly subject to bladder and kidney infections. Without surgery she had virtually no chance of living past the age of two.[71]

At first Mr. and Mrs. Doe decided on surgery. Then, after consulting more physicians, religious advisers, and family members, they changed their minds. "We were told she would have no control over her bladder or rectal functions," her father said. "Her condition for future life is to be bedridden," his wife added, "and she would not have use of her hands. . . . We also know that as she grew older, she would always be an infant. . . . And while she might feel sorrow and joy, her overall condition would be pain."[72] That is how they defined Baby Jane's "best interest." Instead of surgery they chose only feedings, antibiotics, and hygienic care of the exposed spinal sac. The infant wasn't being starved to death. She was being given what the doctors called "conservative" treatment, which would sustain her until she died from her impairments. To pro-life advocates, however, this was nontreatment in disguise, merely killing her more slowly than Infant Doe. Someone on the hospital staff phoned A. Lawrence Washburn, a right-to-life attorney in Vermont, who immediately filed suit in New York courts to compel surgery.[73]

Politically it was the Infant Doe case again, this time with the HHS regulations in place and the pro-life forces steeled by their loss in Bloomington. As the New York Court of Appeals rejected Washburn's suit, denouncing his "offensive" intrusion into "the very heart of a family circle," the Reagan administration took action.[74]

HHS demanded to look into Baby Jane's medical records for evidence of discrimination, and when the hospital refused, the Justice Department sued in federal court. "We're not just fighting for the baby," Surgeon General Koop declared on national television. "We're fighting for the principle of this country that every life is individually and uniquely sacred."[75] Every life, no matter what quality. Seven years earlier, in a booklet against abortion, Koop had described "the dilemmas I have lived through" when deciding whether to operate on infants with no rectum, whose bladder and abdominal organs were inside out, with a cleft spine and with legs so deformed that their feet lay most comfortably next to their ears. But given what the Bible taught, Koop had no doubt about what he should do. "I treated a boy who had half of these things plus a few others," and after twenty-five operations, the family "consider the boy and his problems to be the best experience life has offered them. The boy is a delight."[76] In 1983, talking about Baby Jane, he reiterated that he had "never seen a child like this live a life of pain."[77]

The right-to-life forces were better organized than in the Infant Doe case, but they were no more successful. They lost in court. The U.S. Court of Appeals ruled that Section 504 of the Rehabilitation Act was not intended to apply to newborn infants—a devastating blow to the "Baby Doe regulations." They also lost in the court of public opinion. The surgeon general might invoke the sacredness of life, but even the conservative *Wall Street Journal* said "we are appalled by the hotline brainstorms" created by "the Reagan administration's medico-legal busybodies." Let families decide, not "Big Brother Doe." Dr. Koop, the *New York Times* added, cared less about the infant girl than about "the idea of her."[78]

The conservatives' resort to government power on behalf of family values was backfiring politically, and also emotionally. Baby Jane Doe was not Infant Doe. All families' dilemmas were not alike. To insist on identical treatment was unfair; it was unfeeling. "Who but parents can begin to interpret the meaning of a child born with handicaps?" a journalist argued. "Perhaps it can be said that parents of severely damaged children inhabit a Beirut of the spirit. . . . The rest of us are strangers, and we ought to let the parents consult the doctors, reach their decisions, tend to their babies, grapple with their lives. We ought to respect their heartache and their wishes. We ought to leave them in peace."[79]

But the parents had to make their way through heartrending ambiguity before they could claim any peace of mind. "Where there's life, there's hope," Karen Keatley's father had asserted. "We want to put her in the hands of the Lord," declared Karen Quinlan's father. The clichés scarcely suggest the tortuous calculus by which parents of PVS patients worked them out. For the parents of handicapped newborns, the dilemma was even worse because, however much the doctors' prognoses disagreed, one thing was certain: these children would be conscious. "While she might feel sorrow and joy, her overall condition would be pain," said the mother of Baby Jane Doe. But even this conclusion did not always suffice. Sometimes the decision to let die did not end the story but turned out to be only the middle of a yet more complicated tale.

In April 1984 the parents of Baby Jane allowed surgeons to perform a shunt operation to relieve the pressure on her brain. They didn't explain why, six months after rejecting surgery, they changed their minds. Was it another part of the calculus of minimizing pain? Or a burst of crazy hope? For against medical odds, the spinal opening had healed by itself, with tough leathery skin protecting against infections. The girl, doctors said, was healthy enough to be taken home. And so the young couple took her to the crib they had long ago installed in their bedroom. Four years later a reporter visited the Long Island ranch house and interviewed Dan and Linda A. about Kerri-Lynn. Everything was transformed. Just as the Does had shed some of their anonymity, their daughter had acquired partly normal functions. Although she couldn't walk and had to sit in a wheelchair, she was talking, attending a school for the handicapped, learning to socialize with other children.[80]

It was a disconcerting turn of events. There had been a doomed infant; here was a functional girl. After all the persuasive "best interest" justifications for withholding treatment, five-year-old Kerri-Lynn embodied a powerful refutation. What are we to make of this unexpected outcome?

That depends on who "we" are. A believer in the right to life will read her story as proof that all lives, even the most "deformed," must be protected. To quote an attorney, Victor Rosenbaum, who was working with Americans United for Life: "How is one to determine at birth whether or not you have a Helen Keller?"[81] *One can't*—that's the answer he wrapped inside his rhetorical question. But it's also the answer a believer in the right to die will make. No one can predict with 100 percent certainty at birth, nor at any later point of life. A prognosis offers at best a reasonable probability, says the right-to-die supporter, and so a responsible person decides within a range of uncertainty. In other words, the ethic of ambiguity again. It's a convincing answer as far as it goes. But this general argument seems to falter when it confronts the specific instance of Baby Jane/Kerri-Lynn. She survived "unreasonably," improbably. How ethical is it, then, to say that parents have the right to make mistaken decisions about their children's lives? If she recovered, there must be others who will.

But that's not all there is to say. Debaters of the right to die are, to some extent, the outsiders. Even after they have wrestled with the issue, bringing to bear their keenest analysis and deepest compassion, they ought not be the ones to settle it for an individual patient—a Karen or a Kerri-Lynn. The decision belongs to the parents, the insiders. As that journalist put it, the rest of us are strangers, and we should respect "the Beirut of the spirit" that parents inhabit. Precisely because one can never be certain that a "hopelessly ill" person will not "miraculously" recover, deciding to withhold treatment comes down to an act of faith. Existential. Personal. Notice attorney Rosenbaum's pronouns: "How is *one* to determine at birth whether *you* have a Helen Keller." Outsider pronouns. But Dan and Linda were the ones who "had" Baby Jane. Only they could define what her survival meant to them. It was— had to be—a subjective judgment. They decided, and changed their minds, and changed again, and finally—along with Kerri-

Lynn—they had to live with whatever the consequences turned out to be.

Eight years earlier, Joseph and Julia Quinlan had made a similar act of faith on behalf of their daughter. Now they too were living with the unexpected consequences.

5

Dying on One's Own

SHE WAS EXPECTED to die soon. After her father ordered the physicians to unhook her from the respirator, Karen Ann Quinlan would die within hours, or days, or surely within a few weeks. That's what neurologists had predicted and journalists reported.[1] That's what the New Jersey Supreme Court authorized on March 31, 1976, when it upheld her right of "self-determination," or as courts would later call it, her right of "autonomy." Most people called it her right to die.

Two weeks later nothing had changed. Doctors Morse and Javed, along with the St. Clare's Hospital staff, were continuing essentially the same life-support treatment they had been using all along. "Standard medical protocol," they explained to the Quinlans.

"Does that mean you are going to ignore the Supreme Court?" Joseph Quinlan asked Morse. "You're not going to do anything?"

"Be patient," the doctor replied. "We'll work this out."

Four weeks later Joseph wrote in his diary: "Nothing going on. Nothing. Doubt now whether drs. can carry out our wishes."[2]

Something was being done, but it wasn't what the court or the Quinlans had intended. The doctors and staff were working to "wean" Karen. Every few days they detached the respirator and stood by, ready to reinsert it the moment she seemed in danger of expiring. At first she was able to breathe on her own for an hour, then two hours, then longer. The notes scribbled by Javed and the nurses compose a terse narrative.

MAY 15: Regular breathing pattern with sleep cycle. Off MA-1 for 4 hrs. Did well; will continue weaning process.

MAY 16: Off MA-1, 7 A.M. Sleep cycle with little movement. Later—restless with scream[-]like motions. . . . Put back on MA-1, 11:05. . . . Tolerated well. Will up this period off MA-1 to 8 to 12 hrs. tomorrow.

Weaning. It's a darkly paradoxical term. Karen was being weaned from a machine so that she could live in a persistent vegetative state. If the doctors succeeded, it would be a perverse kind of success, turning the principles of the Supreme Court's decision inside out. Breathing on her own, she would acquire an autonomy that had nothing to do with the usual meaning of self-determination. Her lungs and brain stem would be acting; her consciousness would remain dead.

MAY 17: Color pale. Off MA-1, 8:30. Remains quiet. Respirations remain regular. Awake 10:10, moving head and arching back. Periods shallow breathing. 6:30, respirations irregular and shallow at times. Corrects herself. . . . Off respirator 7 hours. Doing Well.

MAY 18: Off MA-1 for 12 hrs. Restless period. Sleeping, in no apparent distress.

MAY 21: Off MA-1 over 48 hrs.

MAY 22: Doing very well without MA-1. . . . Pt. resting comfortably. Color good. Restful evening. Respiration even and full most of the time.[3]

She was weaned. A few days later the staff moved her out of the intensive care unit to a private room, where she lay with a feeding tube inserted into her nostrils and a catheter into her bladder, along with electric monitors for her heart and breathing. A hose rested on her tracheostomy, emitting distilled air that formed a cloud of misty white vapor over the bed. "That room looked a dream world, almost surrealistic," Julia recalled.[4]

Although Drs. Morse and Javed and the hospital had lost in court, they won in the ICU. They had weaned Karen from the respirator and kept her alive. As Sister Urban, the president of the St. Clare's board of trustees, declared at a meeting with the Quinlans: "You have to understand our position, Mr. Quinlan. In this hospital we don't kill people."

"We're not asking you to *kill* anyone," Joseph shouted.

The story was not ending when it was supposed to. The Quinlans had struggled through grief, anxious conferences with doctors and priests, and the glare of publicity in order finally to let their daughter die naturally, only to find that they—and she—must go on. "I couldn't help but wonder," Joseph remarked, "what could God be using her for now?" The crisis had come and gone. The rest was anticlimax, stretching indefinitely into the future.[5]

For the moment, however, the Quinlans had no time to contemplate that prospect. They needed to transfer Karen to a nursing home, and as they discovered, it was hard to find one that would take a PVS patient. After two hectic weeks and twenty-two rejections, they finally gained consent from Morris View Nursing Home. Next came the problem of how to transport her twelve miles to Morris View without being overrun by voracious journalists. For by this time the media had caught up with the unexpected turn of events. "KAREN'S CASE TANGLED IN WEB OF CONFUSION," proclaimed the *Newark Star-Ledger*.[6] As word spread of the imminent move, reporters and photographers began camping out by the hospital emergency entrance.

In league with the county sheriffs, the Quinlans worked out an escape plan. At 8:45 on a cloudy evening in early June, two of their friends parked an ambulance at the hospital's private entrance, which was hidden by trees, and rushed up to the second floor. With armed sheriff's deputies guarding the elevators and doors, the two men put Karen on a stretcher and took her down to the ambulance. "She was quiet," one recalled, "and so light that it was like handling a sleeping little child." They pulled the curtains tight across the windows to thwart any photographer, the nurse adjusted the bottles feeding Karen, and they sped away into the night, one sheriff's car ahead of them and another following.

Outside the nursing home the media were waiting with floodlights beaming upon the circular driveway. The driver stopped, backed up to the front doors. Photographers sprinted toward the ambulance. But at that very moment a bolt of lightning exploded across the sky, blinding them. Rain gushed down across their camera lenses. "Ready in there?" someone called, and sheriff's men were reaching into the ambulance, rolling the stretcher through the wide entrance doors, across the lobby, up the elevator, and through the heavy metal security door into the bright yellow room on the second floor. As a nurse attached the tubes and bottles, Joseph, Julia, and Father Trapasso stood by the bed, Karen's head rolled slowly side to side, her eyes gazing vacantly at this and that. "It's a nice room, honey," Julia said, kissing her cheek. Joseph set a picture of the Holy Mother on a shelf and hooked a crucifix to the lamp chain above her head. Karen's head slowed, her eyes closed. Father Tom leaned over her and whispered a prayer. With a burst of exhilaration, Julia thought: *You're free, honey.*[7]

Free from the respirator and from the media. But free for what? That was what one couldn't help asking as, day after day, Karen continued breathing. The story turned into a round of tasks, an interminable present.

Joseph visited twice every day, in the morning on his way to work and in the afternoon on his way home. After he and Julia moved to a smaller house forty miles away, he had to wake up at 4:30 a.m. The nurse was usually changing the bed when he arrived. If Karen was in a "wake cycle," he talked to her, "sometimes I even sing," and if she was restless he massaged her back at the top of the spine. "If I see Karen and she's in bad shape, it's upsetting. But if I *don't* see Karen," he said with a shrug, "I just can't relax."

Julia visited once a day. "Hello, Karen, mommie's here." She leaned down to kiss her cheek, stroked her forehead, brushed the dark hair. "I just couldn't imagine lying in a bed for . . . years and not being talked to or held or touched." The little bedside radio was on—it was always on. Some days Julia brought tapes with her daughter's favorite music: Simon and Garfunkel, Judy Collins singing "Amazing Grace." "I know she can't comprehend, but just imagine someone lying in a room with no sound." Some days she brought a nightgown that she cut and sewed, cleaned and pressed, at home the night before.

The nurses turned Karen every two hours, flexed her muscles, administered an anticonvulsant drug, changed the tubes carrying urine and bodily wastes. Every few days the flowers in the vase withered and were replaced with fresh flowers. Summer gave way to fall, winter, spring, a new summer. Karen awoke and slept and awoke again, now and then uttering whimpers, her eyes roving but empty. Her arms and legs were folded tightly against her body, so tightly that her heels made bruises on her buttocks, locked in a fetal position. "She [is] so twisted," a doctor said, "that I couldn't even conceive the pain she would feel if she were to regain consciousness. One could only imagine the feeling if one would take a foot, twist it around a couple of times, and then tie it in that position, curled backward." The nurses bathed and dressed her every day. Her parents talked to her, prayed with her.

As if someone were inside there. Or at least some remnant of Karen. But exactly what kind of existence did she experience? Those on the outside could "imagine." But only she knew whether she saw light, heard music, felt the pain of her heels pressing against her buttocks. It was more consoling to believe that she did not have feelings and especially that she did not know her situation. But when sensation and consciousness were gone, what remained? Ordinary experience offered no answers. "Karen is in limbo," Julia said. "We're all in limbo because she isn't dead, and yet she is not alive, as we think of it." They continued to identify Karen with her body, but what one normally meant by "identity"— her personality—had disappeared. Her body had managed to outlive the person who had inhabited it. "It's a difficult time," Julia said.[8]

After June 1976 the Karen Ann Quinlan story became uneventful. Or it stretched out into one unchanging event hidden behind the locked security door and the lowered window shade on the second floor. But the media kept on talking and writing about her. "Karen Ann still lives, still in a coma," Walter Cronkite announced in October.[9] Her afterlife was the news. As year after year went by, journalists chose different anniversaries for commemoration. The day she fell into the coma; the day doctors weaned her from the respirator; and the favorite choice, her birthday. Curiously, they didn't commemorate the court decision, which had consequences reaching through political, legal, and medical realms. Instead they personified the right to die via the birthday of the woman who lived on. Twenty-three years old in 1977. Twenty-five. Thirty. Thirty-one.[10]

As newspapers and magazines marked each milestone, they often reprinted that familiar high school photograph, increasingly anachronistic. It was even more disquieting to open *People* magazine in April 1985, shortly after her thirty-first birthday, and see Mr. and Mrs. Quinlan holding the framed photo of their teenage daughter. Their faces were jowly and wrinkled while hers remained young and hopeful, as though clocks had stopped. And in every sense but physiological, that was what had happened. Karen's life had stopped on that April night back in 1975, leaving behind a slowly aging simulacrum. The true Karen lay in the past. "I remember a living, vibrant daughter," Julia said in 1985. "Nothing is going to change my memories."[11]

The public also remembered. People from around the globe continued to write to the Quinlans, an average of a dozen letters a day, with the heaviest volume on Karen's birthdays. No more hate mail accusing the Quinlans of killing their daughter. A few writers objected to taking her off the respirator, but most sent support, prayers, even inspirational books. Just as during the trial, the Quinlans remained the saintly protagonists of this prolonged melodrama. They read each letter, saved the children's crayoned prayers, and donated the books by the boxful to the local library.[12]

Only once did the public threaten to strip them of sainthood. In 1977 the Quinlans sold an excerpt of their forthcoming memoir to *Ladies' Home Journal* for twenty thousand dollars. At the same time NBC television broadcast a film titled "In the Matter of Karen Ann Quinlan," with Brian Keith and Piper Laurie playing Mr. and Mrs. Quinlan. (No one portrayed Karen. Again she was the

Joseph and Julia Quinlan,
1985 (Marianne Barcel-
lona, *People*)

invisible presence.) Suddenly the selfless parents seemed to be cashing in on their anguish. "People thought we were taking the money and running to South America," Joseph said. But suspicion evaporated as soon as they made clear that in fact they were using the royalties to establish a home-care program for the terminally ill—the Karen Ann Quinlan Center of Hope. (A few years later Julia would complete a course on counseling the dying and then enroll as one of the initial thirty-two volunteers at the Center.)[13]

Except for this momentary hesitation, the Quinlans retained the sympathy of the vast majority of the public audience. A right-to-life physician might write: "The only once [sic] who wants [sic] to get rid of this burden on their shoulders are the parent [sic] of Karen. Karen is only an adopted child as you know. Who cares about such a thing. A child of your own (not adopted) you have a different feeling from an adopted child." But he confined this malice to an unpublished letter.[14] No one wanted to utter such blasphemy in public. When Shirley MacLaine jokingly described New York City as "the Karen Ann Quinlan of cities" (this was in the middle of New York's fiscal crisis), she hastily apologized in the press as well as directly to the Quinlans by telephone. Whatever accusations and jokes there were, they circulated underground.[15]

But the Quinlans did not escape one basic question. As a *New York Times* editorial phrased it: "Metabolism for what?" If they had unhooked the respirator, why not take the next logical step and remove the artificial nutrition and antibiotics? After all, said the *Times*, these forms of treatment were as "extraordinary" as the breathing machine. The longer they were used, the longer they preserved her "tortured body" and prolonged the "ordeal." And the Quinlans were not the only ones to be considered. "Shall society continue to provide the measures to continue the patient's bodily functions. . . ?"[16]

To Mr. and Mrs. Quinlan the answer was clear and unshakable. "Intravenous is food," Joseph had declared during the trial. "You can't remove that. That would be euthanasia. . . ."[17] Even after she was weaned from the respirator and, contrary to expectations, remained alive, the Quinlans didn't change their minds. Why this apparent inconsistency? In part they were too exhausted, physically and emotionally, to start rethinking their position. But they also had theological reasons, which made their position not at all inconsistent. Having chosen to disconnect the respirator and let God decide her fate, they wouldn't now go on to withdraw the feeding tube. That would be second-guessing God.[18] As their lawyer, Paul Armstrong, announced in May 1976: "[The Quinlans] want especially to assure all who have come to know Karen and wish her well that, until God calls her home, she will be cared for as one of His children and that every need of her sadly weakened body will be ministered to."[19]

There was also a more pragmatic—one might call it "political"—subtext. They were taking public opinion into account. In 1976 they had discussed with Armstrong whether to withdraw the feeding tube and had decided to wait until "cultural acceptance and understanding" caught up with the idea.[20] During the next ten years Americans did just that. To be sure, there was a hue and cry when Infant Doe's parents decided to let their son starve to death.

But he was mentally retarded, not in a vegetative state. He had the prospect of a meaningful life, whereas for Karen there was only expensive, twenty-four-hour-a-day maintenance. By 1985, while the Quinlans continued waiting for God to let her die, the vast majority of physicians, state court judges, bioethicists, and the general public supported the right of families to withdraw life support.[21] Withdrawal not simply of respirators but of artificial food and liquid. And not just from PVS patients but from the elderly.

THANKS TO economic abundance, modern medicine, and Medicare, Americans were living longer. The average life expectancy, which had been sixty-three in 1940, leaped to seventy-one by 1970 and by 1990 rose yet further to seventy-five. The elderly formed, in fact, the fastest-growing age group in the population.[22] It was fitting that Ronald Reagan, just short of his seventieth birthday, became the oldest president ever elected.

Contrary to the usual bleak image, most old people were enjoying their "extra" years. With the combined benefits of Medicare and Social Security, the proportion of elderly Americans in poverty diminished from 35 percent (1959) to 12 percent (1990).[23] Physically they were also doing better than one might suppose. Despite aches and pains and illnesses, few were bedridden. According to a federal survey conducted during 1982–1994, a smaller and smaller percentage of people over sixty-five were unable to feed themselves, take a walk, and otherwise care for themselves. Furthermore, the percentage with chronic diseases like high blood pressure and emphysema had steadily declined. When they did fall ill, the large majority were cared for by spouse or children or friends. A growing number of old people—including 40 percent of elderly women—lived alone but usually not in lonely isolation. Most said they preferred independence rather than being a burden on others. And three of four had seen one of their children during the past week, while one-third had been visited at least three times by relatives.[24]

Nevertheless, the longer they lived, the more hardships they experienced: arthritis, above all; also impaired hearing and vision, hypertension, heart disease, emphysema.[25] Body inexorably deteriorated, and so did mind. In 1994 Nancy Reagan announced that her husband, like more than 10 percent of elderly Americans, was suffering from Alzheimer's disease. So he faced the grim prospect of losing his memory, his speech, his physical mobility—in sum, his personality—while she had to try and take care of him during "the thirty-six-hour day." Because women outlived men, they were more likely to suffer the worst of old age. Wives tended their husbands through illnesses and then were left to live on their own. Only one-third of all widows were cared for by their children. The rest either depended on strangers—nurses, social workers, Meals on Wheels volunteers—or in the case of one-fourth of these women, received no help at all.[26]

For the most helpless there was a nursing home. Although at any one time only 5 percent of people older than sixty-five resided in nursing homes, during their last years 20 percent spent at least a short time there. One of four would die there. But death came late for nursing home residents (their average age was eighty-two), and in the meantime they languished. Physically most were dependent for feeding, bathing, and bodily functions. Socially they were isolated; almost half had no visits by a close relative. They became depressed, incoherent, hunched in their wheelchairs, indifferent to the noisy television and one another's mumblings.[27]

It was not surprising, then, that half of the right-to-die cases in state appellate courts during 1976–1992 involved elderly, incompetent individuals.[28] More surprising was the confusion and controversy these cases stirred up. One might have thought that the Quinlan court had paved a clear judicial route. Once it permitted a young adult to be taken off life-support, presumably other courts would have little difficulty justifying the same for the elderly. But it wasn't to be that simple. When was life no longer worth living, and who should decide? The answers given by *In re Quinlan* didn't settle those questions. Quite the contrary, it opened the way for cases that confronted judges with new questions and deeper ambiguities.

A few months after the *Quinlan* decision, for example, the

Massachusetts Supreme Court was asked to decide whether a profoundly retarded sixty-seven-year-old man should be given chemotherapy for acute leukemia. Joseph Saikewicz had an IQ of ten and a mental age of less than three. During the past forty-eight years he had been living in Belchertown state mental hospital. After the diagnosis of leukemia, the probate court appointed a guardian to decide what should be done. For Saikewicz certainly could not decide for himself. As a social worker reported after visiting him: "He was engaged in observing others watching t.v. while he uttered loud declaration [sic] sentences, which while emphatic were completely unintelligible to me. He shook my hand when I presented it, but otherwise did not relate to me or to what I said." [29]

The leukemia was life-threatening, but treatment was threatening too. Chemotherapy caused pain, nausea, and tingling of the extremities, plus severe anemia and susceptibility to infection. Worse, it had only a 30 to 40 percent chance of producing a remission for only two to thirteen months. Nevertheless most people chose to suffer the side effects rather than allow their leukemia to run its natural course. But Saikewicz was not like most people. Others had to choose for him. The hospital's attorney argued that, weighing suffering against life, the court should "gamble for success which [Saikewicz] can't do for himself." [30] But the doctors painted a grimmer scenario. Because Saikewicz could not understand why doctors would be plunging needles into him, he would probably resist. "You have to see him," one physician testified in probate court. "When you approach him . . . , he flails at you and there is no way of communicating with him and he is quite strong. . . ." So in order to receive the intravenous drugs, he would have to be tied down and kept in restraint for anywhere between twelve and twenty-four hours a day, as long as five days—a kind of torture scene. And medically speaking, such restraint increased the risk of pneumonia.

Here was the classic debate: state's interest in life versus individual rights. At first the guardian had taken the state's side, favoring treatment, but after hearing the doctors' objections he changed his mind. Unlike competent patients, who "know the reason for the pain and their hope makes it tolerable," Saikewicz would never understand. "Not treating Mr. Saikewicz would be in his best interests," the guardian told the court in May 1976. The judge agreed, ruling in favor of the patient's right to refuse chemotherapy, even though it would temporarily save his life.[31]

The hospital administration immediately appealed to the state supreme court. By the time that court issued its decision, Saikewicz had succumbed to pneumonia, but his name remains attached to one of the more enigmatic opinions in the history of the right to die.

Certain premises were clear enough—clearer, in fact, than the reasoning by the Quinlan court. First of all, incompetent persons maintain their right to refuse life-prolonging treatment. Second, that right outweighs the state's interest in preserving life when the person's condition is incurable. It wasn't a question of whether Saikewicz could be saved, but "when, for how long, and at what cost to the individual that life may be briefly extended."[32] In his case the answer was far less ambiguous than in Quinlan's. Her vegetative state was irreversible but not fatal; Saikewicz's leukemia undoubtedly was terminal. He had the right to be allowed to die unimpeded by treatment.

The right may have been clear, but the person was clouded. The court's problem emerged when it turned to the question of what Saikewicz wanted done to him. Quinlan's parents had quoted the preferences she had expressed before she fell into a coma. Saikewicz had been profoundly retarded since birth, so there were no prior wishes (advance directives) for someone to quote. Worse yet, there was no family to speak for him, because two sisters—the only relatives who could be located—refused to become involved.[33] For most of his life Joseph Saikewicz had been in the care of strangers, and now strangers determined his dying. Somehow or other, eight judges would speak for this man with a mental age of less than three.

They could have used the "best interests" criterion, as other courts did when deciding whether to treat a handicapped baby like Infant Doe. That is, subtracting the patient's pain from his pleasure and considering what "a reasonable person" wants, would treatment serve his interests more fully than nontreatment?[34] But even if Saikewicz was like an infant by providing no past testimony, he was also quite different, because at age sixty-seven with leukemia, he had a limited future. So the Massachusetts Supreme Court rejected the ostensibly "objective" best-interests criterion and, citing the *Quinlan* precedent, chose a subjective approach: "substituted judgment." When the Quinlan court put themselves in her place, they had no doubt that "if Karen were herself miraculously lucid for an interval," she would want the respirator disconnected. When the Saikewicz court made the same move, however, they ran into embarrassing trouble.

Given the "pain and fear" that Saikewicz would experience, they said, he would refuse chemotherapy. But how could they imagine what a man with a mental age of two years, eight months, would choose if he could understand what in fact he could never understand? "The decision in cases such as this," declared the justices, "should be that which would be made by the incompetent person, if that person were competent. . . ." This formula was enigmatic enough, but the court didn't stop there. It added to the enigma a baffling paradox. The decision should be what an incompetent person would make if he were competent, "but taking into account the present and future incompetency of the individual as one of the factors that would necessarily enter into the decision-making process of the competent person."[35]

Subjectivity had landed the judges in incoherence. As one legal scholar put it, they had postulated "a miraculously lucid Mr. Saikewicz looking down upon himself and his plight. Yet the miraculously lucid Mr. Saikewicz would not be Mr. Saikewicz at all. He would be someone else entirely—a person who could comprehend complex medical and moral dilemmas."[36] Other commentators were more scathing. The court's approach, a critic said, "is like asking 'If it snowed all summer would it then be winter?'" Constitutional expert Laurence Tribe derided "the fiction" that reached "almost Alice in Wonderland proportions."[37]

It *was* a kind of fiction, but so was what the New Jersey

Supreme Court had constructed on behalf of Karen Ann Quinlan. Given little or no evidence of what an incompetent person would think about invasive treatment, outsiders had to make up a plausible narrative. Or in psychological terms, they had to fill in the blanks of personal identity. "I know she can't comprehend," Julia Quinlan said as she played her daughter's favorite music, "but just imagine someone lying in a room with no sound." For Joseph Saikewicz there were fewer clues from which to construct the narrative. Logically the court would have been on firmer ground if they had simply said: "We want to spare Mr. Saikewicz this useless pain and fear; may he die in peace." Legally that would have been untenable—a Do Not Resuscitate order issued without the patient's consent. Morally it seems very defensible. The court was sparing Saikewicz the trauma of chemotherapy that would have staved off death by an extra few months, a year at most. He had almost fulfilled his biblical quota of three score and ten. Why make him eke out a little more life with a lot of pain and fear?

Very defensible but not absolutely certain, because no one can inhabit someone else's consciousness. Outsiders, whether parents or judges, must construct a kind of "fiction." They can read the signs of pain—the grimaces, the moans—but only the subject himself knows what he is feeling. Only he decides, moreover, the *meaning* of the pain: whether it's chosen (like a marathon runner's pain) or endured (like a patient's after surgery) or unbearable, with no redeeming quality. As Elaine Scarry has brilliantly clarified, pain creates an "absolute split between one's sense of one's own reality and the reality of other persons." Although they may be merely inches apart, the person in pain is absolutely certain of "having pain," but his companion cannot absolutely confirm it.[38]

When the insider is deemed incompetent, the split of uncertainty widens to a gulf, requiring an outsider to construct both parts of the dialogue. So the Massachusetts court presumed to read the mind of a severely retarded man. Even if Saikewicz had once been competent, however, the task would not necessarily have become simple. For then there would have emerged a different kind of split: between what the once competent, younger individual wished and what the now incompetent, elderly patient may or may not wish. History—personal identity—enters the calculation and introduces the challenge of defining who the person is or has become over the twisting course of time. Do we honor the preferences he declared when still in good health, even though he now appears content—or at least resigned—to live as long as medical ingenuity can sustain him? The answer depends on how we understand "identity": whether one's personality remains essentially the same or, on the other hand, changes over time, outdating what one believed at an earlier stage of life. That's the issue in the abstract. In practice, it becomes a matter of whether a relative of an incompetent, terminally ill patient can justifiably say: "I know which treatment my aunt (or wife or daughter) really wants, because I know her." [39]

THIS WAS the dilemma that eighty-two-year-old Claire Conroy personified in 1983 as she lay in a semifetal position in Parklane Nursing Home in Bloomfield, New Jersey. When admitted four years earlier, she had been fairly healthy, although undergoing periods of confusion caused by organic brain syndrome. Since then her condition had deteriorated drastically. She was afflicted by arteriosclerotic heart disease, diabetes mellitus, and incontinence. Following a severe infection of her foot, gangrene had rotted her lower left leg. All these ailments were certainly debilitating, possibly humiliating, but no one could be sure whether she was feeling pain. For she did not speak, although when moved or touched she might moan. Except for minor movements such as scratching, she lay motionless, her legs folded toward her chest. Now and then she followed people with her eyes, but mostly she stared blankly ahead. Sometimes she smiled when a nurse combed her hair. Lately she had been having difficulty swallowing, and for the past four months she was being fed by a nasogastric tube because, as her doctor said, "even a person with great time and patience could probably not have coaxed her into absorbing enough fluids and solid foods by mouth to sustain herself." Several times each day a nurse poured a nutrient formula, vitamins, and medicine through the tube.[40]

Her nephew Thomas Whittemore, who was serving as her guardian, pleaded with the nursing home physician, Dr. Kazemi, to remove the tube. He had known his aunt for more than fifty years, had visited her almost every week before as well as since she entered the nursing home, and had no doubt about what she wanted. She feared doctors—went out of her way to avoid them. When she had pneumonia, Whittemore said, "you couldn't bring a doctor in." Once, when his wife took her to the hospital emergency room, "as foggy as she was she snapped out of it, she would not sign herself in. . . ." All her life she had clung to a narrow but proud independence. For seventy-nine years his aunt had lived with her three sisters in the house where they had been born, and all they wanted "was to . . . have their bills paid and die in their own house."[41] She worked at a cosmetics company from her teens until her early sixties. She never married, had few friends. One by one the sisters died, leaving Claire alone, increasingly confused, until finally Whittemore placed her in the nursing home. A year ago he had refused to let doctors amputate her gangrenous leg, claiming she would not have consented to the surgery. Now he was objecting to the feeding tube as a violation of her wishes—of her personality.

Dr. Kazemi disagreed. "She's a human being," he said, "and I guess she has a right to life if it's possible." Furthermore he believed that withdrawing treatment would violate his ethical obligation not to cause harm. If the nasogastric tube were removed, he predicted that Claire Conroy would die of dehydration in about a week. But before she became unconscious, she would suffer painful thirst.[42]

On January 24, 1983, Whittemore asked the New Jersey Superior Court for authorization to remove the tube and let his aunt die. At first glance *In re Conroy* seems a rerun of *In re Quinlan*. An electrical machine may appear to be more "extraordinary" than a tube, but they were equally invasive of the body, equal interruptions of natural process. And if one is repelled by the idea of letting

Claire Conroy starve to death, how different is the prospect of Karen Quinlan suffocating? But there was a profound difference: Quinlan was vegetative; Conroy was conscious.

This was the quandary that Judge Reginald Stanton pondered during two days of testimony. At the end he remarked, "I think it fair to say that everyone in this case wishes that this poor woman would die." But because modern medicine had postponed that conclusion, physicians and courts must "play God" by exercising "our basic human responsibility to make choices." In working out his existential decision, Stanton had struggled with grave misgivings. ". . . I worried that I was getting perilously close to a straightforwardly wrongful refusal to feed a fellow human being." There was also the danger of the slippery slope. What if a decision to remove Conroy's feeding tube encouraged others to withhold treatment from the senile and retarded? On the other hand, Stanton said, "nature may be telling us something" when a person has lost the ability to swallow. Given the brain damage and all her other ailments, Conroy's life "has become impossibly and permanently burdensome for her." To prolong her life would be "a wrong." Therefore the judge ordered that the nasogastric tube be removed, even though that would lead to a swift and perhaps painful death by starvation and dehydration.[43]

Two weeks later, before the order could be carried out, Conroy died. As Stanton had hoped, nature had taken over for human decision. Because the issues were so significant, however, the case continued on a bizarre, Dickensian journey through the legal system. First to the New Jersey Court of Appeals, which reversed the lower court, then to the New Jersey Supreme Court, which in January 1985, by a vote of 6 to 1, reversed the appeals court. But this ruling didn't double back to Judge Stanton's forthright affirmation of the right to die. As the dissenting justice bitterly complained, the majority narrowed that right while ostensibly expanding it. All this on behalf of a woman who was already dead.

"All Steps to Prolong a Patient's Life, Including Feeding, Can Be Halted," said the front-page headline in the *New York Times*.[44] Feeding certainly was the decision's most radical feature. Nine years after the Quinlan court had struggled to draw a line between ordinary and extraordinary treatment, the Conroy court swept this distinction away. Feeding, with all its emotional symbolism of life and nurture, may seem ordinary—indeed, indispensable. Nevertheless, the justices argued, these presumptions don't necessarily carry over into the ICU. A nasogastric tube is not like bottle-feeding or spoon-feeding. It is a medical procedure, which compensates for what the body cannot do on its own and which entails risks as well as side effects. This definition shifted the burden from the kind of treatment to the patient's choice of whether to be treated. Here the court made a second radical move. ". . . The right we are seeking to effectuate is a very personal right to control one's own life." Where the Quinlan court had anxiously weighed the state's interest in life against the patient's right to refuse treatment, the Conroy court came down emphatically on one side. "A competent patient has the right to decline any medical treatment, including artificial feeding, and should retain that right when and if he becomes incompetent." [45] *Any* treatment, and *in*competent patients. *In re Conroy* appeared to set no limits to self-determination.

But these radical principles turned out to be, in practice, surprisingly conservative. When the justices shifted their attention from the generic patient ("he") to Claire Conroy, they insisted upon criteria that effectively vetoed her right to be allowed to die. (Whatever they ruled, of course, had no consequences for her, because she was dead. They were working out a double fiction: not only what she might have wanted if competent to say it, but what she might have wanted if alive. The historian, in turn, has difficulty figuring out the appropriate verb tense: "she wanted" or "she would have wanted.")

How could one be sure that Conroy wanted the feeding tube removed? A living will would have erased any doubt, but she had never written one and, in her last months, could no longer dictate one. So her nephew had to invoke other evidence if he was to pass what the court labeled its "subjective test." At first his chances seemed good, because—contrary to the Quinlan case—these justices would consider hearsay of Conroy's prior statements about life-prolonging treatment.[46] But such statements alone didn't warrant a substituted judgment. A surrogate must also present a multitude of data: the patient's life expectancy, the risks and benefits of various treatments, the degree of humiliation entailed, the degree of physical pain, and so on. For Claire Conroy the court made yet other requirements. Her nephew should have obtained more information about her ethical and religious beliefs, her feelings about medical treatment and nursing homes, and "her goals in life." [47] The justices may have proclaimed an incompetent patient's right to control his or her life, but, item by item, they were subtracting control. With all these prerequisites, a surrogate had a daunting task to prove that someone wanted to die.[48]

Recognizing this fact, the court supplemented its "subjective test" with two "objective" tests, which posed easier standards of evidence. But they didn't ease the surrogate's obligations. On the contrary, they led into a bioethical cul-de-sac. For the key criterion in both objective tests, the criterion the justices came back to again and again, was pain. "We emphasize that . . . the primary focus should be the patient's desires and experience of pain and enjoyment. . . ." If life-prolonging treatment inflicts unavoidable pain, and if the pain outweighs any physical, emotional, or intellectual gratification, then let treatment end.[49] So said the six justices in the majority. But at this point we need to ask: how does one go about assessing pain objectively?

It's difficult enough to describe our own experience of it. Unlike any other state of consciousness (as Elaine Scarry has noted), physical pain "is not *of* or *for* anything. . . . Because it takes no object . . . , it . . . resists objectification in language." In trying to find words for pain, we resort to metaphors: "splitting, burning, shooting." [50] Nevertheless, even if we can't easily describe our pain, we certainly can assert it and refuse treatment. The trouble comes when we try to define another person's pain. Even with elderly patients who are mentally competent, doctors tend to discredit their complaints, saying that pain is a normal accompaniment to aging and/or that they can find no physical cause. The elderly, in turn, feel stigmatized, confused, even "crazy." [51] If diagnosis in such cases is fraught with ambiguity, it is irreparably so for patients who are demented or cannot speak. When Claire Conroy moaned as nurses moved her, was that a sound of pain or irritation or greeting, or was it merely reflexive noise? When she occasionally smiled as a nurse brushed her hair, was she expressing pleasure? And if so, did this pleasure outweigh the pain that she may have been feeling at other times?[52]

Definition of her present pain was baffling enough; it became quite bewildering when one estimated her pain in the future. If the feeding tube were removed, what then? Dr. Kazemi had predicted Conroy would suffer days of pain until finally becoming unconscious. On the other hand, an internist had testified that, although the dehydration "could be painful," Conroy would become unconscious "long before she died." Given these contradictory signals, the justices produced contradictory conclusions—once again, conservative in practice but radical in principle. On the one hand, they said, Conroy's condition didn't pass the objective tests because medical evidence didn't prove that the pain she felt while fed by tube exceeded the pain she would have felt if the tube were removed. "Guardians—and courts . . . —should act cautiously and deliberately. The consequences are most serious—life or death. . . ."

When they considered treatment in principle, on the other hand, the justices spoke boldly. A nasogastric tube often produces irritation and discomfort, they said, and nurses may have to tie the arms of a patient who tries to pull out the tube. Dehydration, by contrast, "may well not be distressing or painful to a dying patient. . . ." In these last days the patient might simply need ice chips for dry mouth and sips of liquids. "Indeed," the court concluded, "it has been observed that patients near death who are not receiving nourishment may be more comfortable than patients in comparable conditions who are being fed and hydrated artificially."[53]

How could *In re Conroy* expand in principle the right to withdraw treatment but in practice leave Claire Conroy (had she been alive) to die with a nasogastric tube in her body? Something was wrong here. As Justice Alan Handler declared in his dissent, "I harbor the most serious doubts as to the justice, efficacy, or humaneness of a standard that would require a person to die in this fashion." The majority's first fallacy, Handler argued, lay in their emphasis on pain. Drugs and medical techniques can almost always reduce pain to an acceptable level. But some patients abhor dependency as much as pain. Some prefer privacy over nursing care. Some value bodily integrity more than "prolonging life at its most rudimentary level." In short, the issue was not simply pain but suffering. Unless we take into account a dying patient's values, Handler said, we will too easily deny her a "humane, dignified and decent ending. . . ."[54]

Pain was the tip of the iceberg of subjectivity. The justices might try to steer by objective guidelines, but there was no escaping ambiguity. They—or Conroy's nephew, or her doctors—had to interpret her behavior, statements, and values, and then pronounce a life or death sentence. Who can blame the six justices for hesitating and calling for more evidence, as if more evidence would erase the last anxious zone of doubt? But to quote philosopher Thomas Nagel: "Certain forms of perplexity—for example about freedom, knowledge, and the meaning of life—seem to me to embody more insight than any of the supposed solutions to those problems."[55] If outsiders were going to treat dying patients as subjects rather than objects, they would have to make judgments that went beyond the evidence. Physiological data would not suffice, nor even conjectures about the experience of pain. In evaluating how someone would want her life to end, outsiders needed to devise a coherent story of how she had lived it up to now—of who she had been and presumably still was. In other words, understand the personal history that she brought with her to the hospital bed.[56]

Like all narratives, this would be a kind of fiction. Then again, so is the personal identity we claim for who we are now and who we remember having been ever since childhood. In autobiography we recollect and arrange the pieces of our past into a coherent sense of self. In psychotherapy we do the same out loud. An in-

competent patient, however, can no longer testify on her own behalf. She retains the right of privacy but has lost autonomy. She depends upon someone else to devise the proper last chapter—an
ending true to the life she has led up to now. Who should perform
that responsibility, and how should he do it, and when?

THE *Conroy* decision entailed these profound, enigmatic questions about personhood, but the issue of "starving to death" overshadowed them. And even that issue, which had made the cases of
Infant Doe and Baby Jane Doe so notorious, didn't attract the
mass media. Except for a front-page *New York Times* article and an
Associated Press report on page 20 of the *Los Angeles Times*, newspaper readers everywhere else in the country were told nothing.
There were no photographs of Claire Conroy, no interviews with
her nephew or doctors, none of the celebrity heaped upon the
Quinlans. ABC television news did air a story about dying that
evening, but it had an altogether un-Conroy-like heroine and outcome—young and happy. Three-year-old Megan Birmingham, who
had been abandoned by her mother in the snow in Olathe, Kansas,
was revived after hours of exposure and having been declared clinically dead.[57] What this media silence tells us is that an impaired
eighty-four-year-old woman lacked the dramatic appeal of a "sleeping beauty" or an Infant Doe. And by the time the court issued its
ruling, Conroy had died—so it was a drama with an empty stage.

Although this right-to-die sequel didn't have the ingredients to
stir the general public's imagination, within more specialized circles it fanned already heated debates. Predictably, right-to-life
spokespersons were outraged. The *Conroy* decision, according to
the president of the National Right to Life Committee, was
"changing all rules which protected your life and mine." Instead of
the presumption that incompetent patients wanted beneficial
treatment, now the presumption was they did not. "Withdrawing
food and water," said the director of Americans United for Life, "is
allowing the doctor, not the illness, to introduce death." In the

wake of living-will laws and substituted judgment, here was another step toward involuntary euthanasia. "Lord, how quickly awful things are coming to pass," the editor of *The Right to Life News* lamented. It was becoming all too easy, he said, to foresee lethal injections and assisted suicides of Alzheimer victims. ". . . Let us not kid ourselves. We face a pro-death juggernaut that will require every ounce of our creativity, resolve and determination to repulse."[58]

Even though he had been ardently defending patients' rights, abortion, and death with dignity, Daniel Callahan, the liberal director of the Hastings Center, was also dismayed. He felt ambivalent toward the withdrawal of artificial nutrition and hydration. Rationally he could approve it, but emotionally he drew back in "a deep-seated revulsion." Regardless of circumstances, Callahan said, the idea of starving anyone to death was unacceptable. No doubt, he conceded, some people would live on in ways that weren't beneficial to them or others. No doubt their care would be expensive. "That strikes me as a tolerable price to pay to preserve . . . one of the few moral emotions that could just as easily be called a necessary social instinct."[59]

Although removal of a respirator deprived a patient of air, for some reason that action didn't carry the same symbolic weight as withdrawing a feeding tube—perhaps because the respirator is mechanical, hence more "artificial"; perhaps, one can speculate, because nutrient is tangible and connotes infant nursing. Whatever the reason, various bioethicists, law professors, and physicians warned that once you condone the withdrawal of food and drink, you blur the line between letting die and killing.[60] Most state legislators agreed. Even as they enacted permissive living-will laws in the 1980s—some even permitting pregnant women to forgo life-support—they drew the line on feeding. Half the laws didn't mention withdrawal of artificial nutrition, most of the others allowed it only under narrow conditions, and five states passed or amended laws explicitly prohibiting it.[61] In Clearwater, Florida, for example, eighty-five-year-old Estelle Browning specified in her living will that she did not wish to be kept alive by a feeding tube. "Thank God, I've got this taken care of," she said. "I can go in peace when my time comes." But when she suffered a stroke the next year and became permanently comatose, she was kept alive by a feeding tube, because Florida's living-will law allowed patients to refuse food and water only if they were in a "terminal" condition. Browning died, like Conroy, with a tube in her throat and her case being appealed.[62]

When all was said and done, though, the remarkable fact is how sparse the opposition. In 1983, 73 percent of doctors had said they would continue hydrating an incurably ill patient. But opinion leaders in bioethical, judicial, and medical fields took the opposite position. First the president's commission (1983), then the *Conroy* decision (1985), and then the American Medical Association's judicial council (1986) stated that forgoing food and water was no different, morally, from forgoing other life-support procedures. On the contrary, it constituted (to quote one health lawyer) "an intimate final freedom."[63] By the late 1980s, 73 percent of physicians agreed that, if the patient or family requested it, they would *dis*continue hydrating—a complete turnabout. By 1990 they were virtually unanimous.[64]

Even Daniel Callahan resolved his ambivalence. Overcoming his former "deep-seated revulsion," he recognized that the routine use of artificial feeding was "one more case of technology coming to force our hand, leading us to do things we might not otherwise do." As the dying body shuts down, he wrote in 1993, it reduces a person's ability to take food and water. To withdraw the feeding tube, he asserted, isn't to starve the patient but to allow him a peaceful death.[65]

Back in the fifties and sixties the medical profession had been discussing the dilemma of modern dying long before the general public paid attention. In the 1980s public opinion kept pace with the professionals. When asked whether the family of a terminally ill, incompetent patient should be able to tell doctors to remove all life-support, a steadily increasing majority of Americans said yes: 66

percent shortly after the *Quinlan* decision; 73 percent in 1981; and 81 percent in 1985 after the *Conroy* decision. But certain groups held back. Because of their religious beliefs, fewer African Americans and Hispanics agreed. So did high school dropouts and people with lower incomes, perhaps reflecting suspicion of professional authority. And so did people over the age of sixty-five, who feared being denied medical treatment or even being dispensed with. Nevertheless, in each of these categories a solid majority advocated the right to refuse all treatment.[66]

In 1990 the United States Congress reflected this trend when it passed the Patient Self-Determination Act. The law required hospitals, nursing homes, and hospices to inform patients of their right not only to accept or refuse medical treatment but also to execute a living will. If an institution failed to comply it would forfeit Medicare and Medicaid reimbursements. The Department of Health and Human Services installed a nationwide, toll-free telephone number for patients or physicians who had questions. It was a vivid contrast to the "hotline" the Reagan administration had set up eight years earlier to catch doctors or families who wouldn't treat handicapped infants.[67]

In short, pro-life groups spoke for a much smaller constituency than one might suppose. Because of their crusading zeal and the resulting publicity (whether favorable or hostile), they appeared to represent a vast social movement. During the eighties and early nineties, Reagan, Bush, and growing numbers of conservative congressmen were elected, the Equal Rights Amendment was defeated, *Roe v. Wade* was narrowed by subsequent Supreme Court decisions, and abortion clinics were picketed and bombed. By this evidence, the right to life seemed in ascendancy. But on the issue of "dying with dignity," the prevailing trend was moving in the opposite direction. State courts, medical organizations, and public opinion were firmly aligned behind the right to withdraw life-support, now even including nutrition and hydration.

The picture was more complicated, though. Most Americans advocated "the right to die" when they were asked to pay attention to the issue. In their day-to-day experience, on the other hand, they continued to ignore it, even amid a deadly epidemic and even in the face of terminal illness.

STARTING IN 1981, a very unlikely group was forced to contemplate their mortality. Gay men in the prime of life gradually began realizing that a disease was spreading among them. The symptoms were frightening: swollen lymph nodes, weight loss, night sweats, thrush, culminating in bacterial pneumonia, Kaposi's sarcoma, blindness, dementia. In 1982 scientists gave a name to this disease—Acquired Immune Deficiency Syndrome (AIDS)—and two years later they traced it to a virus—the Human Immunodeficiency Virus (HIV)—which was transmitted by semen or blood. But the virus remained latent for years, so for many men the news came too late to avoid infection. And once infected, there was no cure. Reported cases of AIDS in the United States multiplied at stunning speed: 10 new ones each week in 1982, 100 each week in 1984. By 1988, 62,000 cases had been reported, more than half of whom had died. Newspaper obituaries listed men in their forties, thirties, late twenties who had died "of cancer" or "after a long illness," survived by parents, siblings, and sometimes "a companion." Within ten years, AIDS took more American lives than the Korean and Vietnam wars combined.[68]

A lethal epidemic was under way, a plague, and not only among the gay population. Intravenous drug-users, patients who received blood transfusions, women who had sex with HIV-infected men—they too were developing AIDS. Indeed, despite medical experts' assurances, half of all Americans in 1985 believed they could be infected by casual contact: drinking from the same glass of water, for example, as an HIV-positive person. Seventeen percent said they were afraid of contracting AIDS.[69] It seemed as if scientific history was being rolled back thirty or forty years to those days when every parent and child feared being struck by polio. That anxiety had been vanquished in 1955 by the Salk vaccine, but now a new deadly virus was at work, arousing a primitive kind of fear as in

the days of the Black Death. "Fear of AIDS," a *New York Times* reporter wrote in 1985, "has become a kind of disease itself."[70]

Fear quickly took on an edge of panic. These were the years
when airports were installing metal detectors and X-ray machines
to fend off political terrorists. Now some opinion leaders defined
AIDS as biological terrorism.[71] "We must conquer it for the sake [of
the individuals at risk]," Secretary of Health and Human Services
Margaret Heckler declared. "We must conquer it as well before it
affects the heterosexual population and threatens the health of our
general population."[72] Mayor Edward Koch said that no child with
AIDS should be allowed to attend New York City public schools. In
Arcadia, Florida, a minister expelled from the congregation a family whose three hemophiliac sons had acquired AIDS by blood
transfusion, and soon afterward their home was burned to the
ground. When a nursing home in Queens, New York, decided to accept ten AIDS patients, a thousand local residents attended a
protest meeting. "They will be ambulatory!" one man shouted to
cheers of agreement. "They will be walking our streets!"[73] According to a *Los Angeles Times* poll in 1985, 51 percent of the public believed that people with AIDS should be quarantined, and 15
percent said they should be tattooed.[74]

But this was the age of modern science, not the Middle Ages,
and unlike either the Black Death or polio, AIDS was a selective
epidemic. By 1989, when 90 percent of Americans understood they
could not be infected by working closely with an AIDS victim, the
initial panic had subsided.[75] And what followed? One might have
expected AIDS to bring the possibility of death into the center of
cultural awareness. That is what Fenton Johnson, a gay novelist
whose lover had died of AIDS, asserted so confidently in his memoir. "Surely we are all dealing with this, HIV-negative or HIV-
positive, irrespective of our gender or sexualities: incorporating
loss into life; substituting for the myth of control a reality that em-
braces light *and* dark, love *and* grief, life *and* death."[76] No, not all
of us—not even most. The vast majority of Americans—almost 90
percent—believed that AIDS sufferers should be treated with compassion. Basically, though, they were viewing the plague from a

great distance. In 1989, 87 percent didn't personally know anyone with AIDS, and 63 percent were "not very" or "not at all" concerned that they would be infected.[77]

The AIDS epidemic brought awareness of death mainly to those who went through the horrendous dying: gays, homosexual and heterosexual drug-users, and the relatively few people who were infected by heterosexual contact or blood transfusions.[78] Medically and socially they were "the others," who could be pushed away to the margins of concern. Fear of AIDS at first reduced casual sex among college students, for example, but only temporarily. By the mid-1990s a peer health educator at Lehigh University, who provided AIDS information to students, reported: "It hasn't cast a cool breeze at all." Nationwide only one-third of college women demanded that men use a condom for vaginal sex.[79] Despite Johnson's hopes, mainstream Americans embraced love without grief, life without the shadow of death.

ON April 22, 1994, four days after a stroke left him partly paralyzed and virtually unable to speak or see, Richard Nixon died in a New York City hospital. Less than a month later Jacqueline Kennedy Onassis died in her Manhattan apartment shortly after doctors told her that lymphoma had spread to her liver and brain. The media gave lavish attention to their lives, of course, but also to the ways they ended their lives. The former president had instructed his physicians to withhold extraordinary treatment if he were gravely ill, and the former First Lady had done the same via an advance directive. As a *New York Times* headline explained, "The Nixon and Onassis Examples Show the Way to a Dignified Death." Immediately the number of people telephoning Choice in Dying, a national agency furnishing advice on living wills, jumped from an average of one hundred per day to two thousand.[80] But proponents of the right to die should not have felt encouraged. This spurt of public interest produced no improvement in the circumstances of modern dying. "People think advance directives are solving the problem," said one medical researcher in 1995. "We have very good information that they aren't, that nothing has changed—the amount of pain at the end of life, the number of people dying alone attached to machines."[81] Why this gloomy outcome? The answers implicate not only doctors and patients but also the living will itself and ultimately the cultural values imbedded in the right-to-die philosophy.

The first and most tempting answer is to blame doctors, and there is abundant evidence to justify doing so. Equipped with what they call their "armamentarium," physicians all too often battle against disease heroically, relentlessly, defining death as failure, disregarding their patients' suffering and indignity. In one New York state hospital in 1988, for example, patients were revived by CPR as many as fifty-two times in a four- to six-week period.[82] According to a survey of North Carolina doctors a year later, 86 percent would refuse CPR if they themselves were terminally ill, but only 21 percent routinely discussed the issue with their patients. One-third, in fact, believed that, regardless of a patient's preference, it was the doctor who should decide whether to resuscitate.[83]

The vast majority of doctors say they believe in conferring with patient and family about whether to use life-support, but the vast majority don't confer. At Boston's Beth Israel Hospital in 1981, they discussed CPR with only 19 percent of their patients before using it, although 86 percent of the patients were competent. (One-third of the competent patients who survived CPR said they had not wanted it.)[84] Whatever they may profess to opinion pollsters, physicians tend to shy away from talking about death with a terminally ill person. They wait until the last moment, often after the patient is already comatose, and they therefore end up talking with the family. One symptom: most do-not-resuscitate orders are written two or three days before death.[85] Despite physicians' endorsement of the 1973 Patient Bill of Rights, and despite their expedient alliance in the 1980s with patients and ethicists against government regulation, the majority still make their decisions unilaterally.

Even when they take the time to talk with patients and family, doctors often employ techno-language. "The procedure is medically indicated." "He was extubated by conventional criteria." Or else they camouflage their intentions behind euphemisms. "Do you want a little help with your breathing?" the physician asks a patient, and after receiving the intended reply he installs a respirator. "Do you want your grandmother to starve to death?" he asks the relatives, and then surgically inserts a tube into her stomach.[86] Even when a patient has written a living will, chances are that the physicians will be unaware of it. According to a 1994–1995 study of five teaching hospitals, only 47 percent of doctors knew that their patients preferred to avoid CPR.[87]

Medical paternalism also may work in the opposite direction, toward terminating life-support. A doctor at Massachusetts General Hospital, for example, entered a DNR order on the chart of seventy-one-year-old Catherine Gilgunn, who was comatose and irreversibly brain-damaged. He was acting in accord with the judgment by the hospital's health-care committee but against the wishes of Mrs. Gilgunn's daughter. When her mother died three days later, Joan Gilgunn sued the doctors and the hospital. Except for the lawsuit, this episode was less unusual than one might suppose. According to a 1995 survey of doctors in adult ICUs throughout the United States, more than 80 percent had withheld or withdrawn treatment they considered futile, over the objections of family members (and 14 percent without informing the family).[88] Without knowing these facts, many patients—particularly those who were poor or persons of color—feared being deprived of care by cost-cutting hospitals. To sign an advance directive seemed to be saying they had little desire to live, inviting neglect or worse.[89]

In the 1970s the American public had accorded more confidence to the medical system than to any other institution, including even the church. In the make-believe world of television dramas during the eighties and nineties, the men (and some women) in white continued exercising almost mystical authority as they cared for and saved patients.[90] But "St. Elsewhere" and "Chicago Hope" weren't reality. By 1993 the medical profession had slid precipitously in public confidence, ranking lower than seven major institutions (though higher than the media, Congress, and big business).[91] Americans were indignant not only at the staggering cost of health care but also at the arrogance of these highly paid experts. In matters to do with dying, indignation was particularly strong. Patients had won in principle the protection of a living will, but in practice it was nullified when they entered the ICU. So goes one explanation for the failure of living wills.

A second answer, on the other hand, is to blame patients. If health-care costs are high, consumers share much of the responsibility. Doctors order expensive tests—MRIs, CAT scans—sometimes more tests than strictly necessary, because in the era of "patient rights" they need to protect themselves against malpractice suits. Rather than paternalists, they see themselves as beleaguered professionals in an adversarial relationship. And when they discover malignancy, doctors perform exceedingly expensive procedures—chemotherapy or organ transplants—despite low odds of success, because patients insist on "fighting the good fight." A teenage girl with cystic fibrosis, a forty-year-old man with a failing liver, a sixty-year-old woman with metastasized breast cancer: each hopes to salvage some extra years, or at least months, whatever bit of survival their physicians might provide.[92] They want the amazing victory they saw last week on "ER" (which was, tellingly, the most popular TV show during the mid-1990s). All too often it is the doctor who must persuade the patient and family not to prolong futile suffering.

Consider the events surrounding Domenic Ponzo at Boston's Beth Israel Hospital—the same hospital, incidentally, where most doctors in 1981 had performed CPR without consulting their patients. Ten years later, according to *Newsweek*'s cover story, the medical staff were paternalistic in the best sense, compassionately guiding their patients toward difficult decisions. Sixty-nine-year-old Ponzo had had his gallbladder removed, after which things went from bad to worse. Now three doctors and a nurse were sitting with Adeline Ponzo outside the ICU, describing her husband's grim condition: heart weakened by a coronary during the operation; collapsed kidneys; lungs laboring for air; his mind sliding in and out of consciousness. Without massive intervention, they told Mrs.

Ponzo, her husband would die within forty-eight hours—but the intervention would merely prolong his misery.

"Do you mean just let him go?" she asked.

Yes, replied Dr. Scott Weiss, and in the meantime, "we'll do everything short of 'everything.' " That would be the right decision, he added.

"It may be for you, doctor," she replied softly, in sorrow more than anger. "But he's all I have."

In the end she agreed to forgo treatment. The next morning, after she and her husband exchanged "I love yous," he died in her arms.

A few hours later Weiss led interns and residents on morning rounds past the closed door of Ponzo's room. "A peaceful death," he said, far better than the "violent and brutal" experience of being stuck with needles and thumped on the chest. "You have a responsibility," he said, "not to drag out the dying."

Ponzo played a passive role in this end-of-life drama, just as he had during the years leading up to it. He had a history of diabetes, high cholesterol, obesity, high blood pressure, and angina, among other ailments, and for fifty years he had smoked a pack and a half of cigarettes a day. Nevertheless, whenever Adeline, herself a medical assistant, brought up the question of what to do in case of terminal illness, he would say: "I don't want to discuss it."

"He's not a weak-type person," she said, "but he just couldn't discuss this type of thing."

So she ended up discussing it with Dr. Weiss outside the room where Domenic lay dying.[93]

Former President Nixon and Mrs. Onassis may have shown the way toward dying on their own terms, but most Americans hadn't ventured down that path. Like Mr. and Mrs. Ponzo, they swerved. Nearly nine of ten people told pollsters that if they were on life-support with no hope of recovery, they would choose to withdraw treatment and die. In the same spirit, three of four said they would like to have a living will. Yet only 10 to 20 percent in the mid-1990s had actually written one.[94] Whatever they believed in theory, in practice they didn't sit down and face the stark reality that might eventually befall them. Even when that reality arrived, an astounding number of people managed to look the other way. According to an AMA survey of patients *on life-support*, 85 percent still had not written a living will. In fact, 44 percent had not even told family members what they wished done if they suffered an irreversible coma.[95] Doctors deserved to be faulted for ignoring patients' preferences, but all too often their patients had failed to define their preferences. The Patient Self-Determination Act ordered hospital staff to change their paternalistic behavior, but patients continued to shirk self-determination. Despite all the seminars, best-selling books, and television documentaries on "dying with dignity," despite the haunting presence of Karen Ann Quinlan, most Americans didn't write advance directives.

Patients blame doctors, doctors blame patients, and one can also blame the living will itself. The well-known bioethicist and gerontologist Joanne Lynn, for example, created a stir in 1991 with her article "Why I Don't Have a Living Will." Although she supported the Patient Self-Determination Act and encouraged her patients to establish advance directives, she hadn't written one for herself. She wasn't inefficient or imprudent, she said. Rather, "I fear that the effects of having one would be worse, in my situation, than not having one." The standard living will, she explained, fosters the belief that one won't be kept alive like Karen Ann Quinlan or Claire Conroy. But in fact it only protects persons who, with or without treatment, will die soon. Even if one adds clauses to anticipate dreaded contingencies, no one—especially not a layperson—can foretell what will turn out to be desirable or feasible when illness strikes. A respirator for a week or ten days or not at all? CPR once, twice, as often as needed? A feeding tube? Rather than write a self-delusory script of her future, Lynn gave control to her husband. She signed a durable power of attorney, which named him as surrogate. And if she were to become incompetent, it asked doctors and judges to defer to his judgment.[96]

Professional arrogance, personal weakness, and the limitations built into advance directives—each of these explains in part the shortcomings of the right-to-die policy. But only in part. Ultimately we need to recognize that all of them reflect the influence of two American values: abundance and individualism. In other words, how we die, or hope to die, is a cultural construction.

Patients and doctors have joined together in a dance of denial, clinging to the last spasms of life, neither of them wanting to be the first to admit that it would be better to stop. Another round of chemo. CPR. Give heroic treatment to the heroic fighter and never say die. When framed in these terms, anxiety about death becomes a kind of reckless faith, as if there will be more time, more happiness, more reason to hope. It's a medical version of the economic abundance that Americans after 1945 enjoyed and took for granted. The Presidential Commission for the Study of Ethical Problems in Medicine, for example, asserted in 1983 that, unlike other societies, the United States could use life-sustaining treatment without worrying about the price.

But by then that sort of affluent attitude was in fact misguided. Starting in the early 1970s, personal income for all but the wealthiest households leveled off. Unemployment spread across the manufacturing sector and "downsizing" across the white-collar sector. Instead of abundance, Americans began hearing about limits. In "the new constraint environment," one economist said, resources—including health resources—had to be rationed. "It is clear," one political scientist advised in 1988, "that we must . . . regulate our overindulgence of medical care for the individual. . . ."[97] A 1996 television documentary on "Who Plays God?" didn't follow the usual plot line of whether patients should forgo life-support and whether doctors should comply. This time the plot wasn't bioethical but economic. "How do we decide when enough is enough?" asked the program host, George Strait. "And how much care can we really afford?"[98]

Americans aren't ready to accept that stricture—or if at all, they accept it for the society as a whole, not for themselves. Here is the second cultural value underlying the right-to-die policy and the second weakness: self-determination. When asked by Gallup pollsters in 1982 to rate a list of values, six of ten Americans gave "freedom to choose" the highest possible rating, while another 36 percent put it among the top five, ahead of "following God's will" and a "sense of accomplishment."[99] This principle has been a mainstay of the American belief system for more than a century and a half, so entrenched (at least for men) that it has seemed to be an unquestionable truth. "This is a country of *self-made men*," Calvin Colton, a minister and Whig party pamphleteer, declared in 1844, "than which nothing better could be said of any state of society."[100] Those rare men who went from log cabin to White House or rags to riches perpetuated the cultural myth. Nevertheless, when nineteenth-century Americans reached the end of life, they acknowledged the boundary of self-determination and entrusted themselves to the will of God. By the late twentieth century, medical treatment had changed and so had the sense of boundary. Doctors can push back death by means of technological "miracles," such as the respirator, organ transplants, and CPR. Modern Americans, in turn, presume they can determine their dying.

When a person fills out an advance directive, he is predicting—months or years ahead of a life-threatening illness—which medical treatments he will want, under which circumstances, and for how long. Bioethicists call this a claim to "autonomy" or self-determination, which has a comforting sound. An individual is choosing his course of action, free from constraint by others and in accordance with his personal values. Just beneath the surface, however, we should hear the desperate desire to control. The "director" is trying to exert control over how doctors and family treat him when he is helpless. The desperation reflects, in turn, the wishfulness of this process. The author of a living will is writing the last chapter of his autobiography before the intervening chapters have taken place. In contrast to those Victorian deathbed scenes of suffering and resignation, this modern chapter itemizes a painless, "dignified" scenario. Beneath the legal surface lurks fiction.[101]

Self-determination is a fiction not only in advance of dying but even more so in the midst of dying. The principle of autonomy makes sense in the case of a pregnant woman demanding the right to abortion, for example, or a patient claiming the right to a candid diagnosis.[102] When it comes to terminal illness, an individual's right has a very different meaning—or possibly no meaning. For existential freedom stops at the door of death; at best we can exercise autonomy up to the threshold. But modern medicine has made the width of that threshold uncertain. In Joanne Lynn's graphic phrase, "People really die now by inches more than miles," and along the way we will become less and less competent.[103] Like Claire Conroy, we may remain conscious but unable to ask for an end to unendurable pain. Or like Karen Ann Quinlan and as many as 35,000 others now, we may be freed from pain but sentenced to survival.[104] Our fate will rest in the hands of others. By pledging exclusive allegiance to "autonomy," we deny this reality of dying and feed the very dread we're trying to overcome. No wonder so few people have written a living will.[105]

6

A Tapestry of Relatedness

A WEEK BEFORE she fell into a coma, Karen Ann Quinlan came home to report excitedly about her visit to a palm reader. Holding out a hand to her mother, she traced the heart line as it curled all the way down around her wrist. "You know what, Mom?" she said. "I'm going to live forever."[1] Ten years later, on June 11, 1985, at the age of thirty-one, she was dying of pneumonia.

Julia was at the bedside, holding her daughter. ". . . I said the Our Father and the Memorare," she recalled, "and I hid my face next to hers and I cried and cried. . . ." Eventually she called to Joseph, who had stepped out into the hallway, and he returned just in time to hear Karen take her last breath. No more need to play "Amazing Grace" in case their daughter was able to hear. No need to worry whether she was feeling pain. God's will was done at last. Julia went to the next room where Paul Armstrong and Tom Trapasso were waiting. To their surprise, the lawyer and the priest broke down in tears. "I didn't know I'd have as much feeling . . . ," Father Trapasso told a reporter the next day. Then they all gathered around the bedside while he said prayers.[2]

"The death of Karen Ann Quinlan is our top story this morning. . . ." Television and radio newscasters devoted lengthy coverage to the event. "La deuxième mort de Karen Quinlan." Newspapers from Paris to Oregon announced it in front-page headlines. Once again they brought out that photograph from her high school yearbook. The same cartoonist who ten years earlier had drawn a shrouded man carrying a doctor's bag labeled "Abortion on Demand and the Right to Die" now depicted a smiling woman soaring on angel's wings, trailing an electrical cord behind her. "Finally granted the right to die," said the caption. Eulogists proclaimed that, by redefining the meaning of death, she "gave more to humanity than most presidents, physicians or poets."[3] A decade after Joseph Quinlan won the right to turn off the respirator, she had expired.

"Please," Julia Quinlan said to a reporter knocking at their door, "let us mourn in peace."[4] But she and Joseph didn't seclude themselves for long. Although they had shielded their daughter from prurient photographers, they always reached out to people who had comatose relatives. Six weeks after Karen's death they were interviewed on the CBS Morning News. "It's difficult when you ride down the highway and you don't make that turn off to the nursing home . . . ," Julia remarked. But she was consoled by memories: brushing Karen's hair, praying at her bedside. And also the earlier, sweeter memories of the girl always running faster than her friends. "That's right," Joseph added, "memories, beautiful memories, but still they hurt, to look back." He didn't find death fearful, but life was a different matter. Life is "a trial," he said—as though neither the literal trial nor her death had settled the agonizing ambivalence he had felt in those first months of her vegetative state.[5]

Unsettledness also holds true for most Americans. Just as the *Quinlan* case wasn't the first chapter in the history of modern dying, her death doesn't close this book. Troubling questions remain. What is the difference between removing a respirator and removing a feeding tube? If death by suffocation, why not death by dehydration? "We would never stop feeding her," Julia protested. "That would be like actively killing Karen, and we couldn't live with that."[6] It was a revealing reply. *We* couldn't live with that. The subject had shifted from their daughter to themselves. In disconnecting the respirator they had claimed to be carrying out her beliefs. In continuing the feeding tube they were carrying out their own.

Karen Ann Quinlan Is Finally Granted the Right to Die (Paul Conrad, *Los Angeles Times*)

They wrote the remainder of her life story according to their values.

They would have denied self-interest. From the beginning of their ordeal they had insisted they were selfless guardians enacting the will of Karen and of God. But there's nothing wrong with personal interest. On the contrary, it would be wrong if a family were indifferent, like Saikewicz's sisters, leaving the patient to the mercy of strangers—caring professionals but nonetheless professionals. Better that those who know him best, his family and friends, try to interpret what the no-longer-competent person would say. If one thinks of a life as a story, toward the end these surrogates take over for the author and write the last chapter.[7] In so doing they supplement autonomy with what bioethicists call "relatedness." If the right to die is based only on the principle of self-determination, it leaves individuals vulnerable. If it is also based on relatedness, it provides more security and also more care.

AT THE SAME TIME Quinlan died, forty-six-year-old Paul Brophy lay in a vegetative state in a Massachusetts hospital. In 1983 the fireman and emergency medical technician had been in robust health—father of five grown children, a man who hunted deer, fished, and gardened in his spare time. But during the night of March 22 he complained to his wife of a splitting headache, rolled over in bed, and became unconscious with an aneurysm. Three years later a gastrostomy tube was keeping him alive. Cases like Brophy's, wrote nationally syndicated columnist Ellen Goodman, raised questions that "make the original Quinlan case look easy." Was there a difference between pulling the plug and closing the tube? And even if one said there was not, she continued, how did one decide between two "repulsive" options: maintaining him in a vegetative state or starving him to death?[8]

As Brophy entered his third year, his wife Patricia, who was also a registered nurse, telephoned a professor of medical ethics at the College of the Holy Cross and asked those questions. "I told her," John Paris recalled, "that just the day before the *New York Times* had a front-page story on the New Jersey Supreme Court's ruling in the *Conroy* case." To help her make up her mind, Paris sent books and articles for and against withdrawal of tube feeding. A week later Mrs. Brophy called back to thank him and say that she and her children, including Paul's siblings and elderly mother, had reached a decision.[9] Acting as his guardian, she requested the doctors to remove or clamp the tube. When they and the hospital directors refused, she went to probate court. And when the court refused, she appealed to the Massachusetts Supreme Court. Her husband would abhor being kept alive in this condition, she insisted. Ten years ago, for example, when they were discussing Karen Ann Quinlan, he had said: "No way do I want to live like that; that is not living." And again, after rescuing a severely burned man from a truck, he remarked to his brother: "If I'm ever like that, just shoot me, pull the plug." His twenty-five-year-old daughter remembered him saying: "If I can't sit up to kiss one of my beautiful daughters, I may as well be six feet under."[10]

No one disputed this evidence of Brophy's wishes, neither the hospital nor the lower court. But if the higher court went along with him, it would be the first time that any state supreme court authorized withdrawal of artificial feeding from someone who was still alive. (The *Conroy* ruling came posthumously and was hedged with demands for more evidence of the patient's preferences.) On September 11, 1986, over a vociferous dissent by three justices, the court granted Mrs. Brophy's appeal. "In certain, thankfully rare, circumstances," the majority declared, "the burden of maintaining the corporeal existence degrades the very humanity it was meant to save." Given the "fundamental principles of individual autonomy," the state must defer to Brophy's right to direct the course of his life toward "a death with dignity." The three dissenters were outraged, Justice Joseph R. Nolan most of all. Food and water were not medical treatment, he protested. Brophy would not die from the aneurysm or brain damage. "He will starve to death, and the court approves this death." Whatever the majority's "high-blown language" might pretend, "the court today has endorsed euthanasia and suicide," creating "another triumph for the forces of secular humanism (modern paganism)."[11]

That afternoon Patricia Brophy stood outside her neat white bungalow, flanked by three of her children plus five of Paul's seven brothers and sisters, and spoke to the media about her victory. "I have a sense there's a light at the end of the tunnel, and I've been waiting for it for so long." But "victory" was a grossly inappropriate way to describe what she had won. As her husband's doctor remarked, the easiest thing for her was knowing there would now be an end to this ordeal. "And that was the hardest thing, too." When she first learned of the court's ruling, she said, she felt "sick to my stomach," for she had won the right to lose her husband. "Right now I can see Paul. I can touch him. I can wash him." For three years she had been cutting his hair and clipping his nails. "Even though I know he doesn't feel anything, I get a certain benefit from doing these things."[12]

These mundane details brought home the reality of what was at stake in a persistent vegetative state. The Brophy case was as much about Patricia as about her husband. Paul had won the right to die "with dignity," but he hadn't experienced the indignity of life-support. Patricia had experienced it on his behalf. His "individual autonomy" had prevailed, but for three years she had been representing the wishes he no longer was able to express. More than substituting her judgment for his, she was joining her feelings with those he used to have. Pain is private, excluding outsiders, but suffering can be shared between victim and caregivers. Clipping her husband's fingernails and dreading his death, Mrs. Brophy demonstrated how the individual's right to die also inevitably entails a relationship to others. In fact, the full title of the case was *Patricia Brophy v. New England Sinai Hospital, Inc.*

It is an asymmetrical relationship. The caretaker has feelings about a person who has no awareness—who is, in all but body, already dead. Removing the feeding tube doesn't address the patient's awareness but is like posthumously honoring the terms of someone's will. The deceased cannot know, for example, whether his ashes have been scattered in the Atlantic or his diaries will remain closed for fifty years. Cannot know and therefore cannot care. Nevertheless his heirs carry out his wishes because they still care about him, symbolically continuing his identity into afterlife. There are also times when, for the same reasons, heirs disobey the deceased. Emily Dickinson's heirs refused to burn her poems, and Kafka's friend refused to destroy his manuscripts, because such action would have dishonored these artists. We treat the memory of the dead with the same respect we treat their bodies. "That is what he wanted," we say as we keep him alive in memory.[13]

Patricia Brophy, though, was not yet a widow. Before dealing with his absence, she would have to endure his dying. As a nurse, she knew that "seeing anybody die is emotional. It's not going to be easy." That's all she said on the subject, leaving *Boston Globe* readers to imagine what she had in mind. In an adjacent article, two physicians referred more bluntly to "the agony of those who have to stay by the bedside" as their loved one slowly wastes away. If both food and liquids are withdrawn, dying lasts a week or two, ending with kidney failure. If only food is withdrawn, it may last a month, culminating in untreated pneumonia or urinary tract infection.[14] According to neurologists, a patient in a vegetative state or coma will feel nothing. A conscious patient will soon slide into a dulled state, with drugs muting whatever pain he might be experiencing. The survivors—family, friends, and nurses at the bedside—are the ones who suffer.

On October 16, 1986, Patricia Brophy transferred her husband to a cooperative hospital and discontinued feeding (but not liquids). To ward off his body's adverse reactions, she asked nurses to administer anticonvulsants, antacids, and laxatives. She tended him night and day, turning him every two hours, helping to bathe him and change the bed linen, shampooing his hair, rubbing lotion on his back, emptying bedpans and catheter, watching Red Sox games on television, sleeping on a cot. She talked constantly to him. Children and grandchildren visited, played on his bed, and, she recalled, "kissed him goodbye because he was going to heaven." On the eighth day without food, Paul Brophy's breathing became more rapid and shallow. As his wife sat on one side of the bed holding his hand, a grandchild on the other side, he made a peculiar noise, vomited, and stopped breathing. "[It's] the way I would like to die," she said later: "very peacefully."[15] Officially he died of pneumonia.[16]

In stark contrast to Quinlan's death, Brophy's went by almost unnoticed. The newspapers that reported the event did so in a few terse paragraphs on page 2 or 9 or 25, and many didn't report it at all. (The exception was the *Globe* in nearby Boston.)[17] Apparently the withdrawal of life-support, even when it included "the staff of life," no longer was news.[18] Right-to-life spokesmen complained that the media were promoting involuntary euthanasia by blurring the distinction between feeding and medical treatment.[19] But as opinion polls proved, the public clearly understood what was at issue. Even before the *Brophy* ruling, three of four Americans approved the idea of withdrawing life-support, including food and water, when requested by a hopelessly ill patient or family member. By 1990 more than 80 percent endorsed that idea.[20]

Within an astonishingly brief time, the "right to die with dignity" had come to rival or even surpass doctors' "miracle working" in the hierarchy of cultural values. But it still wasn't translated into day-to-day practice. As the family of Nancy Cruzan discovered, powerful pro-life forces raised formidable obstacles.

THE CRUZAN CASE was a virtual replica of Karen Quinlan's. In 1983 twenty-five-year-old Nancy left a group of friends at a Missouri country-music bar after quarreling with her husband. She was driving home alone in her green-and-white Rambler when she went off the left side of the road, hit trees and a mailbox, veered into a field, overturned, and was thrown thirty-five feet from the car, landing facedown in a ditch. By the time the paramedics reached the scene, she had no pulse and hadn't been breathing for at least twelve minutes, probably longer. They began CPR and quickly managed to revive her heartbeat and respiration. But as one of them later remarked, after six minutes without oxygen "the brain . . . goes into what they call biological death of no return."

Lester "Joe" Cruzan and his wife Joyce—he a sheet-metal worker, she a school librarian—were asleep when the phone rang. They were waiting at the Joplin hospital when the ambulance crew carried in their daughter, comatose but at least alive. Three hours later, when a nurse came out of the operating room and told them that Nancy's vital signs were stable, Joe looked at his wife and said: "I feel like I can breathe again."[21] It turned out to be only a brief reprieve, because Nancy never regained consciousness. After ten months she was transferred to a long-term care facility. There she lay, her limbs gradually contracting against her body, her eyes blinking sightlessly, her life sustained by a feeding tube implanted above her navel. "If only the ambulance had arrived five minutes earlier," her father said, "or five minutes later."[22]

A year after the accident, Nancy's husband secured a divorce and her parents became legal guardians.[23] In 1987, more than four years after the accident, they asked the nursing home to remove the feeding tube. "How can you murder your own child?" Joe Cruzan mused. "Our decision is based on what we felt like Nancy would want, and that's all we have to justify [it]. If the decision's wrong, if we're playing God, I'll answer for it."[24] When the nursing home refused, the Cruzans went to the Society for the Right to Die, which put them in touch with a bright, young Kansas City lawyer named William Colby, who agreed to represent them (at no cost) in court.

One would think that *Quinlan* and the numerous subsequent state judicial rulings had cleared the legal path, but the Cruzans faced two special obstacles. A feeding tube was less obviously a form of medical treatment than was a respirator, so their request was vulnerable to accusations of "mercy killing." Furthermore the political atmosphere in Missouri had become markedly conservative during the 1980s. Although the legislature had finally instituted a living-will law, for example, it set stringent criteria. More tellingly it passed an abortion law that declared: "the intention of the . . . state of Missouri is to grant the right to life to all humans, born and unborn. . . ."[25] Before the Cruzans would prevail two years later, they would have to go all the way up to the United States Supreme Court and back down to probate court in Carthage, Missouri.

But to say that they prevailed would leave the wrong impression. This was not a triumphant chapter in the history of "the right to die." On the contrary, the *Cruzan* case exposed the liabilities of that so-called right. On legal grounds the right to die is vulnerable whenever a case involves an incompetent patient whom doctors will not let die and who has not written an advance directive. The family is then dependent on a court's willingness to believe their claims as to the end-of-life treatment he or she would have chosen. This legal limitation points to a cultural one. The principle of autonomy not only may leave an incompetent patient subject to others' dictates. It also ignores the fact that *all* patients are cared for by others, and that their suffering and dying affect those others. For their own sake as well as Nancy's, her family was choosing to let her go. For the same reasons, her nurses objected. "She's like family," said Debbie Schnake. "We go in there and talk to her. We communicate with her."[26] Each allegedly autonomous individual exists within a web of relatedness.[27]

The law recognizes only individual rights, however, and so William Colby had to work within the constraints of that framework. There was, to begin with, the legal problem of establishing that Nancy Cruzan would have wanted the feeding tube removed. Like 90 percent of Americans, she had not written a living will.[28] Even if she lacked that sort of protection, though, she presumably had the constitutional right of privacy. The courts had allowed Joseph Quinlan and Patricia Brophy to withdraw life-support in accord with what Karen would have wanted and what Paul had said he wanted. Unfortunately there was only the slimmest evidence of Cruzan's attitudes. At the trial her former coworker and housemate recounted a conversation in which Nancy said "if she . . . couldn't do for herself things even halfway, let alone not at all, she wouldn't want to live that way and she hoped that her family would know that."[29] The best her family could vouch for was a conversation with her older sister Christy, when Nancy agreed that, compared to constant medical crises, "death is sometimes not the worst situation you can be in."[30]

It's tempting to think about might-have-beens. If only Cruzan, like Paul Brophy, had talked with her family about Karen Ann Quinlan, telling them to "pull the plug" in case she were living like that. But as Joe Cruzan remarked during his testimony, "when you are 25 years old, you don't think about dying. Five and a half years ago, I didn't think I would be in this courtroom. I didn't think I would have a daughter in a vegetative state. I knew that accidents happened, but they happened to other families."[31] Before that January night the Cruzan family had every reason to take for granted that she would live her life as she wanted, and when they discovered they were wrong, it was too late. She had lost the power to say no, and the nursing home denied her parents the power to speak for her.

To compensate for this legal weakness in his case, Colby invoked Nancy's autonomy in psychological terms, as a matter of personal identity, focusing less on what she had said than who she had been. "Well, she was the most independent always and the most vivacious, even when she was little," Joyce Cruzan testified. Again and again the Cruzan lawyers prompted family and friends to describe her in these terms—to recite the script of Nancy as "an independent person" who "lived life to its very fullest."[32] She was energetic, outgoing, fun-loving. She enjoyed sunbathing and wore bright-colored clothing. She took risks and made mistakes: marrying before high school graduation and divorcing two years later; marrying again a construction worker four years older; living briefly in Oklahoma and Florida before coming back to Missouri. She was restless, working in a school for handicapped children, an office supply company, a cheese processing plant. "You have got to assume responsibilities in your life, you have got to grow up," her father told her, and she replied: "I don't want to grow up. I want to have fun."[33] That was the person she used to be. "Nancy would be horrified at the state she is in now," her older sister said.[34] Paralyzed, drooling, bloated by liquid feeding three times a day—the true Nancy was gone, and what remained was a travesty. To keep her alive was to violate her identity.

This evidence convinced Probate Court Judge Charles Teel to grant Mr. and Mrs. Cruzan's petition. But the opposing lawyer chose to appeal, and by a 4 to 3 vote the state supreme court reversed Teel's ruling. Before the Quinlan case, said Justice Edward Robertson, courts had chosen to preserve the lives of incompetents, not to hasten their deaths. "*Quinlan* changed the calculus," he said, by "replacing a concern for life with a concern for the quality of life. . . ." The Missouri court, by contrast, believed that "the state's interest is an unqualified interest in life." Building upon that premise, Robertson constructed piece by piece his rejection of the Cruzans' appeal. Nancy would never again interact meaningfully with her environment, he acknowledged, but a diminished quality of life didn't justify "a decision to cause death." And death was what would follow the withdrawal of the feeding tube. Neurologists and physicians might claim that artificial nutrition was medical treatment, but "common sense tells us that food and water do not treat an illness, they maintain a life." Conceivably a patient might experience such life-support as a burden, but Nancy was unconscious and therefore felt no pain or burden. Her parents nevertheless claimed that she would object to the indignity of being kept alive. But the evidence of her wishes, said Justice Robertson, was "inherently unreliable"—no more than the hearsay of a few recollected conversations. In order for someone to exercise an incompetent person's right of privacy, there must be a written living will or "clear and convincing, inherently reliable evidence" of the person's wishes. Unless there was unarguable indication that Nancy herself would have chosen to do so, no one should remove her life-support. After all, Robertson said, the right of privacy is rooted in autonomy, and autonomy means the ability to decide by oneself. With this disarming gambit, Robertson took the principle of autonomy and turned it against Cruzan's "right to die." By a one-vote margin, then, the court decided to prolong her life in a vegetative state.[35]

The ruling was greeted by a flurry of denunciation in legal and bioethical circles. "This is a regime of rights turned on its head," said the bioethicist Susan Wolf of the University of Minnesota Law School. By setting so high a standard of evidence, the court had made it practically impossible for incompetent persons to have their life-support ended. The court, she said, propounded a "fantasy of a world in which people speak contract-talk about their deaths." But Wolf also made a broader critique, going beyond the pragmatics of living wills to the underlying principle of autonomy. When the court dismissed the evidence offered by family and friends, she said, it presumed "a world in which relationships count for nothing." It thereby cut off Cruzan from the people who loved her and spoke for her, leaving her isolated, helpless, without a voice.[36]

Autonomy as powerlessness, and relatedness as strength:

when we reframe the case this way, we discover new and persuasive justifications for "the right to die." Self-determination is a kind of fiction in the world of law, and even more so in the world of everyday experience. Even if Cruzan had written a living will, her parents and doctors would have had to enact her wishes for her. And even if she had been (to quote *In re Quinlan*) "miraculously lucid for an interval" and had stated the wish to end her life, she would not have existed totally independent of others. An individual right doesn't exist in a vacuum, after all, but plays out against competing rights and values (a Jehovah's Witness's refusal of blood transfusion versus a doctor's responsibility to provide treatment). The same is true outside of hospitals and courtrooms. Everyone except a Robinson Crusoe depends upon others for food, clothing, and a livelihood. Although Americans have traditionally enshrined "the self-made man," he is as much an ideal type—a fiction—as the "invisible hand" behind free-enterprise capitalism. "Autonomy is an odd concept," Dr. Eric Cassell has observed. "It is a goal toward which people strive, which never actually exists. No one is, or can be, totally autonomous. . . ."[37]

The wife of a young historian expressed these ideas with painful eloquence as she was tending him after a near-fatal accident. While rollerblading one summer night in Atlanta, Jon Houghton had collided headfirst with a truck and suffered severe brain damage. Someone set up a home page on the Worldwide Web where friends could send letters and Susan could issue updates on Jon's condition. Two weeks after the accident, she wrote:

> I watch Jon every minute of the day and I think of what a strange society we live in. In the U.S. we have such a strong culture of individualism. A person is defined as a single entity, the indivisible unit of society. . . . I think we have the wrong idea. Jon is so much more than his body in the bed or the words he speaks. He is a woven tapestry made whole by the threads of other lives that weave throughout his own. His tapestry is rich in texture, color and pattern, as we have all experienced by reading this website this last month. Every note and card that I get, every story of Jon

remembered, reinforces this image for me. . . . How could we possibly imagine that a human being is a stand-alone unit? I concur about the nomanisanisland thing.[38]

We are not literally self-sufficient in what we do, nor are we self-determining in who we are. Although philosophers and lawyers find it useful to consider the generic *individual*, in fact we are *persons*. Starting from birth, we develop our personalities—our identities—through interactions with parents, siblings, teachers, and a myriad of friends and acquaintances.[39] When Cruzan's friends and family described her as "independent," they were talking about a type of relationship with them. Now that she was utterly dependent, that relationship prompted them to speak for her in court.

Just as Nancy Cruzan depended on others, they were affected by—interdependent with—her. She had been "the center of the family wheel," according to the psychologist who counseled her parents after the accident.[40] When she was flung out of that car, their lives were wrenched out of shape. Her death would have been traumatic enough, but this vegetative state was worse. "Along with Nancy, we are caught in limbo," Joe Cruzan said.[41] Joyce retreated into a shell of bitterness, sleeping constantly. "I was very angry for a long time," she said. "I didn't know how God could let this happen." Joe couldn't sleep, searching obsessively for a solution to the agony.[42] "My dad has always been a fixer," Christy remarked. "He's always wanted to make things right."[43]

The bearded, dark-eyed sheet-metal worker was the one who dealt with the press while his wife stayed out of the public eye. In his Midwestern accent, sometimes taut with passion, he spoke out bluntly. ". . . I think in a lot of ways, Nancy was like I am," he testified. "Her temperament was like mine is. She was not much to take anything off of anyone. . . ."[44] But he couldn't fix her vegetative state, and the court denied his appeal to let her die, so how could he help her? "There were lots of times I thought about killing Nancy," he said, "and then killing myself."[45] The bond he used to feel with his "independent" daughter he now felt in the dependency they shared. "I know damn well if it were me up there [in the nursing home] I would be furious with the state of Missouri because of what they had done to my family by forcing me to stay alive."[46]

At one point shortly after the accident, the Cruzans considered getting divorced. But with the help of marital counseling over the next five years, they stayed together and, with their daughter Christy, struggled as a family through this ordeal.[47] Every Saturday or Sunday they left their home in Carterville and drove forty-five miles to the Mount Vernon Rehabilitation Center, bringing cards and stuffed animals on Valentine's Day, a jack-o'-lantern and black cat on Halloween, a tiny tree on Christmas. On Nancy's thirtieth birthday they walked into her room singing "Happy birthday to you."[48]

They also found strength from people far beyond their Ozark community of two thousand. They met with their psychotherapist, with the Head Injury Support Group, and with the Society for the Right to Die. They contacted nonexperts, people like Patricia Brophy and the Quinlans, who had gone through the same ordeal. Joe described his encounter, for example, with a professor who had himself gone to court to withdraw life-support from his PVS wife. "There is two guys, he was a professor, I'm a construction worker, . . . and yet . . . the first thing that happened when we walked in the door was we hugged each other, and that's the truth because we had been through very similar circumstances."[49] And most of all, they relied on William Colby, their lawyer and soon their friend. Colby, in turn, called on others for help: lawyers such as Paul Armstrong, bioethicists such as Ronald Cranford.[50]

In 1975 the Quinlans had been pioneers. They had relied on Father Trapasso and their faith for spiritual guidance and on Paul Armstrong for legal guidance, while Armstrong in turn called upon the ethicists at the fledgling Hastings and Georgetown institutes. Ten years later the Cruzans had no religious framework to instruct and nurture them. But by then they and Colby could draw upon a nationwide network—a tapestry—of secular experts and peers.

If they were to win the power to remove the feeding tube, however, it would be in terms of autonomy, not relationships. As Colby said when announcing his appeal of the Missouri ruling, "we will fight to have an individual's constitutional rights vindicated."[51] For the first time the "right to die" would come before the nation's highest court.

THE ORAL HEARING took place on December 6, 1989. At 7:30 that morning Paul Armstrong was walking around the Supreme Court building when he met Joe Cruzan walking toward him, dressed in a suit and tie. "You could see in his eyes that he was at sea," Armstrong recalled. Hours later, inside the large courtroom, the construction worker who was used to fixing things sat with his family behind rows of VIPs and watched lawyers and judges debate his daughter's life.[52] The media were also there: reporters from newspapers across the country and all three television networks. When the case had been argued in Missouri it had seemed simply one more in the line of *Quinlan, Brophy,* and dozens of others, and so the press had given it only perfunctory coverage. Now that it had reached the Supreme Court it became news, though still not front-page news.[53]

At stake was the issue of withdrawing food and water, but lurking behind it was an even more controversial issue: abortion. Outside the Supreme Court building, protesters waved placards showing a fetus curled up on the American flag and the admonition: "Only God has the right to pull the plug."[54] The link was not logical as much as political and emotional. Letting a fetus die differed from ending an incompetent patient's life-support, because the fetus could not express a choice whereas the patient could have. But the two situations overlapped, since both were life-or-death and both dealt with the constitutional "right of privacy." The abortion issue also had a direct bearing on developments inside the courtroom. Three of the justices who had been part of the *Roe v. Wade* majority had recently retired or died. Anti-abortion had served as the litmus test for the persons President Reagan had nominated to sit in those three seats. By 1990 Colby faced a Supreme Court that had been steadily curtailing women's access to abortion and presumably would be less sympathetic to the right to die.[55]

As the justices peppered the attorneys with questions during the hour-long session, one could infer easily enough how some of them would vote. There were the three conservatives: Antonin Scalia, Byron White, and Chief Justice William Rehnquist. At one point Scalia set a trap for Colby. Given that you claimed the state could ignore an "irrational" refusal of food and water, such as by a Jehovah's Witness parent of an ill child, Scalia said, why should the Court necessarily defer to other families' requests? Because, Colby said, those other families may have legitimate reasons. To which the justice replied: These are the kinds of philosophical questions that the state should refuse to answer.

There were the three liberals: Harry Blackmun, William Brennan, and Thurgood Marshall. During a comment by Missouri Assistant Attorney General Robert Presson, Blackmun interrupted with exasperation: "Have you ever seen a person in a persistent vegetative state?" Yes, Presson said, disconcerting Blackmun, I've visited Nancy Cruzan more than once.

And there were the three hard-to-classify justices: Sandra Day O'Connor, John Paul Stevens, and Anthony Kennedy, who formed the "swing" vote. O'Connor's questions offered ambiguous signals. Although parents deserve the opportunity to speak for their child's treatment, she said at one point, isn't a judge ultimately more qualified to determine the child's best interest? Another time she quizzed the Missouri attorney: Is there no federal limitation on how the states regulate a family's choice of treatment?[56]

At the end of the morning a reporter asked Mr. Cruzan if he felt encouraged. "I don't know," Cruzan said with a shrug. Quickly Colby stepped in: "They're pretty stressed out. They're on the edge. This is a pretty emotional day."[57] Now there was nothing the Cruzans could do but go home to Missouri, resume their weekly visits to Nancy's bedside, and wait.

Six months later, on June 25, 1990, the ruling came down, but the potentially "historic" decision turned out to be more equivocal than trailblazing. In sharp contrast to the unanimous *Quinlan* decision, *Cruzan* was split 5 to 4. Not only split, but the majority was itself a patchwork of Chief Justice Rehnquist's opinion (with White and Kennedy) and two concurring opinions (Scalia and O'Connor). A ringing dissent came from the liberal trio of Brennan, Marshall, and Blackmun, with another from Stevens. Tellingly, this lineup duplicated the one in an abortion ruling the Court had issued earlier that year.[58] The justices were warring with one another about the rights of women and fetuses as much as those of incompetent patients. Whereas the *Quinlan* court had leaped ahead of public opinion on the right to die, the *Cruzan* court lagged behind.

On the broadest level of principle, Rehnquist took a surprisingly liberal position. "For purposes of this case, we assumed that the United States Constitution would grant a competent person a constitutionally protected right to refuse life-saving nutrition and hydration." But what seems at first to be a trumpeting assertion of the right to die was actually more muted. The Court didn't declare but merely assumed—and assumed in this case only—and for competent but not incompetent persons.

What did this assertion of principle mean for Nancy Cruzan? When the chief justice addressed the specifics of her situation, his ruling took a very different direction. Being incompetent, she didn't possess the same right of refusal as a competent person. Missouri acted legitimately, therefore, in requiring "clear and convincing evidence" of her wishes, because "there can be no gainsaying [the state's] interest in the protection and preservation of human life." To be sure, Rehnquist conceded, Missouri's rule might have the "erroneous" result of keeping someone in a vegetative state who wanted to die. But the rule prevented the opposite error, which would be an uncorrectable one, of letting someone die against her wishes. No doubt, Rehnquist concluded, Mr. and Mrs. Cruzan were loving and caring parents who sincerely believed their daughter's life was "hopeless, meaningless, and even degrading." But the Constitution didn't protect family decision-making.

"We do not think the Due Process Clause requires the State to repose judgment on these matters with anyone but the patient herself."[59]

There was something paradoxical in this argument, almost perversely so. The Court was defending the exercise of self-determination by a woman who was irreversibly unconscious. To explain this peculiar conclusion, we must first understand it in political terms. The chief justice was enacting a judicial version of the Reagan administration's "neofederalism," transferring powers from the federal government to the states. In addition to a political explanation, though, a philosophical one has to do with the concept of autonomy. Rehnquist was correct to say that the Fourteenth Amendment, like the Bill of Rights, protects individuals, not families. In drafting the Constitution, the Founding Fathers replaced the classical ideal of civic or collective virtue with a modern ideal of individual rights and self-government.[60] But if an individual becomes comatose in a state where the legislature has restricted the refusal of life-support, how can she protect herself?

According to Justice Scalia, she couldn't—even if she were conscious. In his concurring opinion he declared with characteristic vehemence that the state has the power to prevent suicide, "including suicide by refusing to take appropriate measures necessary to preserve one's life."[61] Justice O'Connor, on the other hand, tried to pry open the door of decision-making. To avoid falling into Cruzan's situation, O'Connor said in her concurring opinion, people should write living wills. But in reality, she acknowledged, few do so, and even then states often fail to honor their wishes. A better remedy, therefore, would be to fill out a durable power of attorney, naming a proxy to make decisions if one becomes incompetent. (This is precisely what the bioethicist Joanne Lynn recommended instead of a living will.) "Today we decide only that one State's practice does not violate the Constitution," O'Connor concluded. "In the 'laboratory' of the States," Americans should figure out how to safeguard incompetents' rights.[62]

What was one to make of this discordant trio of opinions? The interpretation varied according to the predispositions of the interpreters. Right-to-life proponents hailed the decision as "a major victory for those who would protect the lives of vulnerable people."[63] Some right-to-die advocates echoed the passionate dissents of Justices Brennan and Stevens. "We should not be invaded by the state that wants to put a tube down our stomachs and keep us in a persistent vegetative state," declared the chairman of the American College of Physicians' board of regents.[64] Physicians will hesitate to start life-support, Joanne Lynn warned, for fear of being unable to withdraw it later.[65] But the director of legal services for the Society for the Right to Die read the decision more positively: "Now the next time I get a call from someone who's competent and in a dispute with a doctor," she said, "I'm going to be able to tell them there is a constitutional right at stake."[66]

Although the experts were divided not simply between right and left hands but between fingers on a hand, the media produced a single interpretation of the *Cruzan* ruling. In almost identical wording, front-page headlines the next morning announced: "High Court Limits 'Right to Die'."[67] At first glance there's nothing in particular to catch one's eye here, other than those quotation marks skeptically hedging the right to die. But notice what is absent from the headlines' narrative—or rather, who is absent. The media featured two impersonal antagonists, a court versus a right, and ignored the woman whose life hung in the balance. Except in her home-state *St. Louis Post-Dispatch*, Nancy Cruzan appeared in none of the headlines. Readers had to proceed to the first or even second paragraph before learning her role in the story. To see her image—the smiling pre-accident photograph—they generally had to turn to page 9 or 10, and sometimes there was no photograph at all.

One has to wonder why the media (with a few exceptions) didn't construct the kind of melodrama they had fashioned around Karen Ann Quinlan. Both cases had the same basic ingredients, after all: a young woman cruelly transformed into Sleeping Beauty, whom her father was protecting against the callousness of men in power. But the Cruzans had two kinds of disadvantages. For one thing, in certain personal details they were not ready-made subjects for a sentimental narrative. Nancy was less "innocent" than Karen, not only five years older at the time of her accident but twice married and divorced. As for her parents, unlike the pious, soft-spoken Quinlans they were angry and nonreligious.[68] A more basic factor was also at work: the Cruzans' story was a sequel, lacking the novelty that had drawn reporters from California, Europe, and Japan to the Quinlans' front yard. Karen's case came first and thereby evoked all the culture's anxieties and confusions about modern dying. Fourteen years later the anxieties and confusions remained but were familiar—news for the inside pages. Even the question of withholding artificial nutrition and hydration was no longer novel, either to the courts (see *Jobes, Conroy,* and *Brophy*) or to the public. Nancy Cruzan's only novelty was that her plight came before the U.S. Supreme Court. In the media's narrative her case became less a human melodrama than a legal—one might even say a technical—problem to be solved in the "laboratory" of the states.

This was not at all true for the protagonists most intimately involved. On the day of the verdict the Cruzans stayed in seclusion, but their next-door neighbor in Carterville had angry words. "The Supreme Court goofed," said Dick Moyer. "If each of those justices walked a mile in Joe and Joyce's shoes," they wouldn't have made this "pitiful" decision.[69] Despite the setback, however, the Cruzans weren't surrendering. ". . . The whole system has tried to almost break us," Joe declared, "but they are not going to succeed as long as Bill Colby sticks with us and when he falls to the wayside then we will keep going because I made a commitment to my daughter that I wouldn't let this go on. . . ."[70]

Colby didn't fall. After the Supreme Court remanded the case to Missouri, he went back to probate court, this time armed with new, hopefully "clear and convincing" evidence. Three of Nancy's former acquaintances had come forward with recollections of her statements that she wouldn't want to be kept alive by respirator or force-feeding. What might have become the fourth round of the legal contest turned out to be an uncontested victory. For in October the Missouri attorney general, William Webster, withdrew the state from the case, claiming that his aim in the original case had been merely to clarify the law on surrogate rights, not to oppose the removal of Cruzan's tube. The real reason, though, was political rather than legalistic. Webster was planning to run for governor in 1992, and he could see that voters sided overwhelmingly with the Cruzans. According to a poll two months after the Supreme Court ruling, 89 percent of Missourians would want to end treatment if they were hopelessly ill or in a vegetative state. Even the governor offered the Cruzan family his prayers and sympathy for their "unfortunate, compound tragedy." To oppose abortion was one thing, but to oppose the Cruzans was a political liability.[71] Once the state withdrew, the way was cleared for Judge Teel to order again, as he had two years earlier, that the feeding tube be removed.

Unlike for Karen Quinlan, who could survive without the respirator, the effect for Nancy Cruzan was certain and foreseeable— a matter of days. On December 15 the Cruzans parked their trailer on the hospital grounds, where they planned to eat and sleep when they weren't sitting at their daughter's bedside. "We walk with her to the door of death," Joe said, "so that she may at last pass through and be free. So fly away little sister and have fun."[72]

Many of the nurses who had been tending her wept and refused to cooperate. "She's their daughter, but she's our patient," one said. Another added: "The Humane Society won't let you starve your dog." On December 16 an anti-abortion leader in Atlanta began fasting in protest. Two days later an anti-abortion group entered the hospital trying to break into Nancy's room and force-feed her. When nineteen of them were arrested, they all gave their names as "Nancy Cruzan." During the following week there were more break-ins and arrests while the protesters camped outside the hospital in fifteen-degree weather and held an overnight prayer session.[73]

Twelve days after the tube was removed, seven years after being thrown from her car, Nancy died. She was thirty-three years old. Now in newspaper headlines she was no longer merely a "comatose woman" but Nancy Cruzan, whose "ordeal" had finally concluded in a "peaceful death." The Cruzans buried her beneath a gravestone that read: "Nancy Beth Cruzan, Most Loved Daughter—Sister—Aunt—Born, July 20, 1957—Departed, January 11, 1983—At Peace, December 26, 1990."[74]

BUT IF THIS marked the end of Nancy Cruzan's story, it didn't end her family's, or my connection to theirs. Four days after I wrote the preceding pages, I was in my living room reading the *New York Times* when I saw a familiar face on the obituary page. I felt a jolt in my chest. Joe Cruzan had hung himself in his carport on August 17, 1996, at the age of sixty-two. I had followed this man through all his anguish, I had formed a bond with him, and now he had killed himself. I felt desolate, and a little frightened.

I read through the article again, looking for some reason. "Miss Cruzan was permitted to die late in 1990. Later, Mr. Cruzan expressed uncertainty about whether the right action had been taken." But I thought he was sure—he said he would go on until he won, and he won. So did he have second thoughts about what he had committed? Or was there nothing left to live for? Or did the sadness finally eat him up?

I stared at the grainy little photograph. He was looking vacantly off to the right, his lips slightly parted as if having just said something, his beard mostly white, a worn-out man.

I had the impulse to go to Carterville. I would stand outside the Cruzans' house gazing at the carport, at the curtained windows, hoping to share some of my sorrow . . . at least as much as an outsider could.[75]

7

Suicide with Assistance

Nancy cruzan's family went through three years of battles in four courts before being allowed to end her life-support. If only she had written a living will, they would almost certainly have been spared their torment, but as Joe Cruzan remarked, at the age of twenty-five who thinks about dying? Still, age was not the main deterrent. The vast majority of Americans, young and old, had not completed an advance directive.

A month after the Supreme Court's *Cruzan* ruling, in which Sandra Day O'Connor had advocated a durable power of attorney, U.S. Senator John Danforth—from the Cruzans' home state of Missouri—took action. He introduced the Patient Self-Determination Act, which would require hospitals to inform incoming patients about their right to make advance directives. The title Danforth chose for his bill was revealing. As one congressman explained during the committee hearings, if Nancy Cruzan could speak she would say "Empower the individual."[1] Congress passed the bill easily while various state legislatures amended their living-will statutes to permit withdrawal of life-support (including food and water) from PVS patients and to authorize a durable power of attorney.[2]

But for some Americans these were feeble protections against their dread of modern dying. A living will, which applied to terminal illness (death within six months), didn't benefit someone with Alzheimer's or multiple sclerosis, who would be slowly devoured by helplessness for years before nearing death. Nor did it benefit someone in a persistent vegetative state who was not dying but who burdened or bankrupted her loved ones. And as stories in the morning newspaper proved all too grimly, both a living will and a proxy could be thwarted by doctors, hospital administrators, or right-to-life groups: Forty-four-year-old Michael Martin, brain-damaged and in need of total care for nine years, wanting to die but kept alive by court order. Thirty-four-year-old Jamie Butcher of Minnesota, unconscious for seventeen years since an automobile wreck, with pro-life attorneys contesting his parents' request to end feeding. Forty-four-year-old Joey Fiori of Philadelphia, in a PVS for eighteen years, his mother unable to have his feeding tube removed.[3] How could anyone be sure of ending life when and how he or she wanted to—the last act of self-determination?

Back in the 1930s small groups in England and the United States had promoted legalization of euthanasia. They wanted to include not only voluntary *passive* euthanasia: a patient choosing to forgo life-sustaining treatment. They also included voluntary *active* euthanasia: a patient asking the doctor to hasten his dying either directly (by injection) or indirectly (by prescription of a lethal dose of drugs). After World War II and disclosure of the Nazi extermination policy—*involuntary* euthanasia—the word "euthanasia" carried only one meaning: extermination of innocent people.

As the right-to-die movement made headway in the 1960s and 1970s, however, discussion of hastening death again became permissible. When Derek Humphry wrote a book about having helped his first wife kill herself to escape the ravages of cancer, he was invited to address professional groups and lay audiences throughout the United States, Canada, even Australia. So Humphry decided in 1980 to found the Hemlock Society, promoting the right of suicide. By the 1990s it had 86 local chapters claiming 57,000 members, most of whom were white, middle-class women over the age of 65. The first issue of the *Hemlock Quarterly* went out to 443 subscribers, but 10 years later to more than 30,000. As one journalist and subscriber described it: "HQ was really a how-to magazine, like *Needlepoint News* or *Bon Appetit*. Its readers were recipe clippers.

They were seeking a recipe they would use only once. . . ." In the letters column, readers not only shared cheerful accounts of relatives who had killed themselves after a glass of champagne or while listening to a favorite piece of classical music or overlooking a patio of homegrown flowers. They also provided practical advice. "My mother's prescription for death was one Dramamine (as antiemetic), then a twenty minutes wait, then tea and dry toast. Another twenty minute wait, then 25 Seconal of 100 mg rapidly taken and washed down with whiskey and soda."[4]

Fearing prosecution for aiding suicide, Humphry himself at first referred vaguely and obliquely to the drugs and dosages. By the late 1980s, when no police had shown up at his door, he became more specific. And in 1991 he came fully out in the open by publishing a small book titled *Final Exit*. It was a suicide manual—or, as the subtitle said more gracefully, *The Practicalities of Self-Deliverance and Assisted Suicide for the Dying*. "I am not for one moment advocating that elderly people, or patients with degenerative diseases, should take their lives," he wrote. Instead he was speaking for "that most important of civil liberties: the option to govern our own lives, which includes the right to choose to die." Chapter Two explained how to "shop for the right doctor," one who will write a prescription for a lethal dose of drugs. A seven-page "Drug Dosage Table" listed eighteen different pills by generic and trade names and specified the maximum usual dose for each. In most cases, Humphry wrote, you will die within twenty minutes to an hour. But given the small possibility of vomiting up the pills or lingering near death for one or two days, he devoted a chapter to "self-deliverance via the plastic bag." It should be large but not huge, firmly tied around the neck by a rubber band or ribbon. As for clear or opaque bags, "that's a matter of taste," Humphry wrote. "Loving the world as I do, I'll opt for a clear one if I have to."[5]

Final Exit jumped onto the *New York Times* best-seller list and stayed there for 18 weeks. Bookstores couldn't keep up with demand and besieged the Hemlock Society with orders for 150,000 additional copies. By the mid-1990s sales totaled over 600,000.[6] Copies were found near the bodies of 12 suicides in New York City.

And the number of deaths by asphyxiation was twice as high in the year after the book appeared as the average during six preceding years.[7] Clearly there was in the America of the nineties a hunger for the knowledge of doing away with oneself. "Our heady dominion," Andrew Solomon called it in his account of how he, along with his brother and father, had helped his mother kill herself before the ovarian cancer killed her.[8]

These desperate acts were part of a nationwide trend. After declining for four decades, the suicide rate among Americans over the age of sixty-five rose nearly 9 percent during 1980–1992. The elderly constituted 13 percent of the population but almost 20 percent of annual suicides, the highest rate of any age cohort.[9] At the same time suicide was spreading even faster among a quite different group: young men infected with HIV. In 1987 the antiviral drug AZT finally became available, but it proved not to be the "magic bullet" that AIDS victims desperately wanted. All the elaborate and expensive treatments merely gave borrowed time. Paul Monette, a thirty-six-year-old poet, began his 1988 memoir by writing: "I don't know if I will live to finish this." An HIV-positive diagnosis was a death sentence, but an indeterminate one. All a man could be sure of was that his body and mind would disintegrate painfully and hideously, maybe this year or the year after ("I've watched too many sicken in a month and die by Christmas," wrote Monette), but one day almost imperceptibly there would be a lesion or a shortness of breath ("it comes like a slowly dawning horror"), only to retreat so that for several months he would feel healthy and want to believe the sixteen or twenty pills a day had killed the virus, except he had to know that sooner or later it would be back ("you fight tough, you fight dirty, but you cannot fight dirtier than it") and he would resume dying.[10]

One choice was to end his life sooner than his body chose to. "At parties we sit around and say 'Let's start accumulating pills now,'" a San Francisco State student told a reporter. "The feeling is 'Let's be squirrels.' Everybody knows what's coming." After George Kingsley, a forty-eight-year-old publishing executive, contracted AIDS, he assembled a fatal amount of drugs but, despite three hospitalizations, hadn't used them. Simply having them "has diminished my horror, as though I was facing an enemy on a battlefield stark naked and now I have armor."[11] The suicide rate among gay men with AIDS was significantly higher than among other men aged twenty to fifty-nine—in New York City, thirty-six times higher.[12] But the risk of failure was also high. One read in the newspaper of men with AIDS who swallowed all their pills and were found in the morning, severely brain-damaged.[13] It was safer to die with the help of friends. "I couldn't do it for just anybody," explained a man who had helped his HIV-positive friend commit suicide. "It would have to be someone I love. . . . After all, friends help friends, because doctors usually won't." In Los Angeles, Marty James founded an organization called Safe Passages. Before his own suicide on Christmas Day, 1991, he openly helped fourteen AIDS victims kill themselves.[14]

One doctor, though, was regularly performing highly publicized assisted suicides, and not only for the elderly or terminally ill. In a public park outside Detroit on June 4, 1990, Janet Adkins lay on a bed in the back of a rusting VW camper while Dr. Jack Kevorkian attached EEG electrodes to her wrists and ankles and inserted a syringe into her arm. A tube led from the syringe to three bottles hanging from a metal and wood frame. The first bottle contained saline solution, the second thiopental, and the third potassium chloride. When everything was set up, Adkins pressed a button and within ten seconds her eyelids began to flicker and droop. "Thank you, thank you," she said. "Have a nice trip," he replied. She became unconscious, and six minutes later the EEG indicated that her heart had stopped beating.[15]

Janet Adkins was fifty-four years old, living in Oregon, married and the mother of three grown sons, a teacher of English and piano, an avid outdoorswoman who enjoyed hang gliding and had trekked in Nepal. A week before her death she had played tennis with her son and won. Why would she want to commit suicide? After several years of forgetting songs and failing to recognize notes as she played the piano, she had recently been diagnosed with Alzheimer's disease. She read in *Newsweek* about Kevorkian

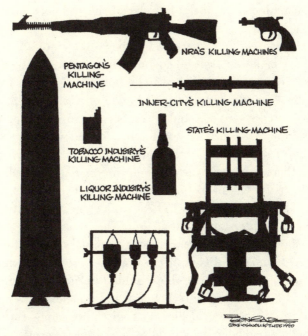

PENTAGON'S
KILLING
MACHINE

NRA'S KILLING MACHINES

INNER-CITY'S KILLING MACHINE

TOBACCO INDUSTRY'S
KILLING MACHINE

STATE'S KILLING MACHINE

LIQUOR INDUSTRY'S
KILLING MACHINE

Dr. Kevorkian's Killing Machine (Paul Conrad, *Los Angeles Times*)

and his "Mercitron" machine, then saw him on the "Donahue" TV show, and with her husband's consent—but over the objections of her doctors and sons—telephoned to arrange to kill herself. As she wrote in a note on the morning of her death, "I don't choose to put my family or myself through the agony of this terrible disease."[16]

Media reaction was immediate, intense, and totally hostile. "Dr. Kevorkian's twisted experiment." "Dr. Death's suicide machine." Zealot, maverick, fanatic. It was a mockery of medical responsibility, critics said, for a pathologist to help a woman die who was not terminally ill, who in fact was still in the early stage of Alzheimer's, and whom he had met only two days before. "If anything, the clandestine administration of a lethal injection in the back end of a rusty van mocks the very phrase: death with dignity." A *Los Angeles Times* cartoonist portrayed Kevorkian's device alongside a machine gun, ballistic missile, electric chair, and other "killing machines." Even the founder of the Hemlock Society objected.[17]

This hue and cry marked the beginning, not the end, of Kevorkian's career in assisted suicide. During the next seven years he became a national celebrity as he helped more than forty-five people die. Countless individuals phoned or wrote him, and some too weak to write sent dictated notes, begging for his help. A quadriplegic from Missouri: "I am totally dependent on people for *everything*. I don't have a life. I am a mind trapped in this dead body. Is there any way you can help me *end* this so-called life? Please!" A palsy victim in Illinois: "This is not living. I am taking up space. I'm eagerly waiting to hear from you. There will never be anyone more understanding than you."[18]

Most of his clients were not in the terminal stage of illness and many—Alzheimer's patients, for example—weren't enduring pain. They wanted to die because they couldn't bear their indignity and envisioned a future yet more helpless and hopeless. A few clients may have had no physical illness at all. Thirty-nine-year-old Rebecca Badger had been diagnosed with multiple sclerosis, but after her death with Kevorkian's assistance in 1996, the autopsy found no evidence of that disease. Following reports of her periodic depressions and drug abuse, her doctor changed his diagnosis to Munchausen syndrome, in which patients fake or induce illness to gain attention.[19] As the deaths mounted, so did outcries from physicians, ethicists, and people with disabilities. "Kevorkian is a grotesque parody of how our society should treat those who can't live without long-term care and community support," exclaimed a man with a progressive disability who used a motorized wheelchair. "His answer is to treat us no better than a horse with a broken leg. When we can no longer run and jump and entertain the king, it's time to be mercifully destroyed."[20]

Law enforcement officials also intervened—in vain. Prosecutors in Michigan indicted Kevorkian three different times for violating the state's law against assisted suicide, and each time the jury acquitted him. "I don't feel it's our obligation," one juror explained, "to choose for someone else how much pain and suffering that they can go through."[21] Some months later a county circuit judge struck down the law, arguing that "it's hard to imagine a state action that would have a greater intrusive effect upon a person's quest to make decisions based upon their personal moral beliefs than the state's blanket proscription on assisted suicide." When Kevorkian helped two women die, prosecutors charged him with murder, but in the absence of a state law against assisted suicide, the judge dismissed the case. The Michigan Supreme Court then ruled in 1994 that physician-assisted suicide could be prosecuted as a common-law felony. Given that loophole, prosecutors indicted the doctor a fifth time, but again the jury voted for acquittal. Yet another attempt at conviction in 1997 ended in a mistrial. At that point both candidates for chief prosecutor in Oakland County, Michigan, said that further prosecutions would be a waste of their time and taxpayers' money.[22]

"It's no longer a question of whether we endorse him or abhor him," a North Carolina columnist remarked. "As the body count rises, Doctor Death is such a tall grim reality we're obliged to deal with him."[23] For a growing majority of the general public, assisted suicide seemed an increasingly desirable option. For leaders of the right-to-die movement, on the other hand, assisted suicide spelled trouble. People such as Paul Armstrong and Daniel Callahan had been successfully persuading judges, medical authorities, and the general public to let patients or their surrogates end life-support. Now they found their success taking forms they hadn't intended and couldn't control. Dr. Kevorkian was like the monster created by Dr. Frankenstein. So, in a peculiar turn of events, right-to-die proponents joined right-to-life proponents in a chorus of alarm. "This is a defining moment in medicine," said the AMA vice-president for ethics standards. "If doctors are allowed to kill patients, the doctor-patient relationship will never be the same again."[24]

Bioethicists, lawyers, and physicians emphasized the distinction between stopping life-support and hastening death either indirectly (prescribing an overdose) or directly (injecting a lethal substance). Omission versus commission. Passive versus active euthanasia. In the first case, the disease kills; in the second case, the doctor kills. Once we cross the line from passive to active euthanasia, opponents argued, how can a patient trust that his doctor is doing everything to heal her? According to surveys, for example, physicians tend to estimate the quality of chronically ill patients' life to be worse than do the patients themselves, and therefore are more inclined to assume patients don't want to prolong treatment.[25] And conversely, how can society protect a patient against completing what might be—and typically is—only a temporary suicidal impulse? For the great majority of elderly patients who ask to be put out of their misery are suffering from depression; when their depression is alleviated, they want to stay alive.[26]

Still more disquieting, critics noted, female patients may be especially susceptible to self-destruction. Consider the fact that American women attempt suicide three times as often as men while succeeding only half as often—the proverbial "cry for help." But Kevorkian provided help for successful suicide. Perhaps not coincidentally, all of his first eight clients were women, as were half of the next twenty. Forty-three-year-old Sherry Miller, for example, was confined to a wheelchair by multiple sclerosis. Five years after her deterioration had set in, her husband divorced her, her children went to live with him, and she had to move into her parents' house. "I am not in any pain," Miller said. "I just can't do anything anymore. I'm just existing, and I no longer care just to exist." In 1991 Kevorkian helped her put on a face mask attached to a canister of carbon monoxide; she pulled a string that opened a valve, and died thirty minutes later.[27] Advocates of assisted suicide claimed that women like Miller were exercising self-determination. Feminists said these women were feeling depressed and helpless.[28]

In the wake of Kevorkian's activities, right-to-die supporters worked with growing frenzy to repudiate assisted suicide. If one person arranges to be killed by another, Callahan argued, that is a perverted version of autonomy. "[It is] self-determination run amok." To legalize it, he warned, is to endanger the most vulnerable members of society. ". . . Once the turn has been made down the road to euthanasia, [it] could soon turn into a convenient and commodius expressway."[29]

AS A SUPPORTER of voluntary *passive* euthanasia, however, Callahan himself had already made that turn. Logically, physician-assisted suicide—an indirect form of voluntary *active* euthanasia—is the next milestone along the path that right-to-die proponents had traveled for more than twenty years. On behalf of Quinlan, Conroy, Cruzan, and other incompetent patients, they had argued that these individuals preferred not to be kept alive. Sherry Miller made the same argument on her own behalf, invoking the same principle of self-determination. The difference was that she asked a doctor to let her die not by ending treatment (passive euthanasia) but by providing treatment—lethal gas or drugs (active euthanasia). Omission versus commission. Critics of assisted suicide consider this the crucial difference, because removing life-support allows a natural process to end in death (the disease kills). But this critique misunderstands the pertinent moral principle. The crucial criterion is not the doctor's action but the patient's wishes. If a doctor lets an injured patient bleed to death, he would be allowing nature to take its course but would be acting immorally. On the other hand, if a patient with an incurable disease pleads for an end to her suffering, it doesn't matter whether the doctor suspends life-prolonging treatment or prescribes a lethal dose of pills, except that the pills will be quicker. Both actions have the same intention: to help the patient die.[30]

Even before Dr. Kevorkian began using his "Mercitron" machine, a few physicians publicly advocated assisted suicide and countless others secretly honored requests of hopelessly ill patients.[31] If a son, husband, or lover was the one who actually crushed the barbiturates and mixed them into yogurt, it was the doctor who had prescribed them, perhaps with a pointed comment that more than so-and-so-many at a time would be fatal. It was a tacit conspiracy, like the one performed among doctors, terminally ill patients, and their families in the days before legalized DNR codes and advance directives. It had to be tacit because although suicide was legal in all fifty states, assisting a suicide was forbidden in all but eighteen.

In 1991 a Rochester, New York, internist named Timothy Quill broke the silence. In the *New England Journal of Medicine* he explained why he had prescribed a lethal dose of sleeping pills for Diane, a forty-five-year-old patient with acute leukemia. Quill had known her for eight years, admiring her courage as she overcame vaginal cancer, alcoholism, and depression. By 1990 she had not only solidified her relationship with her husband and college-age son but had made strides in her artistic work and her career. Still, the verdict of leukemia was more than she could bear. Although Quill said the odds of success with chemotherapy were 25 percent, she refused to undergo the torment of treatment. He was "disturbed" and held long discussions with her about the implications of nontreatment. He described the benefits of pain-relief medication and arranged for a home hospice program, during which she received nursing care and took antibiotics. But Diane was obdurate: no chemo, no hospice. Gradually Quill became convinced that "it was extraordinarily important to Diane to maintain control of herself and her own dignity during the time remaining to her. When this was no longer possible, she clearly wanted to die." He suggested she contact the Hemlock Society. A week later she asked him for the barbiturates. After four months at home with her husband and son, she said her goodbyes to Dr. Quill, to friends, to her family, and asked to be left alone in the living room for an hour. "I wonder whether Diane struggled in that last hour," Quill wrote, "and whether the Hemlock Society's way of death by suicide is the most benign. I wonder why Diane, who gave so much to so many of us, had to be alone for the last hour of her life."[32]

In other words, Quill wanted her autonomy to be supplemented by relatedness. He wanted to extend her tapestry of relationships up to the last moment before she loosed herself. That is how the parents of Nancy Cruzan had arranged her death, and how Patricia Brophy had arranged Paul's: surrounded by family, even though neither Nancy nor Paul had any awareness of the event. All the more reason for Diane, who was entirely aware. But had Diane died in the arms of her doctor or her family, they would have been committing a felony. In fact, Quill's case was presented to a grand jury, but it refused to indict him for having prescribed the pills, and the New York State Professional Review Board refused to declare misconduct.[33]

After reading Quill's account, one has to wonder what is wrong—legally and morally—with his scrupulous form of physician-assisted suicide. He hadn't hooked her up to a "Mercitron" apparatus two days after meeting her, nor was she suffering a nonterminal illness. The prescription of drugs came toward the end of an eight-year relationship following long discussions about options and consequences and in response to an imminently fatal disease. Instead of removing a life-prolonging device, the physician gave his patient a death-hastening means, but either way the purpose was the same: dying on her own terms. Or if one thinks of one's life as a narrative, it was Diane's autobiography completed with the assistance of Timothy Quill.

Although medical organizations continued to object to assisted suicide, individual physicians became more receptive. A 1995 poll of doctors in Michigan found 56 percent in favor of legalizing assisted suicide. A year later a group of San Francisco health-care providers were drafting professional guidelines for handling patients who requested aid in dying, and the Stanford University Center for Biomedical Ethics convened medical professionals for the same objective.[34]

Public opinion moved in the same direction. Whatever their qualms about "Doctor Death," a growing majority of Americans disregarded the bioethicists' distinction between passive and active voluntary euthanasia. "When a person has a disease that cannot be cured," the pollsters asked, "do you think doctors should be allowed by law to end the patient's life by some painless means if the patient and his family request it?" Before the *Quinlan* decision, 53 percent said yes. Shortly afterward, in 1977, 60 percent or more said yes. By the 1990s approval rose as high as 69 percent. Even when pollsters asked more pointedly about permitting doctors to provide lethal drugs or injections to a terminally ill person in pain, 64 percent of Americans were in favor. And when asked what they themselves would want if they were comatose with no hope of recovery,

75 percent of respondents wanted their families to withdraw life-support.[35]

On the West Coast, meanwhile, assisted-suicide laws became not merely a matter of opinion but a real possibility. In the State of Washington in 1991 euthanasia groups put Initiative 119 on the ballot, which would have permitted doctors to help terminally ill patients die either by suicide or by direct intervention such as lethal injection. In California a year later Proposition 161 gave voters the same choice. In certain respects the campaigns seemed an updated enactment of the battle over Barry Keene's Natural Death Act in California fifteen years earlier. State branches of the Catholic Conference and the Right-to-Life Committee again mobilized staunch opposition. The AMA and the Hospital Association declared formal opposition, although they contributed no money and spoke up halfheartedly.[36] In remarkable contrast to the living-will contest, however, bioethicists and some liberal Christians from around the nation also fought against assisted suicide, warning voters that they stood "on the edge of a moral cataclysm."[37]

On the other side of the battle line, the coalition included numerous Protestant denominations, organized labor, the state Democratic party, AIDS activists, the Grey Panthers, and, of course, the Hemlock Society. Moreover, almost half of Washington's doctors said they favored legalizing assisted suicide. According to pre-election polls, so did 60 percent of the likely voters in each state, with 12 percent undecided. But when it came down to the moment of enacting the first euthanasia law in the world, some of those voters flinched. In both Washington and California the measures lost, 54 to 46 percent.[38]

In strictly arithmetical terms, these added up to defeat, but in the perspective of history they marked an extraordinary sea change in "the right to die." Fifteen years earlier—no more than a minute or two of cultural-historical time—Americans had been hesitant to legalize living wills. Now 46 percent voted to legalize not simply passive euthanasia but active euthanasia by doctors. Attitudes were shifting with astounding speed; informal or extralegal behav-

---

PROPOSED BY INITIATIVE PETITION

---

16. ALLOWS TERMINALLY ILL ADULTS TO OBTAIN PRESCRIPTION FOR LETHAL DRUGS —

QUESTION: Shall law allow terminally ill adult patients voluntary informed choice to obtain physician's prescription for drugs to end life?

SUMMARY: Adopts law. Allows terminally ill adult Oregon residents voluntary informed choice to obtain physician's prescription for drugs to end life. Removes criminal penalties for qualifying physician-assisted suicide. Applies when physicians predict patient's death within 6 months. Requires:

   15-day waiting period;

   2 oral, 1 written request;

   second physician's opinion;

   counseling if either physician believes patient has mental disorder, impaired judgment from depression.

Person has choice whether to notify next of kin. Health care providers immune from civil, criminal liability for good faith compliance.

ESTIMATE OF FINANCIAL IMPACT: No financial effect on state or local government expenditures or revenues.

SAMPLE BALLOT
GENERAL ELECTION
JACKSON COUNTY, OREGON
NOVEMBER 8, 1994

An election will be held within Jackson County, Oregon on Novermber 8, 1994 from 7 a.m. to 8 p.m.

Assisted Suicide Ballot, Oregon, 1994

ior was moving almost as fast; sooner or later, legislation surely would catch up.

In Oregon in 1994 a citizen-initiated "Death with Dignity Act" offered voters a less drastic version of assisted suicide—more like Dr. Quill's than Dr. Kevorkian's. Instead of direct assistance by doctors, it allowed a patient to obtain a prescription for a lethal medicine if a doctor determined that the patient had less than six months to live and if a second doctor agreed. The measure also required a fifteen-day waiting period and, if the doctor believed the patient was depressed or demented, it required counseling. The Right-to-Life Committee and the Catholic Conference poured millions of dollars for opposition into Oregon. Significantly, though, the Oregon Medical Association and the state hospice association took a neutral position. On November 8, 1994, by a vote of 52 percent, Oregon became the first jurisdiction in the world to legalize assisted suicide.[39]

Dr. Peter Goodwin, who had campaigned for the measure, was exultant. "The physicians who are presently involved [in assisting suicides] and have kept it secret and so are in the closet so to speak, will now be able to speak to their colleagues and say, 'I will do this in the future because I think it's appropriate care.'" Tim Shuck of Portland, a forty-five-year-old AIDS victim whose brain had been invaded by the virus, said simply: "The biggest gift they could give me is to let me go."[40] Before the law could be implemented, though, the National Right-to-Life Committee filed suit and a federal judge issued a temporary restraining order.

Meanwhile a more potent challenge was taking place at the other end of the country. Three patients and three doctors filed suit in Manhattan Federal District Court against New York State's ban on physician-assisted suicide. The ban, they claimed, not only deprived them of their Fourteenth Amendment guarantee of personal liberty with due process. It also denied them equal protection, because terminally ill patients had the right to hasten death by asking a physician to stop treatment, but they didn't have the right to hasten death by asking a physician to *perform* treatment. One of the patients was George Kingsley, the publishing house director with AIDS, who had collected pills in case he wanted to kill himself. One of the doctors was Timothy Quill.[41] The district court turned them down, but in the spring of 1996 they were upheld unanimously by the Second Circuit Court of Appeals. By coincidence, on the West Coast the Ninth Circuit Court of Appeals simultaneously struck down Washington State's law forbidding assisted suicide. These decisions "would have seemed incredible a few years ago," one constitutional scholar declared, but now they opened the possibility of a "social revolution."[42]

A year later the U.S. Supreme Court voted 9 to 0 to reject both challenges to the state laws that made physician-assisted suicide a crime. But this rejection did not signify defeat. Even though the justices ended up with the same "nay," they reached it via strikingly different arguments. In the principal opinion Chief Justice Rehnquist (whose wife had died in 1991 after a protracted fight with ovarian cancer) said the question was not whether a patient had the right to choose death with a physician's assistance. Rather, he said, it was whether the due process clause protects the right to commit suicide with another's aid. "We are confronted with a consistent and almost universal tradition that has long rejected the asserted right," Rehnquist concluded, "and [that] continues explicitly to reject it today, even for terminally ill, mentally competent adults."

Stephen G. Breyer (whose wife counseled terminally ill children and their families at a cancer institute) framed the issue differently: not as assisted suicide but as "personal control over the manner of death, professional medical assistance, and the avoidance of unnecessary and severe physical suffering. . . ." He didn't believe, however, that the Court needed to decide whether this right belonged among the "fundamental" rights protected by the Constitution. For in both New York and Washington, physicians could prescribe pain-killing medicine, even in lethal doses, so that a patient could die with dignity.

John Paul Stevens kept the door open even more emphatically. He too refused to endorse a categorical right to assisted suicide, but he recognized "the possibility that an individual plaintiff seeking to hasten her death, or a doctor whose assistance was sought, could prevail in a more particularized challenge." Likewise Sandra Day O'Connor and Ruth Bader Ginsburg pointedly refrained from ruling out that possibility.

Justice David H. Souter suggested finding a remedy in a different arena than the courts. Although the Supreme Court should not make a decision on a still uncertain, emerging issue, "legislatures are not so constrained." Let the states experiment in regulating assisted suicide and perhaps the Court could reconsider it at a later time.[43]

What, then, did this myriad of decisions signify? Opponents of assisted suicide pronounced "victory." In terms of medical practice as well as ethical principle, however, that was at best a huge overstatement, and more likely wrong. Regardless of the laws, many doctors would continue discreetly helping terminal patients achieve a "good death." "I think it will be business as usual with regard to the underground practice," Timothy Quill predicted. And in his characteristic style, Jack Kevorkian said the Court's ruling would make "not one damned bit of difference" in what he did.

The practice of assisted suicide would continue and, as Rehnquist himself acknowledged, so would Americans' "earnest and profound debate" about its morality and legality. The Court had handed the dilemma back to the states and had left the hard questions to be answered in the future. As the bioethicist Arthur Caplan declared, "I see this not as the end of anything, but as the beginning of what is going to take years to work through."[44] If this was a victory, it was a victory for the ethic of ambiguity.

Oregon would be the first state to put the ethic to the test. Challengers to the 1994 assisted-suicide law had failed in both the legal and the political arena. The Ninth Circuit Court of Appeals overturned an injunction against the law, and the U.S. Supreme Court refused to hear an appeal. When opponents put the measure on the ballot for a second time, hoping for repeal, they were decisively rebuffed. A huge turnout of Oregonians, the largest in thirty-four years, voted by a 60 percent majority to let doctors help terminally ill patients kill themselves.[45]

8

Cultures of Dying

"THE PAST is a foreign country," the novelist L. P. Hartley has written. "They do things differently there."[1] Distance and differences enable a time traveler to recognize the distinctive features of his own culture. As one closes in on the present, however, perspective and therefore recognition dwindle—like pressing one's face against a mirror.

Now that this book has traveled out of the past into the bewildering questions of our own time, I think it will be useful to make a brief excursion to a literal foreign country, or rather two countries with contrasting cultures of dying.[2] On the one hand is Bali, which is so different that one can't imagine building bridges of comparison with the United States. But that gulf, notably in attitudes toward community, illness, and death, allows us to measure the limits of the American way of dying. The Netherlands, on the other hand, will seem quite familiar, which makes all the more surprising and instructive the official Dutch tolerance not only of physician-assisted suicide but of voluntary euthanasia. If the Dutch have adopted those policies, what would or should prevent Americans from doing likewise? As we'll see, though, in its political and especially its medical culture the Netherlands too is a foreign country. Together these two case studies illuminate, I believe, the need to set "the right to die" within an ethic—a tapestry—of relatedness.

"STRANGE AS IT SEEMS," wrote a North American visitor to Bali, "it is in their cremation ceremonies that the Balinese have their greatest fun."[3] Indeed, by all accounts the event resembles a carnival more than a funeral. Hundreds of people participate: extended family, neighbors, friends, distant acquaintances, nowadays even tourists. There is also an orchestra of drums, gongs, cymbals, and xylophones. This procession accompanies the body of the deceased to the cremation grounds, transporting the coffin upon an elaborately decorated wooden tower with pagodalike tiers rising as high as sixty feet. At times the tower-bearers whirl and spin, fall into ditches, and splash each other with mud so as to confuse any evil spirits that may be pursuing the dead person. When they reach the site, the din subsides to something like a murmur while the priest intones a prayer and casts holy water upon the corpse. But as soon as the first flames lick at the body, the "fun" resumes. The orchestra plays, people prod the corpse with long poles, children snatch tinsel and silks from the tower.[4]

From an American viewpoint this behavior is very "strange." It becomes more comprehensible, though, once we set it into cultural context. The Balinese response to death flows from their lifelong attitudes toward the relationship between body and spirit as well as between individual and community. Death is only one phase of a spiritual journey from birth to rebirth, which a person takes with the assistance of family and community.

They celebrate death boisterously, but the Balinese don't lead carefree lives. On the contrary, they are constantly concerned with maintaining their health. Many take a daily drink of sweetened Javanese *jamu* or Balinese *loloh*, apply a kind of poultice from wrist to shoulder, and use medicines to prolong youth. Everyone bathes morning and night. Ultimately, though, they're worried less about their bodies than about their spirit/life force (*bayu*). When they fall ill, they may go to a doctor for physical treatment, but they certainly will visit the house of a *balian*, or traditional healer, who works upon their soul. The *balian* is cheaper and more accessible than a doctor; most important, he or she is trusted.[5] After listening to the various symptoms and complaints, the *balian* may administer a massage or prescribe potions, or recommend offerings to ancestors whom the patient has offended, or go into trance to communicate with the supernatural realm.[6] Whatever the remedy, it is intended to restore the person's harmony with himself and the world—what Westerners might call centeredness: being well in the larger sense of well-being. "People believe that the doctor can help," a Balinese doctor said, "but only the *balian* can heal. Medicine is a means, not a cure." For cure ultimately depends upon the health of the person's *bayu*.[7]

If someone is beyond cure, the same philosophy applies. When the family of a patient in a hospital is told by his doctor that he is dying, they bring him home, where he is cared for until, ideally, he dies in the arms of his children. Occasionally a person will decide to die on a certain day that fits with other forces in the universe—a full moon, for example—and often that is when he does die. Suicide is a "bad" death, however, because the soul either suffers in limbo or is reincarnated as a lower form of life.[8]

On the day of death, members of the *banjar*, the local community group, take up their responsibility to bring rice, coffee, and other food as well as white cloth in which to wrap the body. They stay for the next three nights, washing the corpse and constructing the bier, the women preparing the food while the men talk and sometimes gamble to stay awake.[9] It is scarcely a heavyhearted scene. "Oh, we sat and talked . . . about her illness and the events surrounding her death," a man said, recounting the night at the house of a friend whose wife had died. "And we laughed and joked a lot to make the family's hearts happy from sadness. We say things like 'what is dead is dead' and 'let bygones be bygones,' and because the husband is still young and should remarry soon, we also advise him that 'the world is bigger than a *kelor* leaf. . . .' "[10] "Good" emotions promote the well-being not only of oneself but of others.

In the end the *banjar* carries the body to the cemetery and helps the family with the burial.[11] Every day for the next twelve days the family visits the grave and places offerings on a small bamboo altar, seeking to purify the soul by erasing character flaws, illnesses, and sins that may hinder its departure from the body. By the forty-second day, when they return with additional offerings, the process is complete.[12]

At this point they consult a priest for a propitious day on which to hold the cremation. Shortly before the chosen date the *banjar* exhumes the body, wraps it in fresh white cloth, and carries it back to the house. Placed on the same pavilion where it once lay, the corpse is strewn with silks, brocades, jeweled krisses (daggers), and family heirlooms.[13] At this point everything else in the community stops while all the members of the *banjar* prepare elaborate effigies made of coconut leaves as well as offerings to speed the soul's departure. As they work, they feast on the rice, eggs, coconuts, duck, pork, coffee, and cigarettes provided by the family. The family spends heavily for a cremation ceremony. But expense is less at stake than mutual obligations. "We all have to die," a Balinese explained. "Imagine if the *banjar* fail to help at a death ceremony. Here you wouldn't pay anyone to take care of your funeral as you do in the West. No matter how wealthy you are, in the end you depend upon your neighbors."[14]

When the cremation ceremony is completed, the dead person's soul is finally liberated from its body and eventually flies to heaven high above Gunung Agung, the volcano looming over the island. There it will live until the time when it is reborn into its family, thus becoming simultaneously an ancestor and his or her own descendant. As this paradoxical status dramatizes, in Balinese culture an individual is not an isolated unit but a nexus of spiritual and natural forces connecting him to others.[15]

It's tempting to envy the Balinese cheerfulness in the face of death, their bonds of community, their belief in the soul's eventual return to the family. If only we imported *banjars* and boisterous cremation ceremonies. But of course they are rooted in an entire cultural context. To transplant them successfully we would need a society that subordinates individual desires to mutual obligations and that sets daily actions and expectations into a spiritual framework. What's more, we would have to uproot life-prolonging treatment and let diseases run their course. In short, there would have to be a cultural revolution, and revolutions of that sort are rare. For more realistic possibilities, we should look closer to home—western Europe—at the Dutch way of dying.

IN THE FALL of 1994, 700,000 Dutch television viewers watched a film of Cornelis "Kees" van Wendel de Joode being put to death by his doctor. "Death on Request," the documentary was titled. Sixty-three-year-old van Wendel had first asked for euthanasia in 1993 after being diagnosed with amyotrophic lateral sclerosis (Lou Gehrig's disease). Within months he grew so weak that he was confined to a wheelchair, at first speaking in a labored, barely audible voice, later working with an alphabet board in his lap to form messages that his wife Antoinette relayed.

On a chilly, wet February afternoon, Dr. Wilfred van Oijen came to the house and questioned van Wendel, as he had several times since December, about his wish to end his suffering. "We mustn't wait any longer," van Wendel mumbled, and began weeping.

"You are upset, Kees, aren't you?" the doctor said. "There, there. Take my handkerchief. . . ."

"Let's change the subject," said Antoinette. "Otherwise he won't stop."

"It's understandable," van Oijen replied. "It's the most essential decision he'll ever take."

Several days later a second doctor arrived and outlined the conditions for euthanasia.

"Yes," van Wendel wrote on his alphabet board. So now the issue was not whether but when.

Van Wendel chose one day, then a later one, then a yet later one, until finally he decided the event should take place on his birthday. Shortly before 8 p.m., sitting in his wheelchair between his wife and his doctor, he sipped a glass of port through a straw.

Antoinette read what her husband spelled out on the letter board: "Let us postpone not any longer."

"If you wish, Kees, we could do it tomorrow," Dr. van Oijen replied.

"No, no," said van Wendel, rolling his wheelchair toward his bed in the next room.

"It is more like a liberation for him," Antoinette said.

She helped her husband into bed and van Oijen gave him an injection. "No bad dreams now," the doctor said. "Just sleep." After van Wendel dozed off, the doctor administered a second injection.

"We've always done everything together," Antoinette said, weeping. "Only I can't come along now. You have to go out on your own."

She then went with the doctor to the next room, where she read aloud a farewell note her husband had written to her.[16]

According to the Dutch penal code, television viewers had witnessed a crime. Since the mid-1970s, however, the courts and the government in the Netherlands have condoned voluntary active euthanasia under three conditions: the patient must have an incurable disease and be suffering unbearable pain; he must have made his request consciously, freely, and repeatedly over time; and finally, the attending doctor must gain consent from a second doctor. By now, active euthanasia has become an established medical option in the Netherlands. Half the physicians there have performed it while only 11 percent would refuse to do so; 75 percent of the public approve, and only 10 percent oppose.[17]

How often it is performed, though, and in what circumstances—these are matters of dispute. The most reliable data come from two studies in 1990–1991, one by the government and the other by an institute of social medicine. Kees van Wendel was one of 9,000 patients each year who asked to have their lives ended. Doctors turned down more than half of these requests and ultimately performed euthanasia in 2,300. The process typically went faster than for van Wendel: in three-fourths of the cases, less than a month elapsed between the first request and death. According to the doctors, the majority of the patients had less than two weeks to live. They accounted for 1.8 percent of all annual deaths. Like van Wendel, the requesters typically were in their mid-sixties and were put to death in their homes, not in a hospital or nursing home. (Assisted suicide, when the patient rather than the doctor performed the lethal action, was relatively infrequent: only 400 of the nearly 9,000 medically induced deaths.)[18]

These data are the most accepted but necessarily approximate. No one knows how many doctors fail to report euthanasia cases, for example, or how many have put patients to death by increasing pain medication to a lethal level. The actual rate, then, may be two or three times higher.[19] More troubling, no one can be sure whether these deaths took place in compliance with the three official guidelines. Were the patients experiencing unbearable pain that could not be relieved by any other means? And did they make their requests freely and repeatedly? One notices, for example, how Antoinette van Wendel translated her husband's replies or perhaps said what she wanted him to say.[20] According to the government's report, Dutch physicians each year hastened the deaths of one thousand patients who were close to death and no longer competent to voice their request. Approximately 60 percent of these patients had previously said something along the lines of "Doctor, please don't let me suffer too long," or "If I can't be saved, you give me something"—an informal advance directive. The other 40 percent underwent unexpectedly rapid deterioration, with great suffering. Nevertheless these were not strictly voluntary euthanasia. For another 5,500 patients, meanwhile, the doctors increased the dosage of pain-killing drugs to levels that would end life.[21]

Given these ambiguities, the Royal Dutch Medical Association in 1995 made a change in its rules. Instead of an injection or an IV drip, it recommended that, whenever possible, doctors should have terminally ill patients swallow the fatal drug by themselves. Basically, though, the medical profession as well as the public remains committed to an individual's right to die with a doctor's active help.[22]

WHEN WE LOOK at the Netherlands' policy toward death, we are looking into the American future—at least so past developments in the United States suggest. In the 1970s and 1980s came permission to let die: first withdrawal of a respirator, then removal of a feeding tube; first from vegetative patients, then from incompetent but conscious ones. In the 1990s court decisions, unofficial medical practices, and public opinion all point toward acceptance of physician-assisted suicide and perhaps even voluntary euthanasia. The meaning of "the right to die" continues to expand. But if that is the lesson of historical retrospect, cross-cultural perspective offers a counterlesson. What works reasonably well in the Netherlands will work poorly, or even maliciously, in the United States until we move closer to the Dutch style of policymaking and to their system of health care.

At first glance the two societies seem alike: prosperous, technologically developed, well educated, and democratic. But the Netherlands is significantly smaller and more homogeneous. Its fifteen million people inhabit an area smaller than West Virginia, and all but 4 percent are white and native-born. Economically the overwhelming majority earn comfortable incomes, in contrast to the widening gap between rich and poor Americans. To be sure, approximately 33 percent are Catholic, 25 percent Protestant, and 40 percent unaffiliated (with a small number of Muslims and Jews), but they coexist according to a long tradition of tolerance and accommodation. Indeed, since 1945 the Catholic and Protestant political parties have usually worked together in a centrist coalition, legislating social welfare programs. By the 1960s there was a welfare state for everyone.[23]

The euthanasia policy has emerged from this same heritage of tolerance and consensus—of "talking it over again."[24] The Dutch had firsthand experience of *in*voluntary euthanasia when the Nazis occupied Holland and demanded that physicians cooperate with the extermination of Jewish and mentally handicapped persons. The physicians refused.[25] During the postwar era, though, life-prolonging technology aroused public discussion of "the right to die." Then in 1973 came a crystallizing event. After her seventy-eight-year-old wheelchair-bound mother repeatedly pleaded for death, a doctor gave her a fatal injection. Instead of punishment, the court imposed a suspended sentence on the doctor and issued guidelines for performing euthanasia. Three grassroots euthanasia groups quickly formed, physicians and judges advocated the idea, and public opinion began to coalesce.[26] The result was characteristically Dutch: euthanasia forbidden by the criminal code while sanctioned by courts and legislature. In contrast to pro-life demonstrators invading Nancy Cruzan's hospital room, Dutch Catholics and Protestants have been equally favorable. Only Catholic bishops and a small group of Calvinists have resisted the consensus.[27]

Successful implementation of euthanasia depended on the political culture in the Netherlands but also the medical culture. Unlike their American counterparts, general practitioners are more important than specialists. Whereas the United States has one GP for every 6.5 specialists, the Netherlands has one for every 1.5. Moreover the Dutch GPs live in the neighborhood of their patients, have their offices at home, and make house calls when the patient is too ill to come in. Dr. Robert Smallhuit, for example, went three or four times a week for three months to the apartment of an elderly woman ("simply for talking," he recalled) before she died of throat cancer. When Andrea de Lang chose to end her life after suffering cancer of the pancreas, her doctor spent the entire night in the living room with her husband, three grown children, sister, and close friends.[28] (Indeed, 40 percent of *all* deaths take place at home, a remarkable contrast to 15 percent in the United States.) Dutch physicians are not "strangers at the bedside." Consequently they enjoy high social esteem and strong trust. Where so many American doctors since the 1970s have contended with the threat of malpractice suits, malpractice is not a part of Dutch culture, so doctors need not practice "defensive medicine."[29]

This trusting relationship between physician and patient is reinforced by the economic structure. Under a combination of private and governmental plans, all inhabitants are insured for virtually all health-care expenses. AIDS patients even receive free doses of AZT. Each Dutch citizen is registered with a *huisarts* (literally, house doctor), and 75 percent see him or her at least once a year. It's a criminal offense for a doctor to refuse or discharge a patient for economic reasons. Nursing homes are publicly funded and are available to all citizens regardless of income.[30]

The structure of American health care, by contrast, makes almost unimaginable the scenario of Mr. and Mrs. van Wendel and Dr. van Oijen. In the United States, family physicians are a minority and house calls an anachronism. Patients see specialists in offices or hospitals, and the more complicated their illness the more specialists they see, until finally they may be lying in an ICU tethered to machines, being monitored by nurses and visited briefly by an overworked oncologist or cardiologist. There are few Timothy Quills.

But even if there were enough doctors to sustain the kind of personalized, ongoing decision-making that takes place in the Netherlands, many Americans couldn't afford them. Every Dutch citizen has health insurance, but at least 15 percent of Americans do not. They visit a doctor only when absolutely necessary, which often means when an illness has become a crisis and they go to the emergency room, where they are treated by doctors who have never seen them before. Insured Americans are more fortunate, but they too face financial obstacles. Insurance premiums have spiraled upward faster than almost all other consumer items, and medical costs faster yet. A catastrophic illness or a nursing home can devour a family's savings. To control this runaway inflation, insurance companies have created a "managed care" system that often restricts patients to certain doctors, a limited number of visits, certain treatments and not others. Depending on your viewpoint, it is a system either of thrift or of deprivation, but certainly it is ruled by bureaucrats whom neither doctors nor patients ever see face to face.

Economics also exerts a more insidious effect. According to an eight-year study, seriously ill patients were 30 percent more likely to refuse life-prolonging care when their illness had caused great financial hardship for their families. As the bioethicist Arthur Caplan commented: "When someone says they don't want to live longer because they don't want to bankrupt their family, that's rationing."[31] Between managed care and the intensive care unit, it's hard for the sick to receive the caring they need. For the dying it's harder yet.

Given this context, legalized assisted suicide or voluntary euthanasia will not function in the United States as it has in the Netherlands. Ideally a future Janet Adkins or Diane would be at home with her loved ones and family doctor during the last hour of her life. More likely, however, she will be in a hospital, and the doctor will be a specialist she has met only recently. Worse yet, if the direst opponents of assisted suicide are correct, some poor, disabled, and elderly patients will succumb not because they choose to die but because they are vulnerable to abuse or coercion by doctors and family members.

Whatever happens, we should remind ourselves that these policies are peripheral to the dilemma of modern dying. For one thing, legalization would not produce an epidemic of hastened deaths. In the Netherlands only 17 percent of the patients who died with doctors' aid did so by voluntary euthanasia either directly (injection) or indirectly (assisted suicide). The other 83 percent died after life-prolonging treatment or withdrawal of that treatment or, in the most desperate instances, pain medication raised to a fatal level.[32] Presumably similar proportions would be true in this country.

More important, for most of us the issue isn't death but what leads up to it. How much pain, how much helplessness, for how long? And how much of a burden, emotionally and financially, to loved ones? These are what most of us dread more than death itself. When asked by pollsters, 75 percent of all Americans (including 83 percent of those above the age of fifty) do not fear death, and the vast majority think about their death only "every now and again" or "almost never."[33] The prospect of painful, hopeless illness, on the other hand, provokes 20 percent to say they would take the shortcut of assisted suicide. (Again, this choice is more favored by the middle-aged than either the young or the elderly.)[34]

Dread, pain, burdening others: these are matters for the *balian* and *banjar*, or the *huisarts*. In the United States they have become the patient's responsibility, the load of his autonomy. En route to death, most American patients and their families must assemble supporters via improvisation, not tradition or institution. In

a culture that espouses individual rights and freedom, even the
ending of one's self is defined as self-determination. As if we can
dictate to our bodies an advance directive. As if we can remain—
or *want* to remain—self-reliant in our last days or weeks, free of
(deprived of) dependence on (care-giving by) others. "Autonomy is
a ravenous concept," the bioethicist Bruce Jennings has written.
"We give it pride of place at the center of our moral imagination
and discourse only at our own peril."[35]

WE NEED NOT LOOK as far as Bali or the Netherlands for reme-
dies to the American way of dying. Alternative forms of moral
imagination and also of medical practice exist along the margins of
the cultural center. Certain ethnic subcultures respond to terminal
illness within a framework of kin and connectedness. So does the
sexual subculture of the gay community. And in what one might
call the medical subculture of hospice, patients are able to die naturally, surrounded by personal and spiritual care-giving.

Korean Americans and Mexican Americans are far less likely
than European Americans to believe that a dying patient should be
told the truth about his diagnosis. According to interviews with two
hundred elderly people in thirty-one senior citizen centers within
Los Angeles County, 35 percent of Korean Americans and 48 percent of Mexican Americans favor telling a patient that he has a terminal illness, in contrast to 69 percent of European Americans.
Nor do these ethnic groups believe that the patient should decide
whether or not to use life-support. Where 65 percent of European
Americans advocate autonomy in this matter, only 28 percent of
Korean Americans and 41 percent of Mexican Americans do so. Instead they believe it's the family's responsibility, not the individual's,
to hear bad news and make life-or-death decisions. Upholding the
patient's self-determination does not empower him; it isolates and
burdens him at a time when he's too sick to make good choices. For
these ethnic groups, then, the recent "reforms" of American medical policy—informed consent and the right to forgo life-support—
are not reforms. Less-educated and poorer persons are more likely

to hold this attitude, but class makes less difference than culture. The more they speak and read English, and the more they associate with European Americans, the more they support patient rights.[36]

Most African Americans (63 percent) agree with European Americans about telling a patient his diagnosis, but their religious beliefs frequently lead them to reject end-of-life options that most whites advocate. While treating a forty-six-year-old black woman with pancreatic cancer, for example, doctors on five separate occasions raised the issue of last-ditch treatment. According to a note in her medical record: "Pt. urged to consider DNR/DNI [do-not-resuscitate / do-not-intubate] given her horrible prognosis." But she would have none of it: death was not a decision for either her physicians or herself to make. ". . . They told me—asked me did I want them to tell me how long I had to live. I told them no, because I said only God has priority over living. That's something man can't tell you—how long you got to live. I said only God can heal you. And they looked at me so funny." If her heart or lungs failed, she insisted on being resuscitated.

Strangers were neither to decide her death nor to nurse her dying. After refusing DNR, the woman also refused "meals on wheels" and hospice. Instead she spent her last few months being cared for by her large extended family.[37] It was a choice that most African Americans would endorse. When a relative is disabled or seriously ill, they are far more likely than whites to call upon a kin network for help—and the kin will oblige. The heritage of oppression has inculcated, as both survival strategy and moral principle, the readiness to put family ahead of self. Indeed, blacks think of the individual as "an extended self" who goes through life and the ending of life in attachment to others.[38]

A similar ethos characterizes the homosexual community. The 1970s had been the "larky" years of self-expression and sexual pleasure, but the HIV virus changed all that. As playwright Scott McPherson wrote in 1991 in the program of *Marvin's Room*: "Now I am thirty-one and my lover has AIDS. Our friends have AIDS. And we all take care of each other, the less sick caring for the more sick. At times, an unbelievably harsh fate is transcended by a simple act of love, by caring for one another."[39] Lacking sufficient support from medical and governmental authorities, gays had to construct their own network and nurse one another. Two years into the AIDS epidemic there were forty-five community-based service groups, within a decade more than six hundred. Meals-on-wheels agencies, for example, with names such as "God's Love We Deliver" (New York City) and "Chicken Soup Brigade" (Seattle). Medical clinics such as Shanti in San Francisco. The Gay Men's Health Center in New York City, with thirty-seven teams of six hundred volunteers who provided support groups, financial advice, medical information. And in every gay community the "buddy system."[40] When Tony Harding died at 5 a.m. in a corner of Washington, D.C., General Hospital, he was indigent, mentally ill, and estranged from his family. But during the preceding months he had received all kinds of care from volunteers at the Whitman-Walker clinic. They delivered hot meals to his apartment, helped pay his rent, and got a pro bono lawyer to clear up a problem with Social Security payments. The Christmas before Harding died, a man he barely knew drove him to Nordstrom's department store and bought him a fancy pair of shoes. In his last weeks, as Harding began falling out of bed at night, a buddy was there to pick him up.[41]

The ethos that gay men and women mustered in response to a sudden lethal epidemic is the same as the one that guided hospice workers' response in the 1970s to the slowly intensifying quandary of modern dying. The United States does not have *banjars* or *huisartsen*, but in hospice it has their modest equivalent: a medical subculture of relatedness. Symptomatically, though, the idea was imported from another country.

During the second year of their daughter's vegetative state, Joe and Julia Quinlan sought an appropriate way of using the $50,000 they had received from their book and the TV film about Karen. So, like hundreds of others from around the world, they traveled to the Sydenham district of south London to see what was being done for the terminally ill at St. Christopher's Hospice.[42]

They entered a place with the atmosphere of an inn more than a medical institution. Outside the main four-storey building was a garden with footpaths and a reflecting pool, a greenhouse, and a play school for staff members' children. Inside, the rooms were spacious, airy, filled with light coming through windows almost reaching the floor. Instead of the smell of antiseptics, the aromas of meat and warm bread floated from the kitchen. Instead of the metallic sound of chimes and names broadcast over a PA system, there was the murmur of conversations, the giggling of children, even a dog trotting down the hall behind a family. The rooms of the fifty-four patients had no IVs or shiny metal machines. In the four-person rooms and in the ward, each bed was surrounded by whatever belongings the patient had brought: reading lamps, armchairs, photographs, books; a bottle of port and two glasses; an ashtray and pack of cigarettes. Nurses sat with patients, chatting, feeding, giving back rubs. A young girl was reading a comic book beside her grandmother.[43]

Besides this solace for the spirit, St. Christopher's also treated the body. To relieve the pain, especially of cancer victims, the staff administered "Brompton's cocktail," an oral mixture of heroin, cocaine, and other ingredients. They prescribed as high and as frequent a dosage as each patient needed. Instead of promoting addiction, though, they found that as the pain subsided, so did the fear of pain, and gradually the patient needed less drugs. In sum, they practiced what is called "palliative care" (the Latin root means "to cover with a cloak") or "comfort care."

In the Middle Ages, hospice was a way station for pilgrims, including the dying. In 1967 Dr. Cicely Saunders established St. Christopher's (with private donations and National Health Service funding) in order to help people travel contentedly through the last stage of their lives. She surrounded them with the feel of home and family—a caring community. More fundamentally her staff—doctors, nurses, social workers, chaplain, volunteers—did not fight against terminal disease but helped people live with it. Healing acquired a different meaning. "Sometimes healing means . . . finding new wholeness as a family—being reconciled," Saunders said. "Or it can mean easing the pain of dying or allowing someone to die when the time comes."[44] In the words of the hospice slogan: Neither hasten nor prolong death.

The Quinlans came home determined to emulate, in some form or other, what they had found in their pilgrimage. After two years of planning, they established in 1980 the Karen Ann Quinlan Center of Hope, a nonresidential facility that sends caretakers to the homes of terminally ill people throughout northwest New Jersey. At the time it was one of only sixty hospices scattered across the United States—almost all of them providing home rather than residential care, relying heavily on volunteers, and each serving an average of thirty-five patients.[45] Even if spread thin, though, this grassroots movement was attracting lavish publicity and praise in professional circles as well as in the popular media. This "radically old-fashioned idea . . . is beginning to catch on in America . . . ," *Newsweek* proclaimed.[46] Elisabeth Kübler-Ross had been convincing millions of Americans to help the dying proceed from denial to acceptance. Hospice translated her approach into institutional form. By 1982, 800 hospice programs were under way. In that same year President Reagan authorized an annual National Hospice Week and, more significantly, Congress permitted hospices to be reimbursed by Medicare. By the 1990s there were at least 1,700 programs serving 200,000 patients a year.[47]

In two different ways hospice helps fill the desperate void that modern medicine all too often creates for the terminally ill. First, rather than choosing heroic treatment or giving up, hospice staff try to control pain with as much narcotics as needed. One would think that hospitals and nursing homes would want to do the same. After all, it is the pain of dying, not dying itself, that most people find unbearable.[48] Nevertheless 80 percent of nurses report that dying patients' pain is undertreated, primarily because doctors have been undertrained. Out of five thousand pages in various textbooks on care of cancer patients, for instance, only twenty deal with relieving pain. If at all, medical students are warned against oversedating and addicting their patients.[49] As a result, 72 percent of physicians in 1996 said they lacked knowledge in pain assessment and treatment.[50]

Palliative care is a matter not only of pharmacology, however, but of personalized relationship. "The terror of illness is loneliness," says the medical sociologist Arthur Frank. If the patient is heard, if he can tell his story to another person, his sense of identity is strengthened.[51] But even if physicians had the time or took the time to listen compassionately, most haven't learned the skill. Medical students rarely observe terminal patients who are being given comfort care, because if trainees aren't "doing something," teaching hospitals consider it a waste of time.[52] For hospice workers, on the other hand, listening is a crucial form of treatment. "It is the only real way we . . . can begin to understand the experience of the dying client," one nurse said.[53]

Hospice works as much with a patient's family as with the patient herself, for terminal illness inescapably involves them too. They have to move her bedroom downstairs and install a hospital bed. They have to take up the housework, cooking, child care, or yard work that she used to do. They need to learn which pills are for which symptoms and how to adjust a breathing tube. They must husband the stamina to carry on through the next weeks or months, no one knows how long. To assist with these multiple problems, hospice staff includes doctors, nurses, social workers, chaplains, and volunteers—a health-care team that incorporates the family as another member. The experience of dying extends beyond the dying person and even beyond her death. "Don't forget," said the director of the New Haven hospice, "that the family lives on after the patient."[54] And so most hospice programs organize bereavement classes or support groups.

Hospice wasn't the only effort to create a familial model of care. At the very time when the movement first took root in America, so did the Lamaze method of childbirth. Until the late 1960s husbands had paced the waiting room while their wives lay in the operating room giving birth. Even if a man wanted to be part of the process, hospitals refused (just as they typically excluded children from visiting hours afterward). Since then, however, birth has involved both spouses in preparatory classes, in labor (with husband as coach), and finally during delivery in the hospital's homelike "birthing center."

Americans deal with life more easily than death. Whereas Lamaze has flourished, hospice has struggled to preserve its small niche in the dominant medical culture. One reason is that comfort care exacts a heavy toll upon hospice workers. "How many deaths and funerals can you actually deal with before it starts to get to you?" said one staff member. Besides the emotional stress, there is also the physical fatigue, especially for home-care nurses, who may have to drive hours a day to visit their widely scattered patients, "and then we're supposed to do bereavements, go to funerals, and visit people in hospitals"—all for a salary that's a fraction of doctors'. Understandably, burnout is frequent and the turnover rate is high. "Two years is really all I can give to this," one nurse confessed.[55]

Another reason is that remarkably few patients take advantage of hospice, and then usually as a last resort rather than a positive alternative. The vast majority of deaths—four of five—take place in acute-care hospitals or nursing homes.[56] As for those terminally ill who do enter a hospice program, they are a minority not only in numerical terms but in socioeconomic terms, being disproportionately upper middle class and white.[57] Even these privileged few, however, are usually referred too late to experience dignified and pain-free dying. Half die within less than thirty-six days, 16 percent within a week.[58] And given that so many have cancer, half of them suffer symptoms so unendurable that they must be sedated during their final two days.[59] Under such circumstances, hospice often doesn't fulfill what a nurse's aide in Tucson, Arizona, promised: "A place to do one's finishing up, to collect one's life together before saying goodbye to all with which one is familiar."[60]

Hospice itself is partly to blame, because it accepts only patients with less than six months to live, thereby excluding Alzheimer's and AIDS patients, whose diseases don't follow a predictable course.[61] Doctors are also to blame, because they tend to continue life-prolonging treatment rather than refer patients to hospice. Most fault, though, lies with the prevailing health-care system. Hospice, especially home care, is cheaper than conventional care for the terminally ill, especially in the last month or two, but both governmental and private insurers limit its accessibility. Medicare covers patients only with a prognosis of less than six months and with someone at home who can function as a primary care-giver. As a result, many people receive hospice care belatedly and millions more, who lack insurance or intact families, don't receive it at all. Medicare also sets a cap on reimbursement, which may cause hospice to refuse patients with expensive needs—those with AIDS, for example. Private insurers, on the other hand, set the opposite limit. Often they won't cover care that is no longer "acute," thereby forcing patients to continue unwanted expensive treatments and to forgo less expensive comfort care.[62] In sum, it's a struggle between different philosophies—medical versus palliative—and the medical has greater power. Consequently the dying suffer more than necessary, and all Americans pay more than necessary.

THE "RIGHT TO DIE" is a cultural phenomenon, incorporating the ambivalences and confusions by which modern Americans shape their lives. We believe every problem can be brought under control if only we try hard enough. But dying has always been the ultimate, uncontrollable uncertainty, and modern dying is no less so. Although (or because) "the right to die" seems to provide a remedy, it gives rise to agonizing uncertainties.

Americans believe in progress, but medical progress has produced the problem of dying by enabling doctors to extend lives into futile suffering or irreversible unconsciousness. In response, patients have claimed the right to stop life-support and to physician-assisted suicide, but that is a grim right. Two centuries ago the Founding Fathers asserted as self-evident truth that all men were endowed with the right to life, liberty, and the pursuit of happiness. Their modern descendants have added the assertion that everyone is entitled to die with dignity, or at least without suffering.

The underlying premise remains the same as Jefferson's: self-determination, or autonomy. No previous generation has had such power to choose whether or not to prolong life. This power entails a dilemma. For with choice comes the dreadful necessity to choose—the shadow side of self-determination. At what point does additional life become more painful or futile than it is worth? Before the twentieth century, Americans left the answer to God. Then, as medical science became more effective, they trusted their doctors to answer. Now they insist on finding their own answers. "As the person's blood pressure is fading," Joanne Lynn notes, "we used to call the Catholic priest to administer the last rites. Now we more often write 'a DNR.' "[63] Uncertainty and anxiety weigh even more heavily when that choice must be made for someone else. "If the decision's wrong, if we're playing God," Joe Cruzan said, "I'll answer for it."

We cannot return to premodern America, nor can we transform ourselves into Balinese. Those "solutions" deny our history and culture. We must contend with the realities of our own time and our own making. Each of us will contend somewhat differently, because Americans bring different experiences and values to the quandary of dying. Still, after pondering the example of the Netherlands as well as the history of the Quinlans, Cruzans, and other families, I am left with two reflections on how we all might have greater opportunity for a death with dignity.

The first has to do with the medical system. For patients afflicted with terminal illness, death is their desperate shortcut, when really they want reassurance or morphine. "It is easier to get antibiotics than eyeglasses," Joanne Lynn states, "and it is certainly easier to get emergency care than to get sustaining and supportive care."[64] Too many patients must cope with pain and loneliness while worrying about bankrupting their families. If hospice were widespread and health care available to all, they could instead attend to living out the last of their lives.

The second reflection has to do with values. It is a cultural illusion that everyone takes care of himself or herself, even in health, much less during illness and dying. People may have written a living will or durable power of attorney, but they depend on doctors, relatives, and friends to honor their wishes at some future time when they no longer can speak for themselves. If they have not written an advance directive and become incompetent, the dependence is all the more obvious. Ailing and demented, Claire Conroy needed her nephew to say she abhorred the indignity of a feeding tube. Karen Ann Quinlan and Nancy Cruzan depended upon their parents to say they wouldn't want to be kept alive this way. Their autonomy was exercised only with the help of others— which isn't autonomy but relatedness. Indeed, these relatives weren't simply serving as agents, like executors of a will. They were speaking for a daughter's or aunt's feelings and beliefs, filling in the blank of her identity.

Relatedness is not only about the one who dies. From birth through dying and in memory after death, everyone makes up the social tapestry. Quinlan and Cruzan may not have felt pain or indignity, but certainly their families and other caretakers did. That is what Joseph and Julia Quinlan exemplified so gently, and Joe Cruzan so vehemently.

As we think about how we hope to die, we need to take into account the perspectives of history and culture. They will help us understand the ambiguities that await us and the choices we want to make or to have made for us, so that each of us can give his or her life the kind of ending it deserves.

Notes

STARTING OUT

1. I'm paraphrasing Clifford Geertz, *The Interpretation of Cultures* (New York: Basic Books, 1973), 5, replacing his metaphor of a web with the tapestry metaphor of Chapter 6. I'm also borrowing from Warren Susman, *Culture and Commitment* (New York: George Braziller, 1973), 1.

2. Arthur W. Frank, "The Language of Principle and the Language of Experience in the Euthanasia Debate," in Ronald P. Hamel and Edwin R. Dubose, eds., *Must We Suffer Our Way to Death? Cultural and Theological Perspectives on Death by Choice* (Dallas: Southern Methodist University Press, 1996), 83–84.

PROLOGUE: A GOOD DEATH

1. In writing this chapter I have greatly benefited from reading Stephen Louis Kuepper, "Euthanasia in America, 1890–1960: The Controversy, the Movement, and the Law" (Ph.D. dissertation, Rutgers University, 1981). See also Henry R. Glick, *The Right to Die: Policy Innovation and Its Consequences* (New York: Columbia University Press, 1992) 54–74.

2. "Death and Dying: Euthanasia and Sustaining Life," in *Encyclopedia of Bioethics,* ed. Warren T. Reich, rev. ed., 5 vols. (New York: Macmillan, 1995), I, 554.

3. Quoted by Harold Y. Vanderpool, "Doctors and the Dying of Patients in American History," in *Physician-Assisted Suicide*, ed. Robert F. Weir (Bloomington: Indiana University Press, 1997), 35.

4. William Munk, *Euthanasia, or Medical Treatment in Aid of an Easy Death* (London: Longmans, Green, 1887; reprinted New York: Arno, 1977), 85–86.

5. Charles B. Williams, "Euthanasia," *Medical and Surgical Reporter*, 70 (June 30, 1894), 909–911.

6. Martha Coffin Wright to Ellen Wright Garrison, February 11, 1870, reprinted in *The Female Experience: An American Documentary*, ed. Gerda Lerner (Indianapolis: Bobbs-Merrill, 1977), 152–153. I thank Joy Kasson for leading me to this source. For a thorough discussion of doctors and dying in England, see Pat Jalland, *Death in the Victorian Family* (New York: Oxford University Press, 1996), 81–83. Although this excellent book focuses on England, it also holds true for the United States.

7. See *ibid.*, 81–93. Quotation on drugs is by Robert Saundby, *Medical Ethics: A Guide to Professional Conduct* (1902), quoted in *ibid.*, 89. Likewise S. D. Williams, "Euthanasia," *Saturday Review*, July 13, 1872; Lionel A. Tollemache, "The New Cure for Incurables," *Fortnightly Review*, 19 (February 1, 1873), 222.

8. Roswell Park in "A Symposium on Euthanasia," *Medical Review of Reviews*, 19 (February 1913), quoted by Kuepper, "Euthanasia," 39.

9. Simeon Baldwin, address to the American Social Science Association, September 1899, published in the *St. Paul Medical Journal*, I (December 1899), 875–899, and excerpted (with editorial commentary) in *Review of Reviews*, 21 (January 1900), 95–96.

10. Kuepper, "Euthanasia," 38.

11. "Shall We Legalize Homicide?" *Outlook*, 82 (February 3, 1906), 252–253.

12. "Euthanasia Once More," *Independent*, 60 (February 1, 1906), 291.

13. Kuepper, "Euthanasia," 107–127.

14. *The Gallup Poll: Public Opinion, 1935–1971*, 3 vols. (New York: Random House, 1972), I, 151.

15. Robert Proctor, *Radical Hygiene: Medicine Under the Nazis* (Cambridge: Harvard University Press, 1988), ch. 7.

16. Foster Kennedy, address to the American Psychiatric Association, 1941, published as "The Problem of Social Control of the Congenitally Defective: Education, Sterilization, Euthanasia," *American Journal of Psychiatry*, 99 (July 1942), 13–16. See also speeches reported in *New York Times*, February 14, 1939, 2:6, and *New York Herald Tribune*, February 4, 1939, 1:31.

17. Kuepper, "Euthanasia," 297–313.

18. Daniel J. Kevles, *In the Name of Eugenics: Genetics and the Uses of Human Heredity* (New York: Alfred A. Knopf, 1985), 251. Likewise Carl Degler, *In Search of Human Nature: The Decline and Revival of Darwinism in American Social Thought* (New York: Oxford University Press, 1991), 203–206.

19. *New York Times*, December 8, 1933, 48:6.

20. "Better Off Dead," *Time*, 33 (January 23, 1939), 24.

21. *New York Times*, February 8, 1950, 1:6; "The Father Killer," *Newsweek*, 35 (February 13, 1950), 21. On the frequency of mercy killings, see " 'Merciful' Killing," *Literary Digest*, 84 (March 21, 1925), 33; "Mercy or Murder?" *New York*

Times, January 8, 1950, IV, 2:5; and "Murder or Mercy?" *Newsweek*, 51 (February 3, 1958), 56. Also Kuepper, "Euthanasia," 119–120.

22. *New York Times*, December 30, 1949, 1:6; January 2, 1950, 25:2; January 9, 1950, 40:2.

23. "The Law of God," *Time*, 55 (January 16, 1950), 20, and "Life and Death," (March 15, 1950), 50.

24. *New York Times*, February 19, 1950, 12:3.

25. Kuepper, "Euthanasia," 225.

26. *New York Times*, March 7, 1950, 1:1, 19:1, and March 10, 1950, 1:6, 23:4.

27. *Ibid.*, March 10, 1950, 23:6.

28. "The Mercy Killing," *New Republic*, 122 (January 16, 1950), 6.

29. "The Right to Die," *Time*, 67 (January 9, 1956), 62.

30. George Annas at Princeton Conference, "Quinlan: A Twenty Year Retrospective," April 1996.

31. E.g., "The Right to Die: A Debate," *The Forum and Century*, 94 (October 1935), 330–334; "The Right to Die," *Journal of the American Medical Association* (hereafter cited as *JAMA*), 105 (November 16, 1935), 1616–1617; "The Right to Die," *Literary Digest*, 120 (November 20, 1935), 17.

32. Joseph Fletcher, *Morals and Medicine: The Moral Problems of the Patient's Right to Know the Truth . . . Euthanasia* (Boston: Beacon Press, 1960; orig. ed., Princeton: Princeton University Press, 1954), 191.

33. Frank J. Ayd, "The Hopeless Case: Medical and Moral Considerations," *JAMA*, 181 (September 29, 1962), 1100.

34. Selig Greenberg, "The Right to Die," *Progressive*, 30 (June 1966), 37–40.

35. "Euthanasia in England: A Growing Storm," *America*, 122 (May 2, 1970), 463.

36. *New York Times*, January 4, 1974, 61:1; *Death with Dignity: An Inquiry into Related Public Issues*, Proceedings Before the Special Committee on Aging, U.S. Senate, 92nd Cong., 2nd Sess., August 7–9, 1972 (Washington, D.C.: Government Printing Office, 1972); *Atlanta Journal*, November 9, 1974, 5-B; Kuepper, "Euthanasia," 311–313.

1. DEATH ON TRIAL

1. Joseph and Julia Quinlan, with Phyllis Battelle, *Karen Ann: The Quinlans Tell Their Story* (Garden City: Doubleday, 1977), xii, 2, 4, 28–29, 41, 44–45, 49–50, 61. Also Joan Kron, "Did the Girl in the Coma Want 'Death With Dignity'?" *New York*, 8 (October 27, 1975), 61.

2. For girlfriends' recollections, *Newark Star-Ledger*, October 27, 1975, 9:1, and September 21, 1975, 1:1, 29. For parties, Quinlans, *Karen Ann*, 28, and quotation on 67.

3. *Newark Star-Ledger*, October 26, 1975, 42:1.

4. Quinlans, *Karen Ann*, 54, and quotation on 29.

5. *Ibid.*, 58, and quotation on 63.

6. *Ibid.*, 70; "Who Was Karen Quinlan?" *Newsweek*, 86 (November 3, 1975), 60.

7. Quinlans, *Karen Ann*, 71.

8. *New York Times*, October 14, 1975, 39:1.

9. Quinlans, *Karen Ann*, 71–76. Quotation on 71.

10. *In the Matter of Karen Quinlan: The Complete Legal Briefs, Court Proceedings, and Decision in the Superior Court of New Jersey* [hereafter cited as *Briefs*], 2 vols. (Arlington, Va.: University Publications of America, 1975), I, 541, says "late 1974 or early 1975." *New York Times*, October 14, 1975, 39:1, says a few weeks before. *Washington Post*, September 19, 1975, A-1, claims a week before. "Who Was Karen Quinlan?" *Newsweek*, 60, says August 1974.

11. Croft quoted in "Who Was Karen Quinlan?" *Newsweek*, 60, and Kron, "Girl in the Coma," 62. See also *Newark Star-Ledger*, October 27, 1975, 9:1.

12. *Newark Star-Ledger*, September 21, 1975, 1:1, 29.

13. "Who Was Karen Quinlan?" *Newsweek*, 60; *New York Times*, October 14, 1975, 50:4.

14. "Life in the Balance," *Time*, 106 (November 3, 1975), 52.

15. "Before Karen's Coma," *Time*, 106 (December 29, 1975), 19.

16. "Who Was Karen Quinlan?" *Newsweek*, 60.

17. Police and hospital records quoted in *Briefs*, I, 341, 310–312; and *New York Times*, October 14, 1975, 39:1.

18. Morse testimony in *Briefs*, I, 215–221; Quinlans, *Karen Ann*, 13–15, 78–80.

19. *Briefs*, I, 236, 312.

20. Quoted in Quinlans, *Karen Ann*, 73.

21. *Newark Star-Ledger*, September 21, 1975, 1:1, 29. *Washington Post*, September 19, 1975, A-1:2. For MA-1 respirator, Quinlans, *Karen Ann*, 295.

22. *Ibid.*, 29.

23. *Ibid.*, 82–86.

24. *Newark Star-Ledger*, October 26, 1975, 42:6.

25. *Washington Post*, September 19, 1975, A-9:2.

26. Quinlans, *Karen Ann*, 81. Quote on 88–89. PVS is not, strictly speaking, a coma, because the person is periodically awake. The original definition of PVS was by W. B. Jennett and Fred Plum, "The Persistent Vegetative State: A Syndrome in Search of a Name," *Lancet*, I (1972), 734–737.

27. Quinlans, *Karen Ann*, 87–92; For Church's position I've drawn heavily on Stanley Joel Reiser, "Therapeutic Choice and Moral Doubt in a Technological Age," *Daedalus*, 106 (Winter 1977), 47–48, and Robert F. Weir, *Abating Treatment with Critically Ill Patients: Ethical and Legal Limits to the Medical Prolongation of Life* (New York: Oxford University Press, 1989),

216–221. Original text is in Pius XII, "The Prolongation of Life," *Pope Speaks*, 4, no. 4 (1958), 393–398.

28. For biographical details, see Quinlans, *Karen Ann*, 34–36, 38–39. Also "Between Life and Death," *Time*, 106 (September 29, 1975), 75. On his mental struggle, Quinlans, *Karen Ann*, 111, and *Briefs*, I, 361–364. For literary reasons I have changed his verbs into the present tense. The order and liability release are in *Briefs*, I, 552. Trapasso's testimony of this conversation is in *Briefs*, I, 395–396.

29. *New York Times*, October 14, 1975, 39:1; *Washington Post*, September 19, 1975, A-2:1. On miscarriages and adoption, Quinlans, *Karen Ann*, 36–39.

30. Reiser, "Therapeutic Choice," *Daedalus*, 106 (Winter 1977), 51–53; Lewis Thomas, "On the Science and Technology of Medicine," *ibid.*, 36–38; Weir, *Abating Treatment*, 30–42.

31. E.g., Tom L. Beauchamp, "A Reply to Rachels on Active and Passive Euthanasia," in *Ethical Issues in Death and Dying*, ed. Tom L. Beauchamp and Seymour Perlin (Englewood Cliffs, N.J.: Prentice-Hall, 1978), 249–250.

32. On fear of malpractice, *New York Times*, September 28, 1975, 1:5.

33. B. D. Colen, *Karen Ann Quinlan: Dying in the Age of Eternal Life* (New York: Nash, 1976), 40–41.

34. Gregory E. Pence, *Classic Cases in Medical Ethics: Accounts of the Cases That Have Shaped Medical Ethics, with Philosophical, Legal, and Historical Backgrounds* (New York: McGraw Hill, 1990), 8–9.

35. Quinlans, *Karen Ann*, 122–126.

36. CBS Evening News, September 19, 1975; NBC covered the story on September 15 and ABC on September 18.

37. *Atlanta Constitution*, September 29, 1975, 4A; editorial, "Medical Dilemma," *New York Times*, September 25, 1975, A-42:2; *Chicago Tribune*, September 21, II, 4:1.

38. Editorial, "Medical Dilemma," *New York Times*, September 25, 1975, A-42:2. For the questions, see *New York Times*, September 25, 1975, A-47:7 and September 21, 1975, IV, 7:1; and "Cruel Questions," *Newsweek*, 86 (September 19, 1975), 76.

39. E.g., "Cruel Questions," *Newsweek*, 76, and "Between Life and Death," *Time*, 59; *Washington Post*, September 19, 1975, A-9.

40. B. D. Colen, reprinted in *Los Angeles Times*, October 19, 1975, IV, 1:6.

41. *Chicago Tribune*, September 21, 1975, II, 4:1; *Newark Star-Ledger*, September 19, 1975, 20:2.

42. CBS Evening News, September 19, 1975; Quinlans, *Karen Ann*, 155; *New York Daily News*, October 27, 1975, p. 3.

43. *New York Times*, October 24, 1975, 41:4; *Louisville Courier-Journal*, October 21, 1975, 1:5; "A Right to Die?" *Newsweek*, 86 (November 3, 1975), 52.

44. "A Right to Die?" *Newsweek*, 86 (November 3, 1975), 58.

45. *Newark Star-Ledger*, October 23, 1975, 15:1.

46. *New York Times*, October 23, 1975, 43:3.

47. *New York Daily News*, October 21, 1975, p. 2. Similarly, one journalist likened Armstrong to Jimmy Stewart in *Mr. Smith Goes to Washington*: Joan Kron, "The Girl in a Coma," *New York*, 8 (October 6, 1975), 33.

48. For the concept of "social drama," see Victor Turner, "Social Dramas and Stories About Them," *Critical Inquiry*, 7, no. 1 (Autumn 1980), 141–168, esp. 150–151 and 157–158: "The social drama, then, I regard as the experiential matrix from which the many genres of cultural performance, beginning with redressive ritual and juridical procedures and eventually including moral and literary narrative, have been generated." Furthermore, "A social drama first manifests itself as the breach of a norm, the infraction of a rule of morality, law, custom, or etiquette, in some public arena. This breach is seen as the expression of a deeper division of interests and loyalties. . . . Sides are taken, factions are formed, and unless the conflict can be sealed off quickly within a limited area of social interaction, there is a tendency for the breach to widen and spread until it coincides with some dominant cleavage in the widest set of relevant social relations to which the parties in conflict belong."

49. On the trial and aftermath, Edward J. Larson, *Trial and Error: The American Controversy Over Creation and Evolution* (New York: Oxford University Press, 1985), ch. 3, and Ronald L. Numbers, "The Creationists," in *God and Nature: Historical Essays on the Encounter Between Christianity and Science*, ed. David C. Lindberg and Ronald L. Numbers (Berkeley: University of California Press, 1986), ch. 16. On Dayton, Willard B. Gatewood, Jr., "From Scopes to Creation Science: The Decline and Revival of the Evolution Controversy," *South Atlantic Quarterly*, 83 (Autumn 1984), 363. I've given the popular version of the trial. In fact, fundamentalists also disagreed with one another about creation. Moreover, religious conservatives and religious liberals of the 1970s were not simply descendants of the 1920s fundamentalists and modernists, respectively. See Ronald L. Numbers, *The Creationists* (New York: Alfred A. Knopf, 1992), ch. 5, and Robert Wuthnow, *The Restructuring of American Religion: Society and Faith Since World War II* (Princeton: Princeton University Press, 1988), 134–139.

50. *Briefs*, I, 198.

51. *Ibid.*, I, 163–167.

52. *Ibid.*, I, 201–203. Likewise, other attorneys, 196–200.

53. Afterward, with the benefit of hindsight, some legal analysts said Armstrong made a mistake by coupling guardianship with the right to die. If he had simply asked the court to appoint Mr. Quinlan as legal guardian, they say, the Quinlans could have transferred Karen to a different hospital and found a physician willing to do what they wanted. In other words, Armstrong should have put pragmatism before principle. See, e.g., Pence, *Classic Cases*, 8–9. Maybe so. But in retrospect, given the context I discuss in Chapter Two, one can argue that sooner or later another right-to-die case would have come before a state court.

54. Weir, *Abating Treatment*, 65–66; Melvin Urofsky, *Letting Go: Death, Dying, and the Law* (New York: Charles Scribner's Sons, 1993), 32–33.

55. Michel Foucault, *The History of Sexuality: An Introduction* (New York: Vintage, 1990), I, 138–145, and *Discipline and Punish* (New York: Vintage, 1979), 135–169. I was guided to Foucault by George J. Annas, "The Long Dying of Nancy Cruzan," *Law, Medicine & Health Care*, 19 (Spring–Summer 1991), 58. See also Mary Douglas, *Natural Symbols: Explorations in Cosmology* (London: Cresset Press, 1970), esp. vii–xiv and ch. 5; Susan Bordo, *Unbearable Weight: Feminism, Western Culture, and the Body* (Berkeley and Los Angeles: University of California Press, 1993). On conflict of authorities, see Bryan S. Turner, *The Body and Society: Explorations in Social Theory* (Oxford: Basil Blackwell, 1984), 211–214.

56. *New York Times*, October 21, 1975, 81:2, says he was thirty-seven. Quinlans, *Karen Ann*, 78 and 179, says he was thirty-two or thirty-seven. According to *Directory of Medical Specialists*, II, 23rd ed. (1987–1988), he was born in 1939.

57. *Briefs*, I, 229–231.

58. Kron, "Girl in a Coma," 34.

59. *Briefs*, I, 239.

60. *Ibid.*, I, 243. I have transposed and combined two of Morse's responses.

61. *Ibid.*, I, 298.

62. *New York Daily News*, October 22, 1975, 3.

63. *France-Soir*, October 22, 1975, 3.

64. *Briefs*, I, 302, 305–306.

65. On traffic jam, *ibid.*, I, 349. On microphone, *ibid.*, I, 359. On voice, *San Francisco Chronicle*, October 22, 1975, 1:2. Quotations are in *Briefs*, I, 360–361, 370, 368.

66. *Ibid.*, I, 368, 369, 387.

67. *Ibid.*, I, 431–435.

68. *Houston Post*, 1 (with photograph), and *Chicago Tribune*, 3:4. Morse's quotation is in *New York Times*, 41:2. For other stories, see *New York Daily News*, p. 1 (with photograph); *Washington Post*, A-4:1; *Baltimore Sun*, 1:1 (with photograph); *Denver Post*, 7:3; *Los Angeles Times*, A-5:1, *Milwaukee Journal*, 3:1; *Times* (London), 1:5—all October 21, 1975. By contrast, CBS Evening News, October 20, 1975, gave fuller coverage to legal arguments.

69. *Atlanta Constitution*, 11-A, and *Baltimore Sun*, A6:1, both October 22, 1975; *Boston Evening Globe*, October 21, 1975, 6:3. *New York Times* and *Washington Post* were untypical in covering legal and bioethical issues: *New York Times*, 1:1, and *Washington Post*, A3, both October 22, 1975.

70. *Boston Evening Globe*, October 21, 1975, 6:3, and *Boston Globe*, October 22, 1975, 1:1; also *New York Daily News*, 3:3, and *New York Times*, 1:1, 49:3, both October 22, 1975.

71. *New York Daily News*, 1; *Boston Globe*, 1:1; *San Francisco Chronicle*,

1:2; *New York Times*, 1:1; *Times* (London), 1:2—all October 22, 1975. By contrast, other papers printed the story farther back: *Cleveland Press*, 4:1; *Milwaukee Journal*, 5:1; *Baltimore Sun*, 6:1; *Atlanta Constitution*, 11:1; *Houston Post*, 12A-3; *Chicago Tribune*, VI, 15:1; *Denver Post*, 27:1—all October 22, 1975. On the television evening news, the story came midway through the half-hour or, on CBS, at the end.

72. *Los Angeles Times*, late final edition, October 22, 1975, 1. Descriptions of Mrs. Quinlan in *Boston Globe*, 2:2; *Los Angeles Times*, 1:6; *Chicago Tribune*, I-3:1, and *Washington Post*, A1—all October 23, 1975. Other coverage: *Atlanta Constitution*, 1:4; *Houston Post*, 11A:6; *Baltimore Sun*, 14:1; *New York Times*, 43:1—all October 23, 1975.

73. Judith Walkowitz, *City of Dreadful Delight: Narratives of Sexual Danger in Late-Victorian London* (Chicago: University of Chicago Press, 1992), 85–86. Also David Grimsted, *Melodrama Unveiled: American Theater and Culture, 1800–1850* (Chicago: University of Chicago Press, 1968), 171–183.

74. *Briefs*, I, 391–411. Quotations from 410, 405. I have rearranged the sequence of the quotations.

75. It was also temporarily a dispute among Catholic spokesmen. In *Osservatore Romano*, the Vatican's official daily, Reverend Gino Concetti wrote: "The case of Karen Ann Quinlan is beyond all doubt harrowing, but life is a gift of God, and only God is the master of life. . . . There is no right to die, but only the right to live." In response, Father Trapasso told reporters: "It's very obvious someone over there is getting the wrong picture." *New York Times*, October 23, 1975, 43:1.

76. *Briefs*, I, 516–518, 23–24.

77. *Ibid.*, I, 533–536.

78. On Muir, see "The Quinlan Decision," *Newsweek*, 86 (November 24, 1975), 107. On mail, see *New York Times*, November 10, 1975, 5:6, and November 11, 1975, 6:8, and Quinlans, *Karen Ann*, 156. On faith healers, see Quinlans, *Karen Ann*, 156–158 (alleging hundreds arrived), and *New York Times*, November 5, 1975, 47:1, which says only thirty to forty.

79. *Ibid.*, December 7, 1975, 10:3.

80. E.g., *Atlanta Constitution*, October 31, 1975, 4-A; Robert E. Hall, "The Gray Zones of Life," *Nation*, 221 (November 1, 1975), 42. Poll is cited in Roy Branson and Kenneth Casebier, "Obscuring the Role of the Physician," *Hastings Center Report*, 6 (February 1976), 9. For West Virginia class, see CBS Morning News, November 10, 1975.

81. *Briefs*, I, 449.

82. *Ibid.*, I, 555–557.

83. Quotations from *ibid.*, I, 561, 559, 560, 567. In general, see 563–568.

84. Quinlans, *Karen Ann*, 235.

85. CBS Evening News, November 10, 1975; *New York Times*, 1:3, *Chicago Tribune*, 1:5, *Los Angeles Times*, 1:2, *Manchester Guardian*, 1:1, *Figaro*, 1—all November 11, 1975; *France-Soir*, November 12, 1.

86. AMA, ABA, and religious leaders in *New York Times*, November 11, 1975, 62:1; "Judicial Restraint in the Quinlan Decision," *Christian Century*, 92 (November 26, 1975), 1068–1069; J. David Blech, "Karen Ann Quinlan: A Torah Perspective," *Jewish Life* (Winter 1976), quoted in Weir, *Abating Treatment*, 29–31; Will in *Los Angeles Times*, November 14, 1975, II, 7:1; African American quoted in *Los Angeles Times*, December 4, 1975, II, 7:1. Also editorial, *Louisville Courier-Journal*, November 13, 1975, A22:3; Thomas C. Oden, "Beyond an Ethic of Immediate Sympathy," *Hastings Center Review*, 6 (February 1976), 12–14.

87. *Los Angeles Times*, November 14, 1975, II, 6:1; *Figaro*, November 11, 1975, p. 1; *Chicago Tribune*, November 24, 1975, II, 2:1. Also editorial, "The Quinlan Quagmire," *New York Times*, November 11, 1975, 31:1; "Sentenced to Life," *Time*, 106 (November 24, 1975), 70. All eight letters printed in the *Los Angeles Times* criticized the decision: November 18, 1975, II, 6:3.

88. Charles M. Whelan, "Karen Ann Quinlan: Patient or Prisoner?" *America*, 133 (November 22, 1975), 346–347, and editorial, "Turning Off the Machine," *America*, 133 (October 11, 1975), 197; editorial, "A Time to Die," *Commonweal*, 102 (November 21, 1975), 547–548. Connery is quoted in *New York Daily News*, November 11, 1975, p. 3.

89. Peter Steinfels, "The Quinlan Decision," *Commonweal*, 102 (December 5, 1975), 584, 604; Roy Branson and Kenneth Casebier, "Obscuring the Role of the Physician," *Hastings Center Report*, 6 (February 1976), 8–11; Robert M. Veatch, *Death, Dying and the Biological Revolution* (New Haven: Yale University Press, 1976), 119.

90. "'Right to Die' Case: Will Anything Change?" *U.S. News and World Report*, 79 (November 24, 1975), 31; *Chicago Tribune*, November 11, 1975, 5:4, and November 19, 1975, III, 4:1; *Washington Post*, November 24, 1975, B-1, B-6.

2. MODERN DYING

1. Lael Wertenbaker, *Death of a Man* (Boston: Beacon Press, 1977; orig. ed. 1957), 143–144. The Wertenbakers were expatriate Americans living in France, and Cartier was a French physician. His attitudes were no different, though, from the doctors in the United States who originally diagnosed Wertenbaker's cancer.

2. Wertenbaker, *Death of a Man*, 175.

3. Robert Fulton, "Death and the Self," *Journal of Religion and Health*, 3 (July 1964), 360; Herman Feifel, "Death," in *Taboo Topics*, ed. Norman L. Farberow (New York: Atherton, 1966), 14; "On Death as a Constant Companion," *Time*, 86 (November 12, 1965), 52; Elisabeth Kübler-Ross, *On Death and Dying* (New York: Macmillan, 1969), 6; Billy Graham, "Through the Valley of the

Shadow," *Reader's Digest*, 98 (April 1971), 107. Also Geoffrey Gorer, "The Pornography of Death," *Encounter*, 5 (October 1955), 49–53; Barney G. Glaser and Anselm L. Strauss, *Awareness of Dying* (Chicago: Aldine, 1965), 3; Jeanne C. Quint, *The Nurse and the Dying Patient* (New York: Macmillan, 1967), 1; David Hendin, *Death as a Fact of Life* (New York: W. W. Norton, 1973), 10; George Dunea, "Death with Dignity," *British Medical Journal*, 1 (April 3, 1976), 824.

4. Jessica Mitford, *The American Way of Death* (New York: Simon and Schuster, 1963); Geoffrey Gorer, *Death, Grief and Mourning* (New York: Doubleday, 1965).

5. E.g., Herman Feifel, ed., *New Meanings of Death* (New York: McGraw-Hill, 1977; orig. ed., 1959); Glaser and Strauss, *Awareness of Dying*; F. Patrick McKegney, Richard A. Iray, and Alan Balsam, eds., "Staff Conference: Problem of the Dying Patient," *New York State Journal of Medicine*, 65 (September 15, 1965), 2356–2366; Leslie Fiedler, *Love and Death in the American Novel* (New York: Laurel ed., 1966); Frederick J. Hoffman, *The Mortal No: Death and the Modern Imagination* (Princeton: Princeton University Press, 1964). For tabulations of popular literature I counted entries in the *Reader's Guide to Periodical Literature*. For tabulations of professional literature, see Robert Fulton, *Death, Grief and Bereavement: A Bibliography, II, 1975–80* (New York: Arno Press, 1981), 1, table 1, and Robert Neimeyer, "Death Anxiety," in *Dying: Facing the Facts*, ed. Hannelore Wass, Felix M. Berardo, and Robert Neimeyer, 2nd ed. (Washington, D.C.: Hemisphere, 1988), 98, fig. 1. See also tabulations on "right to die" articles in Henry R. Glick, *The Right to Die: Policy Innovation and Its Consequences* (New York: Columbia University Press, 1992), 65–66, figs. 3.1, 3.2, and 3.3. For bibliographies, see Austin H. Kutscher, Jr., Martin Kutscher, and Austin H. Kutscher, *A Bibliography of Books on Death, Bereavement, Loss and Grief: 1935–1968* (New York: Health Sciences Publishing, 1969), and Robert Fulton, *Death, Grief and Bereavement: A Bibliography, 1845–1975* (New York: Arno Press, 1977).

6. For overview, see Jeanne C. Quint, *The Nurse and the Dying Patient* (New York: Macmillan, 1967), 11; George L. Engle, "Grief and Grieving," *American Journal of Nursing*, 64 (September 1964), 93–98; Berniece M. Wagner, "Teaching Students to Work with the Dying," *American Journal of Nursing*, 64 (November 1964), 128–131. See also Catherine M. Norris, "The Nurse and the Dying Patient," *American Journal of Nursing*, 55 (October 1955), 1214–1217; Marilyn Folcik and Phyllis Nie, "Nursing Students Learn to Face Death," *Nursing Outlook*, 7 (1959), 510–513; Eleanor Drummond and Jeanne Blumberg, "Death and the Curriculum," *Journal of Nursing Education*, 1 (May–June 1962), 21–28; Cicely Saunders, "The Last Stages of Life," *American Journal of Nursing*, 65 (March 1965), 70–75; editorial, "This He Said, Signifying What Death He Should Die," *Nursing Outlook*, 16 (October 1968), 19.

7. Kutscher, *Bibliography* and *Bibliography: Supplement I, 1968–1972*. See also Fulton, *Death*, and Michael A. Simpson, *Dying, Death, and Grief: A Crit-*

ically Annotated Bibliography and Source Book of Thanatology and Terminal Care (New York: Plenum Press, 1979), vii–viii.

8. Ted Rosenthal, *How Could I Not Be Among You?* (New York: Braziller, 1973); Stewart Alsop, *Stay of Execution: A Sort of Memoir* (New York: J. B. Lippincott, 1973); Gerda Lerner, *A Death of One's Own* (New York: Simon and Schuster, 1978); Lois Wheeler Snow, *A Death with Dignity: When the Chinese Came* (New York: Random House, 1975); Marya Mannes, *Last Rights* (New York: William Morrow, 1974); Kübler-Ross, *On Death and Dying.*

9. *Publishers' Weekly* quoted in *New York Times,* July 21, 1974, 1:5. See also Michael Michaelson, review, *New York Times,* July 21, 1974, VI, 6–8; William Hamilton, review, *New Republic,* 169 (November 24, 1973), 30; and Giles Gunn, review, *New Republic,* 171 (September 21, 1974), 28.

10. *New York Times,* January 4, 1974, 61:1; Mannes, *Last Rights,* 130–131. See also films listed in Simpson, *Dying,* 179–211.

11. E.g., Leon Kass, "Problems in the Meaning of Death," *Science,* 170 (December 11, 1970), 1235–1236; *Atlanta Constitution,* November 9, 1974, I-B, and December 12, 1974, 4-C; William Hamilton, *New Republic,* 169 (November 24, 1973), 30.

12. "Thanatology," *Time,* 101 (January 8, 1973), 36; "How America Lives with Death," *Newsweek,* 75 (April 6, 1970), 81; Edwin S. Shneidman, "The College Student and Death," in *New Meanings of Death,* ed. Feifel, 67–86; Gene Stanford and Deborah Parry, *Death Out of the Closet: A Curriculum Guide to Living with Dying* (New York: Bantam, 1976); Warren Shibles, *Death: The Interdisciplinary Analysis* (Whitewater, Wisc.: Language Press, 1974).

13. *Death with Dignity: An Inquiry into Related Public Issues,* Proceedings Before the Special Committee on Aging, U.S. Senate, 92nd Cong., 2nd Sess., August 7–9, 1972 (Washington, D.C.: Government Printing Office, 1972); *New York Times,* February 17, 1975, 2:7; *Los Angeles Times,* June 7, 1975, A-1:1.

14. On death versus sex, see Mannes, *Last Rights,* 4–5; David Dempsey, *The Way We Die: An Investigation of Death and Dying in America Today* (New York: Macmillan, 1975), 13; *New York Times,* July 21, 1974, 1:5.

15. Edwin S. Shneidman, "You and Death," *Psychology Today,* 5 (June 1971), 43–45.

16. CBS Morning News, November 10, 1975.

17. Daniel C. Maguire, "Death by Chance, Death by Choice," *Atlantic,* 233 (January 1974), 57.

18. Quoted by Paul Boyer, *By the Bomb's Early Light: American Thought and Culture at the Dawn of the Atomic Age* (New York: Pantheon, 1985), 8. This claim was repeated frequently during the next twenty years: e.g., Edward John Carnell, "The Fear of Death," *Christian Century,* 80 (January 30, 1963), 136; Robert Kastenbaum and Ruth Aisenberg, *The Psychology of Death* (New York: Spring, 1972), 234.

19. *Atlanta Constitution,* February 21, 1975, 6-A. Likewise see Michael

Arlen, *Living-Room War* (New York: Penguin, 1982). As media scholars have proved, however, the networks rarely showed the bloodiest scenes sent by their cameramen: Herbert Gans, *Deciding What's News: A Study of CBS Evening News, NBC Nightly News, Newsweek and Time* (New York: Pantheon, 1979), 244; Lawrence W. Lichty, "The War We Watched on Television: A Study in Progress," *American Film Institute Report*, 4:4 (Winter 1973); Daniel Hallin, *The Uncensored War* (New York: Oxford University Press, 1986), 106–108.

20. In the summer of 1946 only 25 percent admitted to being "greatly worried" about nuclear destruction; 65 percent said they were not worried at all or, at worst, "not much." In 1947 a majority thought "it was a good thing that the atomic bomb was developed" (even while believing that other countries were developing bombs of their own): Boyer, *Bomb's Early Light,* 23; and October 1947 polls reported in *Public Opinion Quarterly,* 11 (Winter 1947–1948), 640. Boyer concludes that, following an initial surge, the fear of sudden, irrational death subsided after 1946 into acquiescence and numbness, or perhaps indifference: pp. 277–279, 291–293.

21. A 1951 poll reprinted in *Public Opinion Quarterly,* 37 (Spring 1973), 138.

22. Thirty-eight percent thought "occasionally" about war, 36 percent "occasionally" about death; 12 percent thought "hardly ever" about war, 32 percent "hardly ever" about death: John Riley, "What People Think About Death," in *The Dying Patient,* ed. Orville G. Brim (New York: Russell Sage Foundation, 1970), 34.

23. Shneidman, "You and Death," 75.

24. Isaac S. Barr Penmanship Book, 1852, quoted by Lewis O. Saum, "Death in Pre-Civil War America," in *Death in America,* ed. David E. Stannard (Philadelphia: University of Pennsylvania Press, 1975), 32. On death integrated into daily life, see Gary Laderman, *The Sacred Remains: American Attitudes Toward Death, 1799–1883* (New Haven: Yale University Press, 1996), 23–24.

25. U.S. Bureau of the Census, *Historical Statistics of the United States: Colonial Times to 1970,* Pt. 1 (Washington, D.C.: Government Printing Office, 1975), 54, 55.

26. Beecher, *Autobiography,* and Anna Pierce to Caleb and Emily Carr, November 6, 1856, quoted in James J. Farrell, *Inventing the American Way of Death, 1830–1920* (Philadelphia: Temple University Press, 1980), 33, 39. For background, see James H. Cassedy, *Medicine in America: A Short History* (Baltimore: Johns Hopkins University Press, 1991), 47.

27. Archibald B. Knode Diary, quoted by Saum, "Death in Pre-Civil War America," 34.

28. Beecher, *Autobiography,* quoted in Farrell, *Inventing the American Way of Death,* 40.

29. Quoted by Saum, "Death in Pre-Civil War America," 45. On "beautiful death," see Laderman, *Sacred Remains,* 54–57. On "good death" in En-

gland, where attitudes generally paralleled those in the United States, see Pat Jalland, *Death in the Victorian Family* (New York: Oxford University Press, 1996), ch. 1. On medical care, *ibid.*, ch. 4. On "tamed death" in Europe, see Philippe Aries, *Western Attitudes Toward Death: From the Middle Ages to the Present* (Baltimore: Johns Hopkins University Press, 1974), 11–14, 33–39.

30. On secularization, see Jalland, *Death in the Victorian Family*, 51–58, and Farrell, *Inventing the American Way of Death*, 51–62; Sheila M. Rothman, *Living in the Shadow of Death: Tuberculosis and the Social Experience of Illness in American History* (New York: Basic Books, 1994), ch. 13; Robert J. Glaser, "Innovations and Heroic Arts in Prolonging Life," in *Dying Patient*, ed. Brim, 105–107.

31. U.S. Bureau of the Census, *Historical Statistics*, Pt. I, 55, 57.

32. Robert M. Veatch, *Death, Dying and the Biological Revolution*, rev. ed. (New Haven: Yale University Press, 1989), 3–4; Alsop, *Stay of Execution*, 296.

33. "Twin Transplant," *Time*, 65 (January 3, 1955), 36; Virginia S. Herrick, "He Gave His Kidney to His Brother," *Saturday Evening Post*, 228 (November 19, 1955), 32. During the next fifteen years 2,500 other transplants were performed while dialysis saved innumerable victims of renal failure.

34. "The Ultimate Operation," *Time*, 90 (December 15, 1967); "Future Transplants," *Time*, 91 (January 5, 1968), 60; "The Heart: Miracle in Cape Town," *Newsweek*, 70 (December 18, 1967), 86–87.

35. Glaser, "Innovations and Heroic Acts," 105–107.

36. CBS Evening News, July 30, 1975; Lyn H. Lofland, *The Craft of Dying: The Modern Face of Death* (Beverly Hills: Sage, 1978), 54.

37. Rosenthal, *How Could I Not Be Among You?*, 71–72.

38. Nancy M. P. King, *Making Sense of Advance Directives* (Dordrecht, The Netherlands: Kluwer Academic Publishers, 1991), 29, 31–32; Robert F. Weir, *Abating Treatment with Critically Ill Patients: Ethical and Legal Limits to the Medical Prolongation of Life* (New York: Oxford University Press, 1989), 34–42; Lewis Thomas, *Lives of a Cell* (New York: Viking Press, 1974), 35–42.

39. Where before World War II 63 percent of deaths were at home, by 1958, 61 percent were in a hospital or other institution: Veatch, *Death, Dying*, 3–4. For distinction between process and event, see, among others, Robert S. Morison, "Death: Process or Event," in *Death Inside Out: The Hastings Center Report*, ed. Peter Steinfels and Robert M. Veatch (New York: Harper and Row, 1975), 63–70.

40. Ad Hoc Committee of the Harvard Medical School to Examine the Definition of Brain Death, "A Definition of Irreversible Coma," *JAMA*, 205, no. 6 (August 6, 1968), 337–340; reprinted in *Ethical Issues in Death and Dying*, ed. Tom L. Beauchamp and Seymour Perlin (Englewood Cliffs, N.J.: Prentice-Hall, 1978), 11–18.

41. Veatch, *Death, Dying*, (1976), 21–23; Ronald Converse, "But When

Did He Die?: *Tucker v. Lower* and the Brain Death Concept," *San Diego Law Review*, 12 (March 1975), 424–430.

42. Quotation is from *New York Times*, February 24, 1974, IV, 6:4. For cases, see *Washington Post*, May 24, 1974, A3; *Atlanta Constitution*, October 23, 1974, 2-A, and October 24, 1974, 20-A; and *New York Times*, April 26, 1975, 12:4. In Oakland, California, e.g., Samuel Allen was shot in the head by Andrew Lyons and was declared brain-dead before a transplant team removed his still healthy heart. Lyons pleaded not guilty to a charge of murder, arguing that death was caused by the heart removal rather than the head wound. On bioethicists, see Leslie Rado, "Death Redefined: Social and Cultural Influences on Legislation," *Journal of Communication*, 31 (Winter 1981), 41–44.

43. Robert M. Veatch, "The Definition of Death: Problems for Public Policy," in *Dying: Facing the Facts*, ed. Wass, 44; Alexander Capron and Leon R. Kass, "A Statutory Definition of the Standards of Determining Human Death: An Appraisal and a Proposal," *University of Pennsylvania Law Review*, 121 (November 1972), 87–118. For a lucid synopsis, see President's Commission for the Study of Ethical Problems in Medicine and Biomedical and Behavioral Research, *Defining Death: A Report on the Medical, Legal and Ethical Issues in the Determination of Death* [hereafter cited as President's Commission] (Washington, D.C.: Government Printing Office, 1981), 31–43.

44. President's Commission, 109–114.

45. *Ibid.*, 7–9. For earlier AMA position, see *New York Times*, December 4, 1974, 26:3.

46. Lindsey Prior, *The Social Organization of Death: Medical Discourse and Social Practices in Belfast* (New York: St. Martin's Press, 1989), 4–13; Leonard Isaacs, "Death, Where Is Thy Distinguishing?" *Hastings Center Review*, 8 (February 1978), 5–8; Robert S. Morison, "Death: Process or Event," in *Death Inside Out*, ed. Steinfels and Veatch, 63–70; Veatch, *Death, Dying* (1976), 19–34; Karen Grandstrand Gervais, *Redefining Death* (New Haven: Yale University Press, 1986); Paul Ramsey, *The Patient as Person* (New Haven: Yale University Press, 1970). For arguments against personhood, see Michael Green and Daniel Wikler, "Brain Death and Personal Identity," *Philosophy and Public Affairs*, 9, no. 2 (Winter 1980), 105–123; David Lamb, *Death, Brain Death and Ethics* (Albany: State University of New York Press, 1985), esp. ch. 8.

47. JoAnn Kelley Smith, *Free Fall* (Valley Forge, Pa.: Judson Press, 1975), 25.

48. Surveys cited in Donald Oken, "What to Tell Cancer Patients: A Study of Medical Attitudes," *JAMA*, 175 (April 1, 1961), 1120–1127, and Richard Schulz and David Aderman, "How the Medical Staff Copes with Dying Patients: A Critical Review," *Omega*, 7, no. 1 (1976), 11–21. In 1953, 67 percent of Philadelphia doctors never or rarely told patients. In 1960, 22 percent of a nationwide sample never told, and 62 percent sometimes. In 1961, 90 percent of Chicago doctors did not tell. See also Louis Lasagna, "Physicians' Behavior

Toward the Dying Patient," in *Dying Patient*, ed. Brim, 99, and Louis Lasagna, *Life, Death and the Doctor* (New York: Alfred A. Knopf, 1968), 230. For anecdotal confirmation, see Lerner, *A Death of One's Own*, 56–57.

49. On patients' views, see "Reader Response: What Do You Think of Your Medical Care?" *Life*, 73 (August 11, 1972), 38–39. For physicians' minority views: e.g., Edward H. Rynearson, "You Are Standing at the Bedside of a Patient Dying of Untreatable Cancer," *CA*, 9 (May–June 1959), 85–87; Oken, "What to Tell Cancer Patients," 1120–1127; C. Knight Aldrich, "The Dying Patient's Grief," *JAMA*, 184 (May 4, 1963), 329–331; "Death: 'A Lonely Business,'" *Newsweek*, 57 (May 22, 1961), 56; "Death & Modern Man," *Time*, 82 (November 20, 1964), 92–94; William M. Eason, "Care of the Young Patient Who Is Dying," *JAMA*, 205 (July 22, 1968), 203–207.

50. Quotation is from Milton G. Bohrod, "Uses of the Autopsy," *JAMA*, 193 (September 1965), 810–812. On DeBakey, see Thomas Thompson, *Hearts: Of Surgeons and Transplants, Miracles and Disasters Along the Cardiac Frontier* (New York: McCall, 1971), 45. See also David L. Rabin with Laurel H. Rabin, "Consequences of Death for Physicians, Nurses and Hospitals," in *Dying Patient*, ed. Brim, 174.

51. Quoted by Hendin, *Death as a Fact of Life*, 136–137. See also Oken, "What to Tell Cancer Patients," 1124.

52. Richard Schulz and David Aderman, "How the Medical Staff Copes with Dying Patients: A Critical Review," *Omega*, 7, no. 1 (1976), 14.

53. Herman Feifel, "Physicians Consider Death," paper at American Psychological Association convention, September 1967, cited in Hendin, *Death as a Fact of Life*, 135.

54. Thomas P. Hackett and Avery D. Weisman, "Reactions to the Imminence of Death," in *The Threat of Impending Disaster*, ed. George H. Grosser, Henry Wechsler, and Milton Greenblatt (Cambridge: MIT Press, 1964), 308.

55. Glick, *Right to Die*, 5, fig. 3.1. For exceptions advocating consultation with patients, see Frank J. Ayd, "The Hopeless Case: Medical and Moral Considerations," *JAMA*, 181 (September 29, 1962), 1099–1102; editorial, "When Do We Let the Patient Die?" *Annals of Internal Medicine*, 68, no. 3 (March 1968), 695.

56. Letter by Ronald A. Andree, Roosevelt Hospital, New York City, *Science*, 169 (August 21, 1970), 717, and Howard P. Lewis, "Machine Medicine and Its Relation to the Fatally Ill," *JAMA*, 206 (October 7, 1968), 387–388. Representative articles include: editorial, "Life-in-Death," *New England Journal of Medicine* [hereafter cited as *NEJM*], 256, (April 18, 1957), 760–761. Charles U. Letourneau, "Dying with Dignity," *Hospital Management*, 109 (June 1970), 27–30; Jonas B. Robitscher, "The Right to Die," *Hastings Center Review*, 2 (September 1972), 11–14.

57. See 1961 survey of Chicago internists and surgeons in Arthur Levisohn, "Voluntary Mercy Deaths: Socio-Legal Aspects of Euthanasia," *Journal of Forensic Medicine*, 8 (April–June 1961), 68; 1969 survey of Association of

Professors of Medicine and Association of American Physicians, in Robert H. Williams, "Our Role in the Generation, Modification and Termination of Life," *Archives of Internal Medicine*, 124 (August 1969), 229–230; and survey in *Medical Opinion*, cited in *New York Times*, June 16, 1974, IV, 7:2.

58. Norman K. Brown, *et al.*, "How Do Nurses Feel About Euthanasia and Abortion?" *American Journal of Nursing*, 7 (July 1971), 1413–1416; E. Harold Laws, *et al.*, "Views on Euthanasia," *Journal of Medical Education*, 46 (June 1971), 540–542; Dempsey, *Way We Die*, 110; *Washington Post*, September 25, 1975, A-8. For reports of nurses performing euthanasia, see Norman K. Brown and Donavan J. Thompson, "Nontreatment of Fever in Extended-Care Facilities," *NEJM*, 300 (May 31, 1979), 1246–1250.

59. A. Edward Doudera and J. Douglas Peters, eds., *Legal and Ethical Aspects of Treating Critically Ill Patients* (Ann Arbor: AVPHA Press, 1982), Appendix B, 294.

60. Dr. Paul Beeson, quoted in Sharon A. Kaufman, *The Healer's Tale: Transforming Medicine and Culture* (Madison: University of Wisconsin Press, 1993), 294. See also Jalland, *Death in the Victorian Family*, 77–81, and Edward Shorter, *Bedside Manners: The Troubled History of Doctors and Patients* (New York: Simon and Schuster, 1985), 38–46.

61. Shorter, *Bedside Manners*, 202, 208; Paul Starr, *The Social Transformation of American Medicine* (New York: Basic Books, 1982), 358–359; Boyer, *Bomb's Early Light*, 119–121, 268–271. For "playing God" as common metaphor, see Warren T. Reich, ed., *Encyclopedia of Bioethics*, 5 vols., rev. ed. (New York: Simon and Schuster, 1995), III, 1769. For doctors on "playing God," see Dr. William Zuelzer, 1972, quoted in David Rothman, *Strangers at the Bedside: A History of How Law and Bioethics Transformed Medical Decision Making* (New York: Basic Books, 1991), 196; James P. Carse, "The Social Effects of Changing Attitudes Towards Death," in *Brain Death: Interrelated Medical and Social Issues*, ed. Julius Korein, *Annals of the New York Academy of Sciences*, vol. 315 (1978), 325. For jokes about God and doctors in heaven, Eugene D. Robin, *Matters of Life and Death* (New York: Freeman, 1984), ch. 4 ("The Doctor as God") and 43; Peter J. Berczeller, *Doctors and Patients: What We Feel About You* (New York: Macmillan, 1994), 123–124.

62. "Reader Response," *Life*, 73 (August 11, 1972), 38–39.

63. Thomas L. Haskell, ed., *The Authority of Experts: Studies in History and Theory* (Bloomington: Indiana University Press, 1984), xiii; *Houston Post*, November 11, 1975, 1:1; editorial, "No Right to Die," *Des Moines Register*, November 12, 1975, 8A. Paul Ramsey, *Ethics at the Edges of Life* (New Haven: Yale University Press, 1978), 203; *New York Times*, December 23, 1984, 1:1, 18:1.

64. John Carmody, "A Death, a Radicalization," *Christian Century*, 91 (June 12, 1974), 639.

65. Kübler-Ross, *On Death and Dying*, 19–21 and *passim*.

66. Quotation is from Dempsey, *Way We Die*, 14. On *Life*, see Derek Gill, *Quest: The Life of Elisabeth Kübler-Ross* (New York: Harper & Row, 1980), 308,

and Loudon Wainwright, "A Profound Lesson for the Living," *Life*, 67 (November 21, 1969), 36–43. On seminars, see *New York Times*, January 21, 1973, 44:1. On lectures and letters, see "The Conversion of Kübler-Ross," *Time*, 114 (November 12, 1979), 81, and Gill, *Quest*, xi. On influence, see Carol P. Germain, "Nursing the Dying: Implications of Kübler-Ross's Staging Theory," *Annals of the American Academy of Social Sciences* (1980), 48–50, and Roy Branson, "Is Acceptance a Denial of Death? Another Look at Kübler-Ross," *Christian Century*, 92 (May 7, 1975), 467. On award, see "Women of the Year: 1977," *Ladies' Home Journal*, 94 (June 1977), 77, and Gill, *Quest*, 319.

67. Peter Clecak, *America's Quest for the Ideal Self: Dissent and Fulfillment in the 60s and 70s* (New York: Oxford University Press, 1983), 127–129, 144–156, and Daniel Yankelovich, *New Rules: Searching for Self-Fulfillment in a World Turned Upside Down* (New York: Random House, 1981), esp. 3–8.

68. I adapted the concept of the sacred from Yankelovich, *New Rules*, 7. Leonard L. Lieber, "Parents Anonymous: The Use of Self Help in the Treatment and Prevention of Family Violence"; Virginia Goldner, "Overeaters Anonymous"; and Andy Humm, "The Changing Nature of Lesbian and Gay Self-Help Groups," in *The Self-Help Revolution*, ed. Alan Gartner and Frank Riessman (New York: Human Sciences Press, 1984), 53–64, 65–72, 73–94. Richard Ofshe, "Synanon: The People Business," in *The New Religious Consciousness*, ed. Charles Y. Glock and Robert N. Bellah (Berkeley: University of California Press, 1976), 116–137.

69. Goldner, "Overeaters Anonymous."

70. Joel Henning, *Holistic Running: Beyond the Threshold of Fitness* (New York: Atheneum, 1978), 20.

71. *San Diego Reader*, April 13–19, 1978, quoted by Lofland, *Craft of Dying*, 103.

72. Quoted by Lofland, *Craft of Dying*, 77. The book is better than its cover. Keleman, a practitioner of bio-energetics and Gestalt therapy, has breathless but thoughtful ideas about dying: Keleman, *Living Your Dying* (New York: Random House/Bookworks, 1974).

73. Quotation from David Gutmann, "Dying to Power: Death and the Search for Self-Esteem," in *New Meanings of Death*, ed. Feifel, 336–337. *Chicago Tribune*, December 20, 1975, I, 14:1; Marjorie McClay, *To Die with Style!* (Nashville, Tenn.: Abingdon Press, 1974).

74. "Conversion of Kübler-Ross," *Time*, 114 (November 12, 1979), 81. Also *New York Times*, April 20, 1976, 15:1, and September 17, 1979, B-10; Karen Jacovich, "Sex, Visitors from the Grave, Psychic Healing: Kübler-Ross is a Public Storm Center Again," *People*, 12 (October 12, 1979), 28–29; Ron Rosenbaum, "Turn On, Tune In, Drop Dead," *Harper's*, 265 (July 1982), 32–38.

75. Paul Ramsey, "Death's Pedagogy," *Commonweal*, 100 (September 20, 1977), 497–500; Philip Cushman, *Constructing the Self, Constructing America: A Cultural History of Psychotherapy* (Reading, Mass.: Addison-Wesley, 1995),

240–242; Christopher Lasch, *The Culture of Narcissism: American Life in an Age of Diminishing Expectations* (New York: W. W. Norton, 1979); Peter Marin, "The New Narcissism," *Harper's*, 251 (October 1975), 45–56, and the critique of self-psychology by Yankelovich, *New Rules*, 234–243.

76. Glick, *Right to Die*, 34, table 3:3; *Public Opinion Quarterly*, 44 (Spring 1980), 125; *Los Angeles Times*, April 3, 1975, II, 1:5.

77. Mannes, *Last Rights*, 8. A hostile observer made the same claim: Dempsey, *Way We Die*, 99.

78. *New York Times Index* (1973), 1994; *Gallup Opinion Index, Religion in America, 1977–78*, Report #145, 14; Seymour Martin Lipset and William Schneider, *The Confidence Gap: Business, Labor, and Government in the Public Mind* (New York: Free Press, 1983), 42–43, 67–79.

79. *Gallup Opinion Index*, Report #134 (September 1976), 18. When asked for their opinion of people in eleven occupations in 1976, 1977, and 1980, Americans ranked doctors highest: Lipset and Schneider, *Confidence Gap*, 201.

80. Rothman, *Strangers at the Bedside*, 99–100, 107–108, 140–141. For an early example of complaint, Selig Greenberg, "The Decline of the Healing Art," *Harper's*, 221 (October 1960), 132–137. On malpractice suits, see Fitzhugh Millan, review, *Washington Post Book World*, September 10, 1978, E-5; Dempsey, *Way We Die*, 70; Louise Lander, *Defective Medicine: Risk, Anger, and the Malpractice Crisis* (New York: Farrar, Straus and Giroux, 1978), esp. 103–104; Rothman, *Strangers at the Bedside*, 154–155; and Thomas L. Haskell, ed., *The Authority of Experts: Studies in History and Theory* (Bloomington: Indiana University Press, 1984), xiv.

81. Quotations from the Boston Women's Health Book Collective, *Our Bodies, Ourselves: A Book by and for Women*, 2nd ed. (New York: Simon and Schuster, 1975), 354, 340; see also 344–355. By 1973 it had sold more than 350,000 copies; by 1995 nearly three million in the United States alone: *New York Times*, June 27, 1995, B15:6.

82. See, e.g., Claudia Dreifus, ed., *Seizing Our Bodies: The Politics of Women's Health* (New York: Vintage, 1978).

83. Ellen Frankfort, "Vaginal Politics," *Village Voice*, November 25, 1971, reprinted in Frankfort, *Vaginal Politics* (New York: Quadrangle Books, 1972), xi–xii.

84. Barbara Monty, "Personal Action," *The Second Wave*, 2, no. 3 (1973), 27, quoted by Sheryl Burt Ruzek, *The Women's Health Movement: Feminist Alternatives to Medical Control* (New York: Praeger, 1978), 35.

85. On Downer and Rothman, see Gena Corea, *The Hidden Malpractice: How American Medicine Treats Women as Patients and Professionals* (New York: William Morrow, 1977), 259, and Dreifus, *Seizing Our Bodies*, xxviii. For a listing of groups, see Ruzek, *Women's Health Movement*, Appendix C, 245–264.

86. Emily Mumford, *Medical Sociology: Patients, Providers and Policies*

(New York: Random House, 1983), 160–163. Book titles cited by John D. Stoeckle, ed., *Encounters Between Patients and Doctors: An Anthology* (Cambridge: MIT Press, 1987). See also Herbert Denenberg, *A Shopper's Guide to Surgery: Fourteen Rules on How to Avoid Unnecessary Surgery* (reprinted by Blue Cross, 1972); George J. Annas, *The Rights of Hospital Patients: The Basic ACLU Guide to a Hospital Patient's Rights* (New York: Sunrise Books/E. P. Dutton, 1975); Lowell S. Levin, ed., *Self-Care: Lay Initiatives in Health* (New York: Prodist, 1979); J. Neirenberg and F. Janovic, *The Hospital Experience: A Complete Guide to Understanding and Participating in Your Own Care* (New York: Bobbs-Merrill, 1979).

87. Dr. Willard Gaylin, "The Patient's Bill of Rights," *Saturday Review of Science*, 1 (1973), 22, quoted by William J. Curran, "The Patient's Bill of Rights Becomes Law," *NEJM*, 290 (January 3, 1974), 32. Also *New York Times*, January 9, 1973, 1:6.

88. *New York Times*, January 10, 1973, 24:1, and Glick, *Right to Die*, 108.

89. *New York Times*, September 28, 1975, 50:3.

90. Glick, *Right to Die*, 93–94, 104–108.

91. *Death with Dignity*, Special Committee on Aging, U.S. Senate.

92. *Psychology Today*, 8 (September 1974), 29–30.

3. THE SUBJECTIVITY OF DYING

1. *New York Times*, suburban edition, September 25, 1975, 91:1.

2. "The Right to Live—or Die," *Time*, 106 (October 27, 1975), 40.

3. CBS Evening News, November 6, 1975. Also seventeen-year-old Randy Carmen, in a coma since being injured in a neighborhood football game on September 21, 1975. His parents wanted life-support turned off, but the hospital refused. See NBC Nightly News, October 9, 1975.

4. *Los Angeles Times*, December 3, 1975, I, 5:1. For other cases, *Chicago Tribune*, March 31, 1975, III, 9:1; *Washington Post*, December 17, 1972, B1:1.

5. *New York Times*, November 2, 1975, 55:1, and the obituary on November 10, 1975 (suburban edition), 36:3. *Kansas City Star*, October 26, 4A:1, and November 10, 29:1; *St. Louis Post-Dispatch*, October 26, 1:4, 23A:4, October 27, 3A:3, November 2, 21A:1, November 10, 1:3—all 1975.

6. "Between Life and Death," *Time*, 86 (September 29, 1975), 59.

7. Georgie Anne Geyer, in *Los Angeles Times*, October 27, 1975, II, 7:1.

8. Quotation from *New York Times*, October 24, 1975, 39:1. Also "Before Karen's Coma," *Time*, 106 (December 29, 1975), 19. For a fuller discussion, see Chapter One above.

9. *New York Times*, December 17, 1975, 49:6; December 19, 1975 (New Jersey edition), 48:3; February 25, 1976, 43:8. Two decades later a forty-four-year-old woman wrote to Ann Landers: "I never used any drugs because of Karen's

experience," and she had constantly taught her children the same lesson: *Raleigh News & Observer*, October 6, 1996, 2E:3.

10. Quoted in Vin McLellan and Paul Avery, *The Voices of Guns: The Definitive Story of the Twenty Month Career of the SLA* . . . (New York: Putnam, 1977), 301.

11. For background, see Shana Alexander, *Anyone's Daughter* (New York: Viking Press, 1979); Janice Scheutz, *The Logic of Women on Trial: Case Studies of Popular American Trials* (Carbondale: Southern Illinois University Press, 1994), 161–173, 177–178. For media and Beauty/Beast metaphor, see Elizabeth Walker Mechling, "Patricia Hearst: Myth America 1974, 1975, 1976," *Western Journal of Speech Communication*, 43 (Summer 1979), 168–179; also Bernard M. Timberg, "Patty Hearst and Mercy Short: An Analogue Critique," *Journal of American Culture*, 6 (Spring 1983), 60–64.

12. "Travels with Tania," *Newsweek*, 86 (October 13, 1975), 30.

13. The literature on photography's relationship to the world is large. For some particularly illuminating studies, see Susan Sontag, *On Photography* (New York: Farrar, Straus and Giroux, 1977); Judith Mara Gutman, *Lewis W. Hine, 1874–1940: Two Perspectives* (New York: Grossman, 1974); William Stott, *Documentary Expression and the 1930s* (New York: Oxford University Press, 1973); Alan Trachtenberg, *Reading American Photographs: Images as History, Mathew Brady to Walker Evans* (New York: Hill and Wang, 1989).

14. Sontag, *On Photography*, 15.

15. In reality, the sketches were erroneous. Quinlan's hair had been cut short, and her face was rounder than it had been when she was healthy. In addition, the respirator was on the left side of the bed. See Joseph and Julia Quinlan, with Phyllis Battelle, *Karen Ann: The Quinlans Tell Their Story* (New York: Doubleday, 1977), 222.

16. *Ibid.*, 251, 341–342.

17. *New York Daily News*, October 29, 1975, 61.

18. Quinlans, *Karen Ann*, 250.

19. Editorial, *Milwaukee Journal*, October 26, 1975, II, 5:1.

20. Caryl Porter, "Karen Ann," *Christian Century*, 93 (January 21, 1976), 45.

21. Tabitha Powledge, "Death as an Acceptable Subject," *New York Times*, July 25, 1976, IV, 8:4.

22. For discussion of the military metaphor and disease, see Susan Sontag, *Illness as Metaphor* (New York: Farrar, Straus and Giroux, 1978), 64–65.

23. *In the Matter of Karen Quinlan*, 2 vols., II: *The Complete Legal Briefs, Court Proceedings, and Decision in the Supreme Court of New Jersey* [hereafter cited as *Briefs*] (Arlington Va.: University Publications of America, 1976), 260.

24. *Ibid.*, 214–215, 237–238.

25. *Ibid.*, 267.

26. *Ibid.*, 259.

27. *Ibid.*, 278. See also 254 and 284 for discussion of malpractice.

28. *Ibid.*, 264.

29. Quinlans, *Karen Ann*, 272–273.

30. *Ibid.*, 274–275.

31. *Briefs*, 288–289.

32. *Ibid.*, 561.

33. *Ibid.*, 304, 290.

34. *Ibid.*, 315.

35. *Ibid.*, 313–314.

36. *Ibid.*, 304.

37. *Ibid.*, 305.

38. *Ibid.*, 310–313. Quotations on 310 and 313.

39. *Ibid.*, 302.

40. Robert A. Burt, *Taking Care of Strangers: The Rule of Law in Doctor-Patient Relations* (New York: Free Press, 1979), 162–164.

41. Quoted in Quinlans, *Karen Ann*, 277.

42. CBS Evening News, March 31, 1976.

43. Editorial, *Chicago Tribune*, April 3, 10:1; editorial, *New York Daily News*, April 2, 51:1; *France-Soir*, April 2, 3:1—all 1976. On prayers, see *Milwaukee Journal*, April 1, 1:1, 1976. On "fate," *Boston Globe*, April 1, 1976, 1:1.

44. Virtually every headline used the word "die": *Des Moines Register*, *Newark Star-Ledger*, *New York Daily News*, *Los Angeles Times*, *Portland Oregonian*, *Louisville Courier-Journal*, *Times* (London)—all April 1, 1976, page 1; *Figaro*, April 2, 1976, 1 and 6. On defense appeal, *New York Times*, April 7, 1:5, and April 9, 20:4, 1976.

45. *New York Daily News*, April 1, 1976, p. 2; *New York Times*, New Jersey edition, May 6, 1976, 79:4, and December 14, 1976, 17:1; Michael P. Hamilton, "Karen's Right to Die," *Christian Century*, 93 (April 28, 1976), 404–405; "Karen Ann Quinlan and the Right to Die," *America*, 134 (April 17, 1976), 327. For bitter objections, see Philadelphia *Catholic Standard and Times*, April 8, 1976, quoted by Richard A. McCormick, *How Brave a New World: Dilemmas in Bioethics* (London: SCM, 1981), 353–355.

46. Quoted in *Newark Star-Ledger*, April 1 and April 2, 1976, 1:8. For other doctors' responses, *New York Times*, April 2, 1976, 38:1; *Washington Post*, April 5, 1976, A19:3; and David Rothman, *Strangers at the Bedside: A History of How Law and Bioethics Transformed Medical Decision Making* (New York: Basic Books, 1991), 229. For lawyers, see Joseph V. Reddy, "The Karen Quinlan Case—a Constitutional Right to Die?" *Chicago Bar Record*, 58 (November–December 1976), 120–124; H. Richard Beresford, "The Quinlan Decision: Problems of Legislative Alternatives," *Annals of Neurology*, 2 (July 1977), 74–81.

47. William F. Smith, "In re Quinlan: Defining the Basis for Terminating Life Support Under the Right of Privacy," *Tulsa Law Journal*, 12 (1976), 150–167; Laurence H. Tribe, *American Constitutional Law* (Mineola, N.Y.:

Foundation Press, 1978), 936–937. Also "The Tragic Choice: Termination of Care for Patients in a Permanent Vegetative State," *New York University Law Review*, 51 (May 1976), 285–297. For a completely hostile reaction, see Reddy, "Karen Quinlan Case," *Chicago Bar Record*, 58 (November–December 1976), 120–124.

48. George J. Annas, "In re Quinlan: Legal Comfort for Doctors," *Hastings Center Report*, 8 (June 1976), 29–31; Paul Ramsey, "Prolonged Dying: Not Medically Indicated," *ibid.*, 6 (February 1976), 17; Ramsey, *Ethics at the Edges of Life: Medical and Legal Intersections* (New Haven: Yale University Press, 1978), ch. 7 (quotation on 294).

4. THE POLITICS OF DYING

1. *New York Times*, December 4, 1:1, December 5, 47:1, and December 5, IV, 7:3—all 1976.

2. CBS Morning News, December 27, 1977.

3. "Leslie Rado, "Death Redefined: Social and Cultural Influence on Legislation," *Journal of Communication*, 31 (Winter 1981), 41–47, and in more detail, Rado, "Communication, Social Organization and the Redefinition of Death: A Case Study in the Institutionalization of an Idea" (Ph.D. dissertation, University of Pennsylvania, 1979). On statutes, President's Commission for the Study of Ethical Problems in Medicine and Biomedical and Behavioral Research, *Defining Death: A Report on the Medical, Legal and Ethical Issues in the Determination of Death* (Washington, D.C.: Government Printing Office, 1981), Appendix C.

4. E.g., Dennis Horan, president of American Citizens United for Life, quoted in *ibid.*, 11.

5. California Assembly Committee on Health, *Interim Hearing on Rights of Terminally Ill Patients* (San Francisco, October 8, 1974), 4 [hereafter cited as *Interim Hearing*].

6. For the story of Keene and the California law, I've drawn heavily from Henry R. Glick, *The Right to Die: Policy Innovation and Its Consequences* (New York: Columbia University Press, 1992), 93–97. But I have corrected some of Glick's erroneous details in the light of my interview with Mr. Keene, August 20, 1995, as well as information I read in the bill files, AB 4444, 1974, and AB 3060, 1976, California State Archives, Sacramento. I thank Natalie Fousekis for her invaluable research assistance.

7. David Dempsey, "The Living Will—and the Will to Live," *New York Times Magazine*, June 23, 1974, 12; B. D. Colen, *Karen Ann Quinlan: Dying in the Age of Eternal Life* (New York: Nash, 1976), 160; David Rothman, *Strangers at the Bedside: A History of How Law and Bioethics Transformed Medical Decision Making* (New York: Basic Books, 1991), 239.

8. Dr. Laurens White, *Interim Hearing*, 26 and 26–46 *passim*.

9. *The Gallup Poll: Public Opinion 1986*, 49–51, reviewing polls on abortion since 1974.

10. Steve Bruce, *The Rise and Fall of the New Christian Right: Conservative Protestant Politics in America, 1978–1988* (Oxford: Clarendon Press, 1988), ch. 8; Patrick Allitt, *Catholic Intellectuals and Conservative Politics in America, 1950–1985* (Ithaca, N.Y.: Cornell University Press, 1993), 189–193; J. Holden, "Demographics, Attitudes, and Afterlife Beliefs of Right-to-Life and Right-to-Die Organization Members," *Journal of Social Psychology*, 133 (August 1993), 525.

11. Connie Paige, *The Right to Lifers: Who They Are, How They Operate, Where They Get Their Money* (New York: Summit Books, 1983), 51–64.

12. *Los Angeles Times*, April 3, 1975, II, 1:5 and 6:2. The poll is reprinted (although with incorrect wording) along with other states' polls on euthanasia in *Public Opinion Quarterly*, 44 (Spring 1980), 126–127.

13. Interview with Keene, August 20, 1995.

14. California Legislature, Assembly Health Committee, "Safeguards in AB 3060: The Natural Death Act" (1975); Marc Lappe, "Dying While Living: A Critique of Allowing-to-Die Legislation," *Journal of Medical Ethics*, 4 (1978), 195–199; Michael Garland, "Politics, Legislation, and Natural Death," *Hastings Center Review*, 6 (October 1976), 5–6; Glick, *Right to Die*, 95–97.

15. Most Reverend John S. Cummins to Barry Keene, August 12, 1976, California Legislature, Assembly Health Committee, "Safeguards in AB 3060."

16. Lappe, "Dying While Living," *Journal of Medical Ethics*, 4 (1978), 195–199; Diane Lynn Redleaf, Suzanne Baillie Schmitt, and William Charles Thompson, "The California Natural Death Act: An Empirical Study of Physicians' Practices," *Stanford Law Review*, 31 (May 1979), 919, n.27.

17. Glick, *Right to Die*, 95.

18. Letter from David A. Roberts, *Los Angeles Times*, September 19, 1976, IV, 2:3. Likewise, see letter from D. C. Duggan, Phoenix, Ariz., *Los Angeles Times*, October 12, 1976, II, 6:3.

19. *Ibid.*, September 20, 1976, II, 7:1, and October 4, 1976, II, 7:1.

20. Editorial, "Deathbed Dilemma," *San Francisco Examiner*, April 26, 1976, 30:1.

21. Glick, *Right to Die*, 98; *San Francisco Examiner*, April 26, 1976; KGO-TV editorial, "Right to Die," January 30–February 1, 1976, in California Legislature, Assembly Health Committee, "Safeguards in AB 3060"; Herman Hoth, "'Right to Die' Bill Is Supported," *Sacramento Bee*, May 2, 1976; editorial, "The Right to a Natural Death," *Los Angeles Times*, August 23, 1976, II, 6:1, and editorial, "Humanity in the Law," *ibid.*, October 4, 1976, II, 7:1; Abigail Van Buren ("Dear Abby") also supported: *ibid.*, October 1, 1976, II, 6:4. For letters, see *ibid.*, September 19, IV, 2:3, September 24, II, 2:3, and October 12, II, 6:3—all 1976, and *San Francisco Examiner*, April 2, 1976, 30.

22. Letters from Susan Longworth and Lillian Barker, *ibid.*, April 2, 1976, 31:3.

23. Votes are listed in *California Journal*, July 1976, 247, and October 1976, 543. Quotations from Leah Cartabruno, "Giving the 'Right to Die' to California's Terminally Ill," *ibid.* (July 1976), 218, and *San Francisco Chronicle*, June 18, 1:1, 26:1, and August 27, 1:4, 22:4, both 1976. See also *Los Angeles Times*, June 18, I, 1:3, and August 27, 1:1, both 1976.

24. *Los Angeles Times*, June 18, 1976, I, 1:3.

25. Five of the first seven states were Western neighbors. Meanwhile bills were introduced into all the other legislatures. See Glick, *Right to Die*, 170, table 6-1, and 171–173.

26. On New Jersey, see James M. Hoefler with Brian E. Kamoie, *Deathright: Culture, Medicine, Politics, and the Right to Die* (Boulder, Colo.: Westview Press, 1994), 189; on Connecticut, Stephen A. Wise, "The Last Word—Whose?" *Christian Century*, 98 (September 16, 1981), 395–396; on New York, *New York Times*, October 2, 1983, XXI, 1:1; on Massachusetts, Glick, *Right to Die*, 120–128.

27. For itemized summary of each state law, see Robert F. Weir, *Abating Treatment with Critically Ill Patients: Ethical and Legal Limits to the Medical Prolongation of Life* (New York: Oxford University Press, 1989), 434–442; for comparative analysis, see Hoefler with Kamoie, *Deathright*, ch. 8.

28. *Washington Post*, February 4, A1:5; February 7, B7:4; February 8, C7:4; February 22, C3:1; February 24, B4:2—all 1983. *National Right to Life News* [hereafter *NRL News*], 10 (February 24, 1983), 1, 5. *Richmond Times-Dispatch*, February 4, A6:1; February 7, B1:1; February 8, A5:4—all 1983.

29. Hoefler with Kamoie, *Deathright*, 202–205, 362–364.

30. Paige, *Right to Lifers*, 125–153.

31. Jerry Falwell, *Listen, America!* (Garden City: Doubleday, 1980), 7, 243. For excellent analysis, see Robert Wuthnow, *The Restructuring of American Religion: Society and Faith Since World War Two* (Princeton: Princeton University Press, 1988), 195, 203–207; also, Erling Jorstad, *Holding Fast/Pressing On: Religion in America in the 1980s* (New York: Praeger, 1990), 68; Glick, *Right to Die*, 21–22; Matthew C. Moen, *The Transformation of the Christian Right* (Tuscaloosa: University of Alabama Press, 1992), 25–31 and table 4-1; Wuthnow, *Restructuring of American Religion*, ch. 8; James Davison Hunter, *American Evangelicalism: Conservative Religion and the Quandary of Modernity* (New Brunswick: Rutgers University Press, 1983), ch. 7; Donald Mathews and Jane De Hart, *Sex, Gender and the Politics of ERA: A State and the Nation* (New York: Oxford University Press, 1990).

32. For exceptions, see C. Everett Koop, "The Right to Die," *Human Life Review*, 2 (Spring 1976), 44–45, 52–53; Thomas O'Sullivan, "Active and Passive Euthanasia: An Impertinent Distinction," *ibid.*, 3 (Summer 1977), 40–46; and James P. Csank, "The Right to a Natural Death," *ibid.*, 4 (Winter 1978), 44–54.

33. *Louisville Courier-Journal*, April 16, 1982, 1:1 and 12:1, and *Washing-*

ton Post, April 17, 1982, 1:4. For a convenient synopsis, see Robert F. Weir, *Selective Nontreatment of Handicapped Newborns: Dilemmas in Neonatal Medicine* (New York: Oxford University Press, 1984), 128–129.

34. Headline from *Washington Post,* April 16, 1982, A16:1. Quotation from editorial, "The Bloomington Baby," *Washington Post,* April 18, 1982, B6:1.

35. Quoted in Nat Hentoff, "The Awful Privacy of Baby Doe," *Atlantic Monthly,* 255 (January 1985), 54–62; letter from Ronald P. Prishivalko, *Washington Post,* April 24, 1982, A1:2.

36. For disease rates, see Siegfried M. Pueschel, "The Person with Down Syndrome: Medical Concerns and Educational Strategies," and Langford Kidd, "Cardiorespiratory Problems in Children with Down Syndrome," in *Down Syndrome: Advances in Medical Care,* ed. Ira T. Lott and Ernest E. McCoy (New York: John Wiley and Sons, 1992), 55 and 61. For life expectancy in 1960s, Christof Wunderlich, *The Mongoloid Child: Recognition and Care* (Tucson: University of Arizona Press, 1977), 7–9. On recent mortality, see Mark Selikowitz, *Down Syndrome: The Facts* (New York: Oxford University Press, 1990), 88. On surgery, see introduction and Kidd, "Cardiorespiratory Problems," in *Down Syndrome,* ed. Lott and McCoy, xi, 61.

For doctors' recommendations in 1970s, see Alan J. Weisbard, "Comment on 'Science and Controversy in the History of Infancy in America,'" in *Which Babies Shall Live? Humanistic Dimensions of the Care of Imperiled Newborns,* ed. Thomas H. Murray and Arthur L. Caplan (Clifton, N.J.: Humana Press, 1985), 48 and 55, n.3; Diana Crane, *The Sanctity of Social Life: Physicians' Treatment of Critically Ill Patients* (New York: Russell Sage Foundation, 1975), 45, table 3.4; Anthony Shaw, Judson G. Randolph, and Barbara Manard, "Ethical Issues in Pediatric Surgery: A National Survey of Pediatricians and Pediatric Surgeons," *Pediatrics,* 60 (October 1977), 588–599; and "Treating the Defective Newborn: A Survey of Physicians' Attitudes," *Hastings Center Review,* 6 (April 1976), 2. But in a 1985 survey of neonatal doctors and nurses, 87 percent advocated surgery: Betty Wolder Levin, "Consensus and Controversy in the Treatment of Catastrophically Ill Newborns: Report of a Survey," in *Which Babies Shall Live?,* ed. Murray and Caplan, 177–178.

37. Max L. Hutt and Robert Gwyn Gibby, *The Mentally Retarded Child: Development, Education and Treatment,* 2nd ed. (Boston: Allyn and Bacon, 1965), 68, and Hutt and Gibby, *Mentally Retarded Child,* 4th ed. (Boston: Allyn and Bacon, 1979), 95–96. When the New York Academy of Sciences held an international conference on Down's syndrome in 1969, it still included "Mongolism" (in parentheses) in the title: "Conference on Down's Syndrome (Mongolism), 1969," *Annals of the New York Academy of Sciences,* 171, Article 2 (September 24, 1970), 303–368.

38. *Washington Post,* April 17, 1982, 10:1.

39. CBS Evening News, April 16, 1982, reported simply the death of a "severely retarded week-old infant." *Chicago Tribune,* April 16, 1982, I, 19:2, mentioned the esophagus only in the eighth paragraph. *Washington Post,* April 16,

1982, A16:4, mentioned it in the sixth paragraph. Nat Hentoff, "Awful Privacy," *Atlantic Monthly*, 255 (January 1985), 55, mentioned "a routinely operable intestinal obstruction" only on the third page. See also letters from Thomas Gannon, Washington, D.C., and Jo Lombard, McLean, Virginia, which say nothing at all about the esophagus: *Washington Post*, April 24, 1982, A16.

40. See the letter from Dr. John E. Pless, Bloomington Hospital, *NEJM*, 309 (September 15, 1983), 664.

41. Letters from Karen E. Murray, Arlington, Virginia; Elizabeth G. Haselton, Washington, D.C., and Arthur C. Sabin, Falls Church, Virginia, *Washington Post*, April 24, A16, and April 29, A28, both 1982.

42. *Washington Post*, April 17, 1982, 1:4.

43. Editorial, "'Infant Doe': In Such a Heart-rending Case, No Easy Answers," *Louisville Courier-Journal*, April 20, 1982, A6; Richard Cohen, "It Depends," *Washington Post*, April 20, 1982, B1:1.

44. Quotations from *Washington Post*, April 17, 1982, 10:1; CBS Evening News, April 15, 1982; and George F. Will, "The Killing Will Not Stop," *Washington Post*, April 22, 1982, A29:3. Conservative congressmen reprinted Will's article six times: *Congressional Record*, 97th Cong., 2nd Sess., vol. 128, Pt. 6, 7454, 7624, 7699, 7879, 8117, and Pt. 9, 11936. Many people offered to adopt Infant Doe: *Chicago Tribune*, April 16, 1982, I, 19:2.

45. John D. Arras, "Ethical Principles for the Care of Imperiled Newborns: Toward an Ethic of Ambiguity," in *Which Babies Shall Live?*, ed. Murray and Caplan, 98–99.

46. Stephen Chapman, "From Abortion to Infanticide," *Chicago Tribune*, April 22, I, 24:3; "Introduction," *Human Life Review*, VIII (Summer 1982), 2; David Staton (W. Va.), *Congressional Record*, 97th Cong., 2nd Sess., vol. 128, Pt. 7 (May 13, 1982), 9610. Jeremiah Denton, *ibid.*, Pt. 9 (May 26, 1982), 11926.

47. Henry Hyde (Ill.), *ibid.*, Pt. 6 (April 20, 1982), 7143.

48. *National Right to Life News*, 9 (June 10, 1982), 2.

49. Russell Shaw (secretary for public affairs of the U.S. Catholic Conference), quoted in *Washington Post*, May 15, 1982, A19; Chapman, *Chicago Tribune*, April 22, 1982, I, 24:3; editorial, "Write Now," *National Right to Life News*, 10 (August 4, 1983), 2.

50. Joseph R. Stanton, "From Feticide to Infanticide," *Human Life Review*, 8 (Summer 1982), 39.

51. Editorial, "Deeper into Infanticide," *National Right to Life News*, 10 (April 28, 1983), 2.

52. George F. Will, "Unfashionable Civil Rights," *Washington Post*, November 13, 1983, C7:2, reprinted in *National Right to Life News*, 10 (December 8, 1983), 4. See also J. C. Wilke, president of the National Right to Life Committee, May 26, 1982, condemning the "elitist 'quality of life' argument. . . .": cited in Weir, *Selective Nontreatment*, 135.

53. Duff and Campbell, "Moral and Ethical Dilemmas in the Special-

Care Nursery," *NEJM*, 289 (October 25, 1973), 890–894. For instructive context, see Rothman, *Strangers at the Bedside*, 194–204. For more detailed analysis, see Weir, *Selective Nontreatment*, ch. 3.

54. Duff and Campbell received 102 letters in the year after their article, 23 percent of them disapproving, mostly from a pro-life premise. Duff and Campbell, "Moral and Ethical Dilemmas: Seven Years into the Debate About Human Ambiguity," *Annals of the American Academy of Political and Social Science*, 447 (January 1980), 24. Among the few published nonprofessional references: Arthur J. Snider, "Should Doctors Let Deformed Babies Die?" *Science Digest*, 75 (February 1974), 47–48.

55. *Congressional Record*, 97th Cong., 2nd Sess., vol. 128, Pt. 9 (May 26, 1982), 11931–11934.

56. C. Everett Koop, "The Right to Die," *Human Life Review*, 2 (Spring 1976), 33–38 (quotation on 38); "The Slide to Auschwitz," *Human Life Review*, 3 (Spring 1977), 106–108; "The Silent Domino: Infanticide," 1979 address, reprinted in *Congressional Record*, 97th Cong., 2nd Sess., vol. 128, Pt. 9 (May 26, 1982), 11927–11930; *The Right to Live, The Right to Die* (Wheaton, Ill.: Tyndale House, 1976).

57. On TV series, *National Right to Life News*, 10 (March 24, 1983), 8. Nat Hentoff, "The Awful Privacy of Baby Doe," *Atlantic Monthly*, 255 (January 1985), 57–58.

58. Nancy Rhoden and John D. Arras, "Withholding Treatment," *Milbank Quarterly*, 63 (Winter 1985), 21; Helga Kuhse and Peter Singer, *Should the Baby Live? The Problem of Handicapped Infants* (New York: Oxford University Press, 1985), 21–47, 180–181.

59. Rhoden and Arras, "Withholding Treatment," 18–20 (quotations on 20 and 24); Weir, *Selective Nontreatment*, 133. For size of signs, Peter Singer and Helga Kuhse, "The Future of Baby Doe," *New York Review of Books*, 31 (March 1, 1984), 21.

60. *National Right to Life News*, 10 (August 4, 1983), 2. On letters, see Kuhse and Singer, *Should the Baby Live?*, 43.

61. Marcia Angell, "Handicapped Children: Baby Doe and Uncle Sam," *NEJM*, 309 (September 15, 1983), 660. Of the 141 pediatricians who wrote to HHS about its regulations, 72 percent opposed. (Kuhse and Singer, *Should the Baby Live?*, 43).

62. I'm indebted to Rhoden and Arras, "Withholding Treatment," esp. 27 and 39–40, for their lucid analysis. See also Weir, *Selective Nontreatment*, 137–138, and Kuhse and Singer, *Should the Baby Live?*, 21–47.

63. *American Academy of Pediatrics v. Heckler*, No. 83-0774, U.S. District Court, D.C., April 14, 1983, quoted in Weir, *Selective Nontreatment*, 136, and Earl E. Shelp, *Born to Die?* (New York: Free Press, 1986), 183–184.

64. Quoted in Weir, *Selective Nontreatment*, 136, and Rhoden and Arras, "Withholding Treatment," 20–21. In 1986 the U.S. Supreme Court invalidated these regulations. By that time, however, right-to-lifers had succeeded in

putting their objectives into federal law. A coalition of liberal and conservative congressmen in 1984 passed the Child Abuse Amendments, which defined nontreatment of infants with life-threatening conditions as a form of child abuse: Melvin Urofsky, *Letting Go: Death, Dying, and the Law* (New York: Charles Scribner's Sons, 1993), 112–115.

65. George J. Annas, "Disconnecting the Baby Doe Hotline," *Hastings Center Review*, 13 (June 1983), 16; Thomas Scully and Celia Scully, *Playing God: The New World of Medical Choices* (New York: Simon and Schuster, 1987), 201.

66. *Washington Post* / NORC 1980 poll, cited in Anson Shupe and William A. Stacey, "Public and Clergy Sentiments Toward the Moral Majority: Evidence from the Dallas-Fort Worth Metroplex," in *New Christian Politics*, ed. David G. Bromley and Anson Shupe (Macon, Ga.: Mercer University Press, 1984), 91–100; *Gallup Poll, Public Opinion, 1982*, 22, 24. On abortion, see "Religion in America," *Gallup Report*, nos. 201–202 (June–July 1982), 161.

67. Glick, *Right to Die*, 85–87 and 84, table 3.

68. *Ibid.*, and Robert J. Blendon, Ulrike S. Szalay, and Richard A. Knox, "Should Physicians Aid Their Patients in Dying?" *JAMA*, 267 (May 20, 1992), 2659–2660.

69. Gallup Poll, *Public Opinion 1988*, 206–209, summarizing polls from 1975 to 1988.

70. *Gallup Report* no. 213 (June 1983), 12. Forty percent favored, 43 percent opposed, and 17 percent had no opinion.

71. Jeff Lyon, *Playing God in the Nursery* (New York: W. W. Norton, 1985), 45–47.

72. *New York Times*, November 6, 1983, I, 45:1.

73. Marcia Chambers, "Advocates for the Right to Life," *New York Times Magazine*, December 6, 1984, 105.

74. Quoted by Lyon, *Playing God*, 50.

75. CBS "Face the Nation," quoted in *New York Times*, November 7, 1983, II, 4:3.

76. Koop, *The Right to Live, The Right to Die*, 23–25.

77. *New York Times*, November 7, 1983, II, 4:3. Koop also took less extreme positions: see Kuhse and Singer, *Should the Baby Live?*, 25.

78. Editorial, "Big Brother Doe," *Wall Street Journal*, October 31, 1983, 30:1; editorial, "Baby Jane's 'Defender,'" *New York Times*, November 11, 1983, I, 30:1. Also editorial, "Baby Jane's Big Brothers," *ibid.*, November 4, 1983, I, 26:1.

79. Fred Bruning, "The Politics of the Right to Die," *MacLean's* (December 12, 1983), 17. See also John J. Paris, "Right to Life Doesn't Demand Heroic Sacrifice," *Wall Street Journal*, November 28, 1983, 30:3.

80. *Newsday*, December 7, 1987, quoted in Gregory E. Pence, *Classic Cases in Medical Ethics: Accounts of the Cases That Have Shaped Medical*

Ethics (New York: McGraw-Hill, 1990), 158–160. Looking in *Newsday* of that date and throughout that week, however, I didn't find the article.

81. *New York Times*, October 25, 1983, II, 4:3.

5. DYING ON ONE'S OWN

1. *In the Matter of Karen Ann Quinlan: The Complete Legal Briefs, Court Proceedings, and Decision in the Superior Court of New Jersey*, 2 vols. (Arlington, Va.: University Publications of America, 1975), I, 481, 483; CBS Morning News, October 17, 1975; *Chicago Tribune*, October 22, 1975, VI, 15:1.

2. Quotations in Joseph and Julia Quinlan, with Phyllis Battelle, *Karen Ann: The Quinlans Tell Their Story* (Garden City: Doubleday, 1977), 282–283, 185. For literary reasons I have resequenced his diary notes.

3. Quoted in Quinlans, *Karen Ann*, 297–298. For literary reasons I have rearranged the sequence of notes within each day.

4. *Ibid.*, 302.

5. Sister Urban quoted in *ibid.*, 291; Joseph in *ibid.*, 300.

6. *Star-Ledger* quoted in *ibid.*, 299.

7. *Ibid.*, 321–326; Phyllis Battelle, "Karen Ann Quinlan Ten Years Later," *Ladies' Home Journal*, 102 (April 1985), 119.

8. Joseph is quoted in Quinlans, *Karen Ann*, 179–180; Julia quoted in *New York Times*, January 24, 1985, II, 4:4; doctor quoted in Quinlans, *Karen Ann*, 311. Twenty years later Julia said: "She was still a person": interview on "Fresh Air," National Public Radio, April 9, 1996. For narrative details, see Battelle, "Karen Ann Quinlan," 118–119, 174–180; Julia and Joseph Quinlan, "Karen Ann Quinlan's Parents Quietly Mark a Decade of Watching and Waiting," *People*, 23 (April 15, 1985), 90–92; *New York Times*, January 24, 1985, II, 4:4; *Washington Post*, May 26, 1981, A1, A9; and Gregory Pence, *Classic Cases in Medical Ethics: Accounts of the Cases That Have Shaped Medical Ethics* (New York: McGraw-Hill, 199), 20.

9. CBS Evening News, October 1, 1976. In considering the "best interests" of the PVS patient, the philosopher Joel Feinberg argues that they have none because they lack awareness, desires, and purpose: "The Rights of Animals and Unborn Generations," in *Philosophy and Environmental Crisis*, ed. William T. Blackstone (Athens: University of Georgia Press, 1974), 43, 61.

10. For example, *New York Times*, New Jersey edition, March 28, 1977, 63:5; April 11, 1977, 1:6; April 10, 1978, II, 3:1; March 29, 1979, III, 14:5. CBS Morning News, May 15, 1978; "Karen Ann Quinlan Still Lingers On," *Newsweek*, 95 (March 3, 1980), 14; *Washington Post*, May 26, 1981, A1:1; *Atlanta Constitution*, March 24, 1985, 10:1.

11. *New York Times*, January 24, 1985, II, 4:4.

12. *New York Times*, April 11, 1977, 1:6, 42:5, and January 25, 1991, B1:1.

13. Quotation and details in *New York Times*, September 24, 1977, 10:1. For Julia's work, "Karen Ann Quinlan Still Lingers On," *Newsweek*, 14.

14. Dr. Alejandrino O. Lola, Newark, Calif., to Barry Keene, April 22, 1976, in bill file 1976, California State Archives, Sacramento. I thank Natalie Fousekis for locating this letter.

15. *New York Times*, April 22, 1976, 29:3. MacLaine alleged that the joke was going around Washington, D.C. And in a review of the Quinlans' book, Andrew Greeley claimed that Karen, like Patty Hearst, was the target of vicious prejudices: Greeley, *New York Times*, October 9, 1977, VII, 10.

16. Editorial, "Metabolism for What?" *New York Times*, June 4, 1976, 36:1. Also *ibid.*, May 27, 1976, 22:3.

17. *In the Matter of Karen Ann Quinlan*, I, 369.

18. Interviews with the Quinlans and with Paul Armstrong, May 30, 1996.

19. *New York Times*, May 29, 1976, 20:5.

20. Conversation with Paul Armstrong, March 15, 1996.

21. For Quinlans on feeding, see *New York Times*, January 24, 1985, II, 4:4.

22. U.S. Bureau of the Census, *Historical Statistics of the United States: Colonial Times to 1970* (Washington, D.C.: Government Printing Office, 1975), Pt. 1, 55; U.S. Bureau of the Census, *Statistical Abstract of the United States: 1994* (Washington, D.C.: Government Printing Office, 1995), 87, 32; Allen E. Buchanan and Dan W. Brock, *Deciding for Others: The Ethics of Surrogate Decision Making* (Cambridge: Cambridge University Press, 1989), tables 6.1 and 6.2, 269. The relative increase in cohort size was an effect not only of improved mortality but of the higher number of births during 1900–1920 than during 1921–1945. See Jacob S. Siegel and Cynthia M. Taeuber, "Demographic Dimensions of an Aging Population," in *Our Aging Society: Paradox and Promise*, ed. Alan Pifer and Lydia Bronte (New York: W. W. Norton, 1986), 79–81.

23. *Statistical Abstract: 1994*, 476, table 731. For effects of Medicare on hospital and nursing home admissions, see Elizabeth W. Markson, "Psychological Changes, Illness, and Health Care Use in Later Life," in *Growing Old in America*, ed. Beth B. Hess and Elizabeth W. Markson, 4th ed. (New Brunswick, N.J.: Transaction, 1992), 182–183.

24. On illness, see M. Powell Lawton, Miriam Moss, and Allen Glicksman, "The Quality of the Last Year of Life of Older Persons," *Milbank Quarterly*, 68, no. 1 (1990), 20. On independence, see Pamela Doty, "Family Care of the Elderly: The Role of Public Policy," *ibid.*, 64, no. 1 (1986), 42–43, and *New York Times*, February 27, 1996, 1:5, B10:4. On visiting, see Ethel Shanas, "Social Myth and Hypothesis: The Case of Family Relations of Old People," *Gerontologist*, 19 (February 1979), 3–9, and "The Family as a Social Support System in Old Age," *ibid.*, 19 (April 1979), 169–174.

25. Lois M. Verbrugge, "Longer Life But Worsening Health? Trends in Health and Morality of Middle-aged and Older Persons," *Milbank Quarterly*, 62 (Summer 1984), esp. 484–485, 490–491. During 1982–1994 the overall incidence of chronic diseases declined among people over sixty-five, according to the National Long Term Care Surveys, but it increased for each older age cohort: *New York Times*, February 27, 1996, 1:5, B10:4.

26. On Alzheimer's, see Denis Evans, *et al.*, "Estimated Prevalence of Alzheimer's Disease in the United States," *Milbank Quarterly*, 68, no. 2 (1990), 267–289. On care, see Nancy L. Mace and Peter V. Rabins, *The 36-Hour Day: A Family Guide to Caring for Persons with Alzheimer's Disease, Related Dementing Illnesses, and Memory Loss in Later Life* (Baltimore: Johns Hopkins Press, 1981); Shanas, "Family as Social Support System," 169–174, and Siegel and Taeuber, "Demographic Dimensions," 96–99.

27. *Ibid.*; Subcommittee on Long-Term Care of Special Committee on Aging, U.S. Senate Nursing Home Care, *Nursing Home Care in the United States: Failure in Public Policy*, S. Rep. No. 1920, 93 Cong., 2nd Sess., 16 (December 1974), 5, 14–17; *Statistical Abstract: 1994*, 132.

28. James M. Hoefler and Brian E. Kamoie, "The Right to Die: State Courts Lead Where Legislatures Fear to Tread," *Law & Policy*, 14 (October 1992), 370, n.9; Henry R. Glick, *The Right to Die: Policy Innovation and Its Consequences* (New York: Columbia University Press, 1992), 27. For a thorough synopsis and comparative analysis, see Robert F. Weir, *Abating Treatment with Critically Ill Patients: Ethical and Legal Limits to the Medical Prolongation of Life* (New York: Oxford University Press, 1989), 110–169.

29. Quoted from Hampshire County Probate Court, in Robert A. Burt, *Taking Care of Strangers: The Rule of Law in Doctor-Patient Relations* (New York: Free Press, 1979), 148.

30. Quoted in *ibid.*, 156–157.

31. *Superintendent of Belchertown State School v. Saikewicz*, 373 Mass. 728, 370 N.E. 2d 417 (1977). On effects of chemotherapy, 420–421, incl. n.5. Guardian quoted in *ibid.*, 430, and Weir, *Abating Treatment*, 111. For helpful commentaries, see *ibid.*, 110–112, and Nancy K. Rhoden, "Litigating Life and Death," *Harvard Law Review*, 102 (1988), 385.

32. *Superintendent of Belchertown State School v. Saikewicz*, 426.

33. *Ibid.*, 420.

34. For a helpful discussion of "best interests," see Buchanan and Brock, *Deciding for Others*, 122–124. They make clear that, because the criterion is patient-centered, it must take into account quality-of-life judgments and therefore cannot avoid some subjectivity. For a more complex critique, see Joanna K. Weinberg, "Whose Right Is It Anyway? Individualism, Community, and the Right to Die: A Commentary on the New Jersey Experience," *Hastings Law Journal*, 40 (1988), esp. 163–165.

35. *Ibid.*, 431.

36. Rhoden, "Litigating Life and Death," 386.

37. Legal expert quoted in *In re Storar*, 52 N.Y. 2d 380, 420 N.E. 2d 72–73; Laurence H. Tribe, *American Constitutional Law*, 2nd ed. (Mineola, N.Y.: Foundation Press, 1988), 1369. See also John D. Arras ("the bioethical equivalent of squaring the circle"), "Quality of Life in Neonatal Ethics: Beyond Denial and Evasion," in *Ethical Issues at the Outset of Life*, ed. Martin Benjamin and William B. Weil (Boston: Blackwell Scientific Publications, 1987), 166; and Buchanan and Brock ("a heroic but confused attempt . . ."), *Deciding for Others*, 115.

38. Elaine Scarry, *The Body in Pain: The Making and Unmaking of the World* (New York: Oxford University Press, 1985), 4.

39. For background, see "Special Issue: The Problem of Personhood: Biomedical, Social, Legal and Policy Views," *Milbank Quarterly*, 61 (Winter 1983), esp. Judith P. Swazey, "Introduction," 1, and Ruth Macklin, "Personhood in the Bioethics Literature," 35–57; also Sanford H. Kadish, "Letting Patients Die: Legal and Moral Reflections," in *In Harm's Way: Essays in Honor of Joel Feinberg*, ed. Jules L. Coleman and Allen Buchanan (New York: Cambridge University Press, 1994), 298–311; Ronald Dworkin, "Autonomy and the Demented Self," *Milbank Quarterly*, 64 (Supp. II, 1986), 4–16.

40. *In re Conroy*, 457 A.2d 1232 (N.J. Super. Ct. 1983), 1233–1234, and 486 A.2d 1209 (N.J. 1985), 1217.

41. *Ibid.*, 1218.

42. *Ibid.*, 1217.

43. *In re Conroy*, 1983, 1236.

44. *New York Times*, January 18, 1985, 1:1.

45. *In re Conroy*, 1985, 1219, 1225, 1234–1236.

46. "In this respect, we now believe that we were in error in *Quinlan* . . .": *ibid.*, 1230.

47. *Ibid.*, 1243, 1231–1232.

48. I borrowed this analysis from Robert C. Cassidy, "Conroy on Appeal: Two Contrasting Perspectives by the Appellate Court and the State Supreme Court," in *By No Extraordinary Means: The Choice to Forgo Life-Sustaining Food and Water*, ed. Joanne Lynn (Bloomington: Indiana University Press, 1986), 238–241.

49. *In re Conroy*, 1985, 1232–1233.

50. Scarry, *Body in Pain*, 5–8; Ronald Melzack, *The Puzzle of Pain* (New York: Basic Books, 1973), 41–45.

51. Andrew Cook and Ranjan Roy, "Attitudes, Beliefs, and Illness Behaviour," and Bruce A. Sorkin and Dennis C. Turk, "Pain Management in the Elderly," in *Chronic Pain in Old Age: An Integrated Biopsychosocial Perspective*, ed. Ranjan Roy (Toronto: University of Toronto Press, 1995), chs. 2 and 4.

52. For discussion along these lines, see Rhoden, "Litigating," esp. 399, 404–407. For a contrary view, see Rebecca Dresser, "Life, Death, and Incompetent Patients: Conceptual Infirmities and Hidden Values in the Law," *Arizona Law Review*, 28, no. 3 (1986), 373–405.

53. Justices' quotations from *In re Conroy*, 1985, 1243–1244, 1236. Internist quoted on 1217. The court cited three articles: Joyce V. Zerwekh, "The Dehydration Question," *Nursing83*, 47 (January 1983), 47–51; John J. Paris and Anne B. Fletcher, "Infant Doe Regulations and the Absolute Requirement to Use Nourishment and Fluids for the Dying Infant," *Law, Medicine and Health Care*, 11 (October 1983), 210–213; and Joanne Lynn and James F. Childress, "Must Patients Always Be Given Food and Water?" *Hastings Center Report*, 13 (October 1983), 17–21. On ice chips and liquids, see Ronald A. Carson, "The Symbolic Significance of Giving to Eat and Drink," in *By No Extraordinary Means*, ed. Lynn, 87.

54. *In re Conroy*, 1985, 1246, 1248–1250.

55. Thomas Nagel, *The View from Nowhere* (New York: Oxford University Press, 1986), 4.

56. Linda R. Hirshman, "The Philosophy of Personal Identity and the Life and Death Cases," *Chicago-Kent Law Review*, 68 (Winter 1992), 91–108.

57. *New York Times*, January 18, 1985, 1:1; *Los Angeles Times*, January 18, 1985, 20:1; ABC News, January 18, 1985. A month later the *Chicago Tribune* published a feature column on the decision: Ronald Kotulak, "Cutting Off Food to the Hopelessly Ill: Merciful or Merciless?" February 17, 1985, V, 1:2.

58. *National Right to Life News*, February 1985, quoted by Derek Humphry and Ann Wickett, *The Right to Die: Understanding Euthanasia* (London: Bodley Head, 1986), 175; *Moral Majority Report on Human Life*, 7 (May 1985), quoted in *ibid*.; editorial, "Who Is Next?" *National Right to Life News*, 13 (May 15, 1986), 219. For a less alarmed interpretation, see Thomas J. Marzen, "The Claire Conroy Case: A Fragile New Compromise," *ibid*., 12 (February 14, 1985), 9, and 12 (February 28, 1985), 2, 9.

59. Daniel Callahan, "On Feeding the Dying," *Hastings Center Report*, 13 (October 1983), 22. Also Callahan, *Setting Limits: Medical Goals in an Aging Society* (New York: Simon and Schuster, 1987), 187–193. On ambivalence, Callahan to Peter Filene, March 13, 1996.

60. Alan J. Weisbard and Mark Siegler, "On Killing Patients with Kindness: An Appeal for Caution," in *By No Extraordinary Means*, ed. Lynn, 112–113; Yale Kamisar, "The Right to Die," *Michigan Law Quadrangle News*, 33 (1988), 7–8, and "Right to Die, or License to Kill?" *New Jersey Law Journal*, 124 (1989), 1359; Herbert D. Hinkle, Department of the Public Advocate, quoted in *New York Times*, November 6, 1983, XI, 40:1; John Finnis, "The 'Value of Human Life' and 'the Right to Death': Some Reflections on *Cruzan* and Ronald Dworkin," *Southern Illinois University Law Journal*, 17 (Spring 1993), 566. Also see the synopsis in Weir, *Abating Treatment*, 239–245.

61. Hoefler and Kamoie, "The Right to Die," 361; Nancy M. P. King, *Making Sense of Advance Directives* (Dordrecht, The Netherlands: Kluwer Academic Publishers, 1991), 145, n.3.

62. Quoted in Fenella Rouse, "Does Autonomy Require Informed and Specific Refusal of Life-Sustaining Medical Treatment?" *Issues in Law and*

Medicine 5 (Winter 1989), 331–335; *New York Times*, July 19, 1985, 15:1; Melvin Urofsky, *Letting Go: Death, Dying, and the Law* (New York: Charles Scribner's Sons, 1993), 140–141.

63. Quotation from Larry Gostin, "A Right to Choose Death: The Judicial Trilogy of *Brophy, Bouvia and Conroy*," *Law, Medicine and Health Care*, 14 (September 1986), 200. President's Commission for the Study of Ethical Problems in Medicine and Biomedical and Behavioral Research, *Deciding to Forego Life-Sustaining Treatment: A Report. . . .* (Washington, D.C.: Government Printing Office, 1983), esp. 88–90. *JAMA*, 256 (July 25, 1986), 471. For other bioethicists, see Hastings Center, *Guidelines on the Termination of Life-Sustaining Treatment and the Care of the Dying* (Bloomington: Indiana University Press, 1987), 59–62; Lynn, "Must Patients Always Be Given Food and Water?" reprinted in *By No Extraordinary Means*, ed. Lynn, 52–53; Dan W. Brock, "Forgoing Life-Sustaining Food and Water: Is It Killing?" in *ibid.*, 117–131; Alexander Morgan Capron, "Ironies and Tensions in Feeding the Dying," *Hastings Center Report*, 14 (October 1984), 34; John J. Paris, "When Burdens of Feedings Outweigh Benefits," *ibid.*, 16 (February 1986), 31–32; Robert M. Veatch, *Death, Dying and the Biological Revolution: Our Last Quest for Responsibility*, rev. ed. (New Haven: Yale University Press, 1989), 84; Richard McCormick, "Caring or Starving? The Case of Claire Conroy," *America*, 152 (April 6, 1985), 269–273; for a synopsis, see Weir, *Abating Treatment*, 245–252. For legal profession: Bernard L. Siegel, "Perspectives of a Criminal Prosecutor," in *By No Extraordinary Means*, ed. Lynn, 157–158; *Delio v. Westchester County Medical Center*, 129 A.D. 2d 1, 19, 516, N.Y.S. 2d 677, 689 (1987); Harvey Rothberg, editorial, "Re: Claire Conroy—A Medical and Societal Perspective," *New Jersey Law Journal*, 112 (October 20, 1983), 4, 19.

64. *New York Times*, December 2, 1986, C10, and June 5, 1988, 23:4; American Academy of Neurology, "Position . . . on . . . the Persistent Vegetative State Patient," *Neurology*, 39 (January 1989), 125–126; Charles L. Sprung, "Changing Attitudes and Practices in Forgoing Life-Sustaining Treatments," *JAMA*, 263 (April 25, 1990), 2212; The Multi-Society Task Force on Persistent Vegetative State, "Medical Aspects of the PVS," *NEJM*, 330 (August 26, 1994), 1499; and Norman L. Cantor, "The Permanently Unconscious Patient, Non-Feeding and Euthanasia," *American Journal of Law and Medicine*, 15 (Winter 1989), 385–386 and sources cited in n.15; Sabine M. Von Preyss-Friedman, Richard F. Uhlmann, and Kevin C. Cain, "Physicians' Attitudes Toward Tube Feeding Chronically Ill Nursing Home Patients," *Journal of General Internal Medicine*, 7 (January–February 1992), 46–51.

65. Quotations from Callahan to Peter Filene, March 13, 1996, and Daniel Callahan, *The Troubled Dream of Life: Living with Mortality* (New York: Simon and Schuster, 1993), 80–82.

66. Lou Harris's question: "There have been cases where a patient is terminally ill, in a coma and not conscious, with no cure in sight. Do you think that the family of such a patient ought to be able to tell doctors to remove all

life-support services and let the patient die, or do you think this is wrong?" Gallup's question: "The New Jersey Supreme Court recently ruled that all life sustaining medical treatment may be withheld or withdrawn from terminally ill patients, provided that is what the patients want or would want if they were able to express their wishes. Would you like to see such a ruling in the state in which you live, or not?" See Glick, *Right to Die*, 82–88, and George Gallup, *Gallup Report*, no. 235 (April 1985), 29. For impressionistic confirmation, see Charles Seabrook, "Live and Let Die," *Atlanta Constitution Magazine*, January 27, 1985; Joan Beck, *Chicago Tribune*, January 16, 1985, 14:3.

67. John La Puma, *et al.*, "Advance Directives on Admission," *JAMA*, 266 (July 17, 1991), 402.

68. Mirko D. Grmek, *History of AIDS: Emergence and Origin of a Modern Pandemic* (Princeton: Princeton University Press, 1990), 32, 41; Institute of Medicine, National Academy of Sciences, *Confronting AIDS: Update 1988* (Washington, D.C.: National Academy Press, 1988), 51.

69. *New York Times*, September 12, 1985, B11:3. On media coverage, see Aran Ron and David B. Rogers, "AIDS in the United States: Patient Care and Politics," in *Living with AIDS*, ed. Stephen R. Graubard (Cambridge: MIT Press, 1990), 110–111, 117.

70. *New York Times*, August 30, 1985, I, 1:2.

71. Monroe E. Price, *Shattered Mirrors: Our Search for Identity and Community in the AIDS Era* (Cambridge: Harvard University Press, 1989), esp. 109–110, 114; Allan M. Brandt, "Aids and Metaphor: Toward the Social Meaning of Epidemic Disease," in *In Time of Plague: The History and Social Consequences of Lethal Epidemic Disease*, ed. Arien Mack (New York: New York University Press, 1991), 104.

72. Heckler at International AIDS Conference, Atlanta, April 15, 1985, quoted by Sandra Panem, *The AIDS Bureaucracy* (Cambridge: Harvard University Press, 1988), 120.

73. *New York Times*, August 30, I, 1:2, September 2, A25:3, and September 10, II, 1:2—all 1985.

74. *Ibid.*, December 20, 1985, A24:1.

75. *Gallup Report*, no. 290, November 1989, 15–16.

76. Fenton Johnson, *Geography of the Heart: A Memoir* (New York: Scribner, 1996), 231.

77. Gallup Poll, *Public Opinion*, 1991, 114; *Gallup Report*, no. 290, November 1989, 13–14. According to Gallup, "a striking shift in public attitudes" took place in the summer of 1987: *Gallup Report*, nos. 268–269, January/February 1988, 30.

78. Of the cases in 1988, 63 percent were homosexuals or bisexuals, 19 percent heterosexual intravenous drug users, 7 percent homosexual drug users, 4 percent via heterosexual contact, and 3 percent via blood transfusions (3 percent were undetermined): Institute of Medicine, National Academy of Sciences, *Confronting AIDS: Update 1988*, 51.

79. Trip Gabriel, "Pack Dating: For a Good Time, Call a Crowd," *New York Times*, IVA (Education Life section), January 5, 1997, 23.

80. *New York Times*, June 4, 1994, 1:4 and 8:4.

81. Dr. William Knaus, quoted in *New York Times*, November 22, 1995, 1:1.

82. Rhoden, "Litigating," 420–423 and n.200. See also Mildred Z. Solomon, *et al.*, "Decisions Near the End of Life: Professional Views on Life-Sustaining Treatments," *American Journal of Public Health*, 83 (January 1993), 14–23.

83. Louis L. Brunetti, *et al.*, "Physicians' Attitudes Toward Living Wills and Cardiopulmonary Resuscitation," *Journal of General Internal Medicine*, 6 (July–August 1991), 323–328.

84. Susanne F. Bedell and Thomas L. Delbanco, "Choices About Cardiopulmonary Resuscitation in the Hospital," *NEJM*, 310 (April 26, 1984), 1089–1093.

85. On attitudes, see George M. Burnell, *Final Choices: To Live or to Die in an Age of Medical Technology* (New York: Plenum, 1993), 82; and Renee M. Goetzler and Mark A. Moskowitz, "Changes in Physician Attitudes Toward Limiting Care of Critically Ill Patients," *Archives of Internal Medicine*, 151 (August 1991), 1537–1540. According to earlier studies, three of four CPR orders were written three days before death: Susanne Bedell, *et al.*, "Do-Not-Resuscitate Orders for Critically Ill Patients in the Hospital," *JAMA*, 256 (July 11, 1986), 233–238; Palmi, V. Jonsson, *et al.*, "The 'Do Not Resuscitate' Order: A Profile of Its Changing Use," *Archives of Internal Medicine*, 148 (November 1988), 2373–2385. A more recent study claims that 46 percent of CPR orders were written two days before death: SUPPORT, "A Controlled Trial," *JAMA*, 274 (November 22, 1995), 1591–1598.

86. Papers by Vivian Sanks King and Mildred Solomon, at "The Quinlan Case: A Twenty-year Retrospective," Princeton, N.J., April 1996.

87. "A Controlled Trial," 1591–1598. See also an earlier study in a nursing home, Marion Danis, *et al.*, "A Prospective Study of Advance Directives for Life Sustaining Care," *NEJM*, 324 (March 28, 1991), 882–888.

88. *New York Times*, April 3, 1995, A1:1 and C10:1.

89. Nancy Neveloff Dubler, "Commentary: Balancing Life and Death—Proceed with Caution," *American Journal of Public Health*, 83 (January 1993), 24.

90. George Gerbner, Larry Gross, Michael Morgan, and Nancy Signorielli, "Health and Medicine on Television," *NEJM*, 305 (October 8, 1981), 901–904.

91. *Gallup Poll Monthly*, April 1993, no. 331, p. 23. For earlier rankings, see Chapter Two, above.

92. "Who Plays God?" WETA-TV (Mercury Productions, 1996).

93. "Choosing Death," *Newsweek*, 118 (August 26, 1991), 43–44.

94. *Gallup Poll Monthly* (January 1991), 55; *New York Times*, June 5, 1988, 23:4. On living wills, Richard P. Vance, "Autonomy's Paradox: Death, Fear, and Advance Directives," *Mercer Law Review*, 42 (Spring 1991), 1051–1068; Allen S.

Joseph and Charles E. Grenier, "The Right to Die: Public Perceptions and Attitudes in Metropolitan Baton Rouge," *Journal of Louisiana State Medical Society*, 142 (November 1990), 18–24; Elizabeth R. Gamble, Penelope J. McDonald, and Peter R. Lichstein, "Knowledge, Attitudes, and Behavior of Elderly Persons Regarding Living Wills," *Archives of Internal Medicine*, 151 (February 1991), 277–280; *New York Times*, June 4, 1994, 1:4; SUPPORT, "Do Formal Advance Directives Affect Resuscitation Resources for Seriously Ill Patients?" *Journal of Clinical Ethics*, 5 (Spring 1994), 23.

95. Linda L. Emanuel and Ezekiel J. Emanuel, "Decisions at the End of Life: Guided by Communities of Patients," *Hastings Center Report*, 23 (September–October 1993), 7–8.

96. Joanne Lynn, "Why I Don't Have a Living Will," *Law, Medicine & Health Care*, 19 (Spring–Summer 1991), 101–104.

97. Robert H. Blank, *Life, Death, and Public Policy* (DeKalb, Ill.: Northern Illinois University Press, 1988), 133. Also John H. Knowles, "Introduction," *Daedalus*, 106 (Winter 1977), 4–5; Henry J. Aaron and William B. Schwartz, *The Painful Prescription: Rationing Hospital Care* (Washington, D.C.: Brookings Institute, 1984); *New York Times*, January 18, 1985, B1, B2; Marion Davis, "Following Advance Directives," *Hastings Center Report Supplement*, 24 (November–December 1994), 521–523.

98. Economist Uwe Reinhardt and George Strait, in "Who Plays God?" WETA-TV (Mercury Productions, 1996). See also *New York Times*, January 18, 1985, B1, B2; Davis, "Following Advance Directives," 521–523.

99. Robert Wuthnow, *The Restructuring of American Religion: Society and Faith Since World War II* (Princeton: Princeton University Press, 1988), 260.

100. Quoted in *Ideology and Power in the Age of Jackson*, ed. Edwin C. Rozwenc (New York: Anchor, 1964), 356. For an overview, see Robert N. Bellah, *et al.*, *Habits of the Heart: Individualism and Commitment in American Life*, updated ed. (Berkeley: University of California Press, 1996), esp. 44–48, 55–56.

101. Autonomy is an ambiguous, much-debated concept. My simplified definition is based upon Gerald Dworkin, *The Theory and Practice of Autonomy* (Cambridge: Cambridge University Press, 1988), ch. 1, and Roger B. Dworkin, "Medical Law and Ethics in the Post-Autonomy Age," *Indiana Law Journal*, 68 (1993), 727–742. On control, see Callahan, *Troubled Dream*, 34–37. For a succinct synopsis of the issues, see "Advance Directives: Implications for Policy," *Hastings Center Report Supplement*, 24 (November–December 1994), 52–54.

102. Robert M. Veatch, "Autonomy's Temporary Triumph," *Hastings Center Report*, 14 (October 1984), 38.

103. *New York Times*, June 4, 1994, 8:6.

104. Estimates differ. There were between 15,000 and 20,000 PVS patients, according to the Council on Scientific Affairs and the Council on Eth-

ical and Judicial Affairs, AMA, "Persistent Vegetative State and the Decision to Withdraw or Withhold Life Support," *JAMA*, 263 (January 16, 1990), 427. According to *New York Times*, May 26, 1994, A11:1, there were as many as 35,000.

105. Vance, "Autonomy's Paradox," 1060, 1068.

6. A TAPESTRY OF RELATEDNESS

1. Julia Quinlan, quoted in Phyllis Battelle, "Karen Ann Quinlan Ten Years Later," *Ladies' Home Journal*, 102 (April 1985), 180.

2. *Washington Post*, June 13, 1985, A3; CBS Morning News, July 25, 1985.

3. Quotations from CBS Morning News, June 12, 1985; *Le Figaro*, June 13, 1985, 1:1; and *Atlanta Constitution*, June 16, 1985, C3:3. On her legacy, see Bob Simon, CBS Evening News, June 12, 1985; editorial "Karen Ann's Legacy: Affirming Life's Mystery," *New York Daily News*, June 13, 1985, 51:1; *Chicago Tribune*, June 13, 1985, 5:3; Father Trapasso, *Newark Star Ledger*, June 15, 1985, 9:5; *New York Times*, June 16, 1985, IV, 22:3. On the evening of June 12, 1985, ABC and NBC evening news stories were each longer than two minutes, while CBS gave two-and-a-half minutes to Quinlan and another two minutes to the ethics of withholding treatment. For typical front-page stories, most with the photograph, see *Portland Oregonian*, *Louisville Courier-Journal*, *Houston Post*, *Atlanta Constitution*, *New York Daily News*—all June 12, 1985, and *Le Monde*, June 13, 1985.

4. *Washington Post*, June 13, 1985, A3.

5. CBS Morning News, July 24, 1985. His comment on "trial" comes from *Washington Post*, June 13, 1985, A3.

6. Quoted in Battelle, "Karen Ann Quinlan Ten Years Later," 176.

7. Linda R. Hirshman, "The Philosophy of Personal Identity and the Life and Death Cases," *Chicago-Kent Law Review*, 68 (Winter 1992), esp. 105–108.

8. On Brophy, see *Brophy v. New England Sinai Hospital, Inc.*, 398 Mass 417, 497 N.E. 2d 626 (Mass 1986,), 628–629. Goodman in *Boston Globe*, June 13, 1985, 3:1. On unanswered questions, see also Daniel Callahan, quoted in *Chicago Tribune*, June 13, 1985, 5:3; *New York Times*, June 16, 1985, IV, 22:3.

9. John J. Paris, "When Burdens of Feeding Outweigh Benefits," *Hastings Center Report*, 16 (February 1986), 30–32.

10. Quotations in *Brophy v. New England Sinai Hospital, Inc.*, 632 n.22. On CBS Evening News, June 12, 1985, daughter quotes him saying "*two* of my beautiful daughters."

11. *Brophy v. New England Sinai Hospital, Inc.*, 633, 635–636, 640.

12. *New York Times*, September 12, 1986, 10:5, and *Boston Globe*, September 12, 1986, 87:1; doctor is quoted in *Boston Globe*, October 24, 1986, 39:4.

13. Anthony Preus, "Respect for the Dead and Dying," *Journal of Medicine and Philosophy*, 9 (November 1984), 412–413; Nancy K. Rhoden, "Litigat-

ing Life and Death," *Harvard Law Review*, 102 (1988), 418. See also the communitarian argument for giving priority to family over patient: John Hardwig, "What About the Family?" *Hastings Center Report*, 20 (March/April 1990), 5–10.

14. *Boston Globe*, September 12, 1986, 87:2.

15. From Mrs. Brophy's testimony at Cruzan trial: trial transcript, *Cruzan v. Harmon*, Circuit Court of Jasper County, Missouri, Probate Division at Carthage, March 9–11, 1988, Case No. CV384-9P, 467-71 [hereafter cited as Trial transcript, 1988].

16. *Boston Globe*, October 24, 1986, 1:1, 39:4.

17. *Houston Post*, 2:1; *Des Moines Register*, 2:1; *Atlanta Constitution*, A4:1; *Los Angeles Times*, 25:4; and *New York Times*, II, 9:4—all October 24, 1996. *Boston Globe*, front-page headline. There was no obituary in the *Washington Post, Louisville Courier-Journal, Chicago Tribune*, or *New Orleans Times-Picayune*.

18. Quotation from "To Feed or Not to Feed?" *Time*, 127 (March 31, 1986), 60.

19. Dave Andrusko, ed., *A Passion for Justice: A Pro-Life Review of 1987 and a Look Ahead to 1988* (National Right to Life Committee, 1988), 123–124.

20. (AMA poll in May–June) *New York Times*, November 29, 1986, 32:1; and June 26, 1990, A18:1. For similar responses by nursing-home residents, see Peter J. Greco, *et al.*, "The Patient Self-Determination Act and the Future of Advance Directives," *Annals of Internal Medicine*, 115 (October 15, 1991), 641.

21. Most details from trial transcript, 1988, 25–26, 30–49. Paramedic quotation is on 44. For other details, see Deborah Beroset Diamond, "Private Agony, Public Cause," *Ladies' Home Journal*, 107 (June 1, 1990), 127. Quotation from Joe is from television documentary by "Frontline" (with Media and Society Seminars), *The Right to Die?*, December 6, 1989. I thank Jeffrey Obler for providing a videotape.

22. "Whose Right to Die?" *Time*, 134 (December 11, 1989), 80.

23. Trial transcript, 1988, 435–437.

24. "Frontline," *Right to Die?*

25. Quoted by George Annas, "The Long Dying of Nancy Cruzan," *Law, Medicine & Health Care*, 19 (Spring–Summer 1991), 54; *New York Times*, November 27, 1989, B9:3.

26. "Frontline," *Right to Die?*

27. One of the earliest statements was Richard A. McCormick, "To Save or Let Die: The Dilemma of Modern Medicine," *JAMA*, 229 (July 8, 1974), 172–176.

28. Even if she had written a will, probably it would not have mattered. The living-will statute in Missouri, as in most states, permitted withdrawal of life-support only from patients who were "terminally" ill. One might argue that PVS was terminal because the patient would never recover. But Missouri's law, like that of twelve other states, specified that "terminal" meant that, even with

life-sustaining treatment, death would occur within a short time. What's more, Missouri specifically excluded artificial nutrition and hydration from the definition of "death prolonging procedure." And in any case, the living-will law was passed after her accident, so it wouldn't have benefited her. James M. Hoefler and Brian E. Kamoie, "The Right to Die: State Courts Lead Where Legislatures Fear to Tread," *Law & Policy*, 14 (October 1992), 356–358, and *Cruzan v. Harmon*, 760 S.W.2d 408 (Mo. banc 1988), cert. granted sub nom *Cruzan v. Director*, Missouri Department of Health, *et al.*, 109 S. Ct. 3240 (1989), 420.

29. Trial transcript, 1988, 388–389.

30. *Ibid.*, 541.

31. *Ibid.*, 448.

32. Joyce Cruzan quoted in *ibid.*, 511. On "independence," see 437, 524, 542. On "full life," see 415, 437, 511, 532, 557.

33. *Ibid.*, 411.

34. Christy quoted in *ibid.*, 535. Also 526, 548.

35. *Cruzan v. Harmon*, 412, 422–425.

36. Susan Wolf, "Nancy Beth Cruzan: In No Voice at All," *Hastings Center Report*, 20 (January 1990), 38–41. See also Susan R. Martyn and Henry J. Bourgignon, "Coming to Terms with Death: The *Cruzan* Case," *Hastings Law Journal*, 42 (March 1991), 817–858, and Nancy Rhoden, quoted in *New York Times*, July 25, 1989, A15:5.

37. Eric J. Cassell, "Life as a Work of Art," *Hastings Center Report*, 14 (October 1984), 36.

38. Susan Houghton to "Everyone," August 2, 1996, 9:30 p.m., Website posting.

39. Eric J. Cassell, *The Nature of Suffering and the Goals of Medicine* (New York: Oxford University Press), 211–212; Charles Taylor, *Philosophy and the Human Sciences: Philosophical Papers*, 2 (Cambridge: Cambridge University Press, 1985), 204–209; Philip Selznick, "Personhood and Moral Obligation," in *New Communitarian Thinking: Persons, Virtues, Institutions and Communities*, ed. Amitai Etzioni (Charlottesville: University Press of Virginia, 1995), 110–125; Robert A. Burt, *Taking Care of Strangers: The Rule of Law in Doctor-Patient Relations* (New York: Free Press, 1979), ch. 5, esp. 95–103.

40. Barbara Carter, Trial transcript, 1988, 503.

41. "Nancy Cruzan's Parents Want to Let Her Die—And Are Taking the Case to the Supreme Court," *People*, 32 (December 4, 1989), 135.

42. Diamond, "Private Agony, Public Cause," 180.

43. "Frontline," *Right to Die?* Likewise, psychotherapist in Trial transcript, 1988, 508.

44. *Ibid.*, 447.

45. Diamond, "Private Agony, Public Cause," 180.

46. *New York Times*, November 27, 1989, B9:1.

47. Trial transcript, 1988, 493, 511; Diamond, "Private Agony, Public Cause," 127–129; also Christy's testimony, Trial transcript, 1990, 186–187.

48. "Nancy Cruzan's Parents Want to Let Her Die," *People*, 32 (December 4, 1989), 135; "Frontline," *Right to Die?*

49. Trial transcript, 1990, 174–175.

50. According to Armstrong, lawyers and bioethicists constantly telephone one another and review one another's briefs. Interview with Paul Armstrong, May 29, 1996. On Colby's friendship, I'm citing Christy Cruzan's presentation at "The Quinlan Case: A Twenty-Year Retrospective," Princeton, New Jersey, April 1996.

51. *New York Times*, November 17, 1988, A25:2. I've combined two sentences into one.

52. Interview with Paul Armstrong, May 29, 1996; Diamond, "Private Agony, Public Cause," 181.

53. ABC Evening News, October 1 and 17, December 6; NBC Nightly News, October 1 and December 6; CBS Evening News, December 6—all 1989. *Chicago Tribune*, 3:2 and 27:1; *Atlanta Constitution*, A8:1; *Washington Post*, 4:1; *Houston Post*, A19:1; *Portland Oregonian*, A14:1; *Boston Globe*, 1:1; *Los Angeles Times*, 32:1; *Minneapolis Star-Tribune*, 1:4—all December 7, 1989.

54. *St. Louis Post-Dispatch*, December 7, 1989, 17A:2.

55. Ronald Dworkin, *Life's Dominion: An Argument About Abortion, Euthanasia, and Individual Freedom* (New York: Knopf, 1993), esp. 152–153.

56. *New York Times*, 1:1; *Washington Post*, A4:1–A5:1; and *Los Angeles Times*, A32:1—all December 7, 1989. Marcia Coyle, "Fast, Furious Questioning Marks Session on Coma Case," *National Law Journal*, 12 (December 18, 1989), 8.

57. *St. Louis Post-Dispatch*, December 7, 1989, 17A:2.

58. *Webster v. Reproductive Health Services Incorporated of Missouri.*

59. *Cruzan v. Director, Missouri Department of Health*, 110 S. Ct. 2841 (1990), 279–284, 286.

60. David A. J. Richards, "Autonomy in Law," in *The Inner Citadel: Essays on Individual Autonomy*, ed. John Christman (New York: Oxford University Press, 1989), 246–258.

61. *Cruzan v. Director*, 293.

62. *Cruzan v. Director*, 289–292.

63. James Bopp, Jr., and Thos J. Marzen, "Cruzan Decision Pivotal Pro-Life Victory," *National Right to Life News*, July 12, 1990, 8.

64. *Chicago Tribune*, June 26, 1990, 11:4.

65. CBS Evening News, June 25, 1990.

66. M. Rose Gasner, quoted in *New York Times*, June 27, 1990, A16.

67. *Portland Oregonian*, June 26, 1990. See also, e.g., *Louisville Courier-Journal, Chicago Tribune, Washington Post, Boston Globe, Minneapolis Star-Tribune, St. Louis-Post Dispatch.*

68. For irrelevance of religion to the Cruzans, see Trial transcript, 1988,

455; Diamond, "Private Agony, Public Cause," 180; and Joe Cruzan's comment quoted earlier from "Frontline," *Right to Die?*

69. *Minneapolis Star-Tribune*, June 26, 1990, 8:2.

70. Trial transcript, 1990, 177.

71. Governor quoted in *Kansas City Times*, December 15, 1990, A18. On Webster, see *New York Times*, October 12, 1990, A15:3, and *Washington Post*, October 16, 1990, Health Section, 7. On poll, see Colby's statement in Trial transcript, 1990, 8.

72. *Kansas City Star*, December 15, 1990, 1:6.

73. Nurses quoted in *New York Times*, December 16, 1990, 29:6. On protesters, see *St. Louis Post-Dispatch*, December 18, 7A:1; December 19, 1A:2; December 20, 4C:1; and December 22, 4B:1; *New York Times*, December 27, A15:2; *Washington Post*, December 28, B2:2—all 1990.

74. *Portland Oregonian*, 1:2; *St. Louis Post-Dispatch*, 1; *Chicago Tribune*, 3:1; *Louisville Courier Journal*, 1; for impersonal headlines, *Washington Post*, A3:1, and *Los Angeles Times*, 17:1—all December 27, 1990. One of the few hostile comments was in *Chicago Tribune*, December 28, 1990, 16:1. Gravestone inscription is in "The Cruzans Talk About Nancy, the Critical Care Experience and Their New Mission," *Critical Care Nurse*, 12 (December 1, 1992), 87.

75. *New York Times*, August 19, 1996, C10:1.

7. SUICIDE WITH ASSISTANCE

1. Representative Sander Levin (Mich.), in *Hearings on Living Wills*, U.S. Senate, Subcommittee on Medicine and Long-Term Care, Committee on Finance, July 20, 1990, 6.

2. Holly Caldwell Gieszl and Peggy Addington Velasco, "The Cruzan Legacy: Legislative and Judicial Responses and Insights for the Future," *Arizona State Law Journal*, 24 (Summer 1992), 742–750; James M. Hoefler and Brian E. Kamoie, "The Right to Die: State Courts Lead Where Legislatures Fear to Tread," *Law & Policy*, 14 (October 1992), 357–358; Henry R. Glick, *The Right to Die: Policy Innovation and Its Consequences* (New York: Columbia University Press, 1992), 205.

3. *New York Times*, February 18, 1996, A6:1; *Minneapolis Star-Tribune*, October 6, 1994, 1B:1; *New York Times*, June 6, 1994, A12:1. I thank Elaine Tyler May for sending me some of these articles.

4. For pre-1960 see Derek Humphry and Ann Wickert, *The Right to Die: Understanding Euthanasia* (London: Bodley Head, 1986), 11–59. For background and quotations on Hemlock Society, I've relied heavily on Anne Fadiman, "Death News: Requiem for the Hemlock Quarterly," *Harper's*, 288 (April 1994), 74–81. Also Donald W. Cox, *Hemlock's Cup: The Struggle for Death with Dignity* (Buffalo: Prometheus Books, 1993), 47–49. For demography, J.

Holden, "Demographics, Attitudes, and Afterlife Beliefs of Right-to-Life and Right-to-Die Organization Members," *Journal of Social Psychology*, 133 (August 1993), 521–527. For 1990s membership see James M. Hoefler with Brian Kamoie, *Deathright: Culture, Medicine, Politics, and the Right to Die* (Boulder, Colo.: Westview Press, 1994), 139.

5. Derek Humphry, *Final Exit: The Practicalities of Self-Deliverance and Assisted Suicide for the Dying* (Eugene, Ore.: Hemlock Society, 1991), 106, chs. 2 and 19, appendix, and 97–98.

6. Katherine Ames, "Last Rights," *Newsweek*, 118 (August 26, 1994), 40, and Lonny Shavelson, *A Chosen Death: The Dying Confront Assisted Suicide* (New York: Simon and Schuster, 1995), 11, 230.

7. Peter M. Marzuk, *et al.*, "Increase in Suicide by Asphyxiation in New York City After the Publication of *Final Exit*," *NEJM*, 329 (November 11, 1993), 1508–1510, and Marzuk, *et al.*, "Increase in Fatal Suicidal Poisonings and Suffocations in the Year *Final Exit* Was Published: A National Study," *American Journal of Psychiatry*, 151 (December 1994), 1813–1814.

8. Andrew Solomon, "A Death of One's Own," *New Yorker*, 71 (May 22, 1995). Quotation is on 69.

9. Herbert Hendin, *Suicide in America*, rev. ed. (New York: W. W. Norton, 1995), 81–82, 132; *Raleigh News & Observer*, January 12, 1996, 5A:1.

10. Paul Monette, *Borrowed Time* (San Diego: Harcourt Brace Jovanovich, 1988), 1–2.

11. Student quoted in *New York Times*, May 24, 1989, I, 25:4. Kingsley quoted in *ibid.*, June 14, 1994, C12:3.

12. Peter M. Marzuk, *et al.*, "Increased Risk of Suicide in Persons with AIDS," *JAMA*, 259 (March 4, 1988), 1333–1337; Timothy R. Cote, *et al.*, "Risk of Suicide Among Persons with AIDS," *JAMA*, 268 (October 21, 1992), 2066–2068; Shavelson, *Chosen Death*, 46.

13. *New York Times*, June 14, 1994, C12:3.

14. Quoted in Fadiman, "Death News," 81. See also Nancy Gibbs and Andrea Sachs, "Love and Let Die: In an Era of Untamed Medical Technology . . . ," *Time*, 135 (March 19, 1990), 65.

15. Jack Kevorkian, *Prescription: Medicine: The Goodness of Planned Death* (Buffalo, N.Y.: Prometheus Books, 1991), 208–209, 221–230.

16. Her note is quoted in *ibid.*, 228, fig. 7. For background, *New York Times*, June 6, 1990, A1:3 and B6:1, and June 7, 1990, A1:1 and D22:1; "The Doctor's Suicide Van," *Newsweek*, 115 (June 18, 1990), 46–49.

17. Editorial, "When Right-to-Die Issue Is Done Wrong," *Los Angeles Times*, June 11, 1990, B6:3; "Dr. Death's Suicide Machine," *Time*, 135 (June 18, 1990), 69–70; "The Doctor's Suicide Van," *Newsweek*, 115 (June 18, 1990), 46–49; Clarence Page, " 'Dr. Death' and His Grim Machine," *Chicago Tribune*, June 10, 1990, IV, 3:2; Patrick J. Buchanan, "Gadget to Help Suicide Opens Pandora's Box," *Los Angeles Times*, June 10, 1990, M7:6; Marcia Angell, "Don't Criticize Doctor Death," *New York Times*, June 14, 1990, A27:1; David Neff,

"The Suicide Machine," *Christianity Today*, 34 (August 20, 1990), 14. Derek Humphry, quoted in "The Doctor's Suicide Van," *Newsweek*, 47. Cartoon is in *Los Angeles Times*, June 10, 1990, M7.

18. *New York Times*, February 22, 1993; A12:2.

19. *Washington Post*, July 29, 1996, A1:1, A12:1; Michael Betzold, "The Selling of Doctor Death," *New Republic*, 216 (May 26, 1997), 26. See also the controversy over Judith Curren, who suffered fibromyalgia and chronic fatigue syndrome. Three weeks before her assisted suicide, she had accused her husband of dragging her out of bed and pulling her hair to force her to take her antidepressant medicine. The *Boston Herald* later reported that Franklin Curren owed $355,000 in back taxes because of the costs of caring for her. Raleigh *News & Observer*, August 17, 1996, 1:1; *New York Times*, August 20, 1996, A11:6; Timothy E. Quill and Betty Rollin, "Dr. Kevorkian Runs Wild," *New York Times*, August 29, 1996, A19:1; *Washington Post*, August 24, 1997, A2:4.

20. Mike Ervin in Raleigh *News & Observer*, December 20, 1996, 23A:1.

21. Quoted by Abigail Trafford, "Why They're Not in Jail," *Washington Post*, August 19, 1997, WH6:3.

22. For a detailed synopsis up to 1993, see Hoefler with Kamoie, *Deathright*, 151–157. Judge Richard C. Kaufman, Wayne County Circuit Court, is quoted on 156. For further information, *New York Times*, April 28, 1996, 18:3, May 5, 1996, 27:1, May 15, 1996, A9:1, and June 13, 1997, A13:1; *Washington Post*, August 24, 1997, A2:4.

23. Hall Crowther, "Man of the Year," [North Carolina] *Independent Weekly*, XIV (December 11–18, 1996), 7.

24. For Paul Armstrong, my interview, May 29, 1996. Linda Emanuel quoted in Paul Wilkes, "The Next Pro-Lifers," *New York Times Magazine*, July 21, 1996, 25, 50. For Callahan and other opponents, see *ibid*.; Susan Wolf, "Holding the Line on Euthanasia," *Hastings Center Report*, 19 (January–February 1989), 13–15; David Orentlicher, "Physician Participation in Assisted Suicide," *JAMA*, 262 (October 6, 1989), 1844–1845; Peter A. Singer and Mark Siegler, "Euthanasia—A Critique," *NEJM*, 322 (June 28, 1990), 1981–1983; Richard McCormick, "Physician-Assisted Suicide: Flight from Compassion," *Christian Century*, 108 (December 4, 1991), 1132–1134; Council on Ethical and Judicial Affairs, AMA, "Decisions Near the End of Life," *JAMA*, 267 (April 22/29, 1992), 229–233. Not all bioethicists opposed assisted suicide: e.g., Margaret Pabst Battin, *The Least Worst Death: Essays in Bioethics on the End of Life* (New York: Oxford University Press, 1994), 123–125, chs. 5 and 8; Robert F. Weir, "The Morality of Physician-Assisted Suicide," *Law, Medicine & Health Care*, 20 (Spring–Summer, 1992), 116–125.

25. Dr. Alan B. Astrow, letter to *New York Times*, December 26, 1995, A14:5. For surveys: Richard F. Uhlmann, *et al*., "Physicians' and Spouses' Predictions of Elderly Patients' Resuscitation Preferences," *Journal of Gerontology*, 43 (September 1988), M115–121; Richard F. Uhlmann and Robert A. Pearlman, "Perceived Quality of Life and Preferences for Life-Sustaining

Treatment in Older Adults," *Archives of Internal Medicine*, 151 (March 1991), 495–497; Lawrence J. Schneiderman, *et al.*, "Do Physicians' Own Preferences for Life-Sustaining Treatment Influence Their Perceptions of Patients' Preferences?" *Journal of Clinical Ethics*, 4 (Spring 1993), 28–33; Steven H. Miles, "Physicians and Their Patients' Suicides," *JAMA*, 271 (June 8, 1994), 1786–1788.

26. Yeates Conwell and Eric D. Caine, "Rational Suicide and the Right to Die," *NEJM*, 325 (October 10, 1991), 1100–1103; Ezekiel Emanuel, "Whose Right to Die?" *Atlantic Monthly*, 279 (March 1997), 75.

27. Miller quoted in Cox, *Hemlock's Cup*, 107–108. I've combined two of her statements. For an annotated list of Kevorkian's first twenty clients, plus narrative details, see Hoefler with Kamoie, *Deathright*, 157–159.

28. I've drawn upon the analysis by Susan Wolf, "Gender, Feminism, and Death," in *Feminism and Bioethics*, ed. Susan Wolf (New York: Oxford University Press, 1996), 289; Stephanie Gutmann, "Death and the Maiden," *New Republic*, 214 (June 24, 1996), 20–28; and Nancy Osgood and Susan A. Eisenharder, "Gender and Assisted and Acquiescent Suicides: A Suicidologist's Perspective," *Issues in Law & Medicine*, 9 (Spring 1994), 361–374.

29. Callahan, "When Self-Determination Runs Amok," *Hastings Center Report*, 22 (March–April 1992), 52–55. Also Callahan, *The Troubled Dream of Life* (New York: Simon and Schuster, 1993), 93, 103–108; Dr. Alan B. Astrow, letter to *New York Times*, December 26, 1995, A14:5–6; Wilkes, "The Next Pro-Lifers," *New York Times Magazine*, July 21, 1996, 50.

30. Robert Dworkin, Thomas Nagel, Robert Nozick, John Rawls, Thomas Scanlon, and Judith Jarvis Thomson, "Assisted Suicide: The Philosopher's Brief [before the U.S. Supreme Court]," *New York Review of Books*, 44 (March 27, 1997), 45.

31. Sidney Wanzer, *et al.*, "The Physician's Responsibility Toward Hopelessly Ill Patients," *NEJM*, 320 (March 30, 1989), 848. See also *New York Times*, May 24, 1989, A1:1. Stephen Jamison cites a JAMA study that 24 percent of patients who asked for aid in dying received lethal prescriptions: Jamison, "Dead Right (Physician-Assisted Suicide)," *The Nation*, 262 (April 29, 1996), 4.

32. Timothy Quill, "Death and Dignity: A Case of Individualized Decision Making," *NEJM*, 324 (March 7, 1991), 691–694. Also Quill, *Dignity*, 104–105.

33. Weir, "Morality of Physician-Assisted Suicide," *Law, Medicine & Health Care*, 20 (Spring–Summer, 1992), 119.

34. Council on Ethical and Judicial Affairs, AMA, "Decisions Near the End of Life," *JAMA*, 267 (April 22/29, 1992), 229–233; Jerald Bachman, *et al.*, "Attitudes of Michigan Physicians and the Public Toward Legalizing Physician-Assisted Suicide and Voluntary Euthanasia," *NEJM*, 334 (February 1, 1996), 303–309; *Raleigh News & Observer*, September 27, 1996, 22A:5.

35. Depending on the polling agency, numbers differ but the trend is the same. Floris W. Wood, ed., *An American Profile—Opinions and Behavior,*

1972–1989 . . . National Opinion Research Center (Detroit: Gale Research, 1990), 626–628; Andrew Greeley, "Live and Let Die: Changing Attitudes," *Christian Century*, 108 (December 4, 1991), 1124–1125; Glick, *Right to Die*, 84, table 3:3. For fullest data, including the more specific questions, see Robert Blendon, Ulrike S. Szalay, and Richard A. Knox, "Should Physicians Aid Their Patients in Dying?" *JAMA*, 267 (May 20, 1992), 2658–2662, esp. fig. 1; *New York Times*, June 9, 1990, 6:4; Jerold Bachman, *et al.*, "Attitudes of Michigan Physicians and the Public Toward Legalizing Physician-Assisted Suicide and Voluntary Euthanasia," *NEJM*, 334 (February 1, 1996), 303–309.

36. *New York Times*, October 9, 1992, A18:3.

37. Quotation by Albert R. Jonsen, "Initiative 119: What Is at Stake?" *Commonweal*, 118 (August 9, 1991), 466–468. Likewise, Carlos T. Gomez, "Euthanasia: Consider the Dutch," *ibid.*, 469–472; Leon R. Kass, "Why Doctors Must Not Kill," *ibid.*, 472–476; Daniel Callahan, "Aid-in-dying: The Social Dimensions," *ibid.*, 476–480; Anthony B. Robinson, "Death with Dignity in Washington State," *Christian Century*, 108 (October 30, 1991), 988–989; McCormick, "Physician-Assisted Suicide," *ibid.*, 108 (December 4, 1991), 1132–1134. Bioethicists were not unanimous. Some endorsed the measure: *New York Times*, October 28, 1991, A1:2, B7:1.

38. George M. Burnell, *Final Choices: To Live or to Die in an Age of Medical Technology* (New York: Plenum, 1993), 274; Hoefler with Kamoie, *Deathright*, 146–147; Joseph P. Shapiro, "A Vote on Legal Euthanasia: The Right-to-Die Movement Makes Its Mark in Washington," *U.S. News and World Report*, 111 (September 30, 1991), 32–33; Thomas W. Case, "Dying Made Easy," *National Review*, 43 (November 4, 1991), 25–26.

39. Courtney S. Campbell, "Oregon's Fight over the Right to Die," *Hastings Center Report*, 24 (March–April 1994), 3, and Campbell, "The Oregon Trail to Death: Measure 16," *Commonweal*, 121 (August 1994), 9–10; *New York Times*, October 16, 1994; 18:5. Quotations from *ibid.*, November 11, 1994, 28:5.

40. *New York Times*, November 11, 1994, A28:5.

41. *New York Times*, July 22, 1994, B3:2; April 3, 1996, A1:6, C18:5.

42. Ronald Dworkin, "Sex, Death, and the Courts," *New York Review of Books*, 43 (August 8, 1996), 44. For positive analysis, see Dworkin. For negative analyses: George J. Annas, "The Promised End—Constitutional Aspects of Physician-Assisted Suicide," *NEJM*, 335 (August 29, 1996), 683–687; Jeffrey Rosen, "What Right to Die?" *New Republic*, 214 (June 24, 1996), 28–31.

43. *New York Times*, June 23, 1997, A1:6, A15:1–3, A14:1–5.

44. Quotations from *ibid.*, A14:3–6 and A15:6. Likewise, Dr. Robert Brody, quoted by Ellen Goodman, "Guidelines for Assisted Suicide," in *Boston Globe*, September 27, 1997.

45. *New York Times*, November 6, 1997, A22:1.

8. CULTURES OF DYING

1. L. P. Hartley, *The Go-Between* (New York: Alfred A. Knopf, 1954), 3.

2. I thank Margaret Wiener, Department of Anthropology, University of North Carolina, for inspiring this cross-cultural comparison and tutoring me about Bali. On medical cultures, see Arthur Kleinman, *Patients and Healers in the Context of Culture: An Exploration of the Borderland Between Anthropology, Medicine and Psychiatry* (Berkeley: University of California Press, 1980), esp. 24–70.

3. Miguel Covarrubias, *Island of Bali* (New York: Alfred A. Knopf, 1937), 359.

4. *Ibid.*, 370–377; Carol Warren, *Adat and Dinas: Balinese Communities in the Indonesian State* (New York: Oxford University Press, 1993), 82–83.

5. Unni Wikan, *Managing Turbulent Hearts: A Balinese Formula for Living* (Chicago: University of Chicago Press, 1990), 179–180, 191, 230–231, and ch. 8. Wikan interprets this behavior as a fearful warding-off of danger. I have instead followed Margaret Wiener's more positive interpretation.

6. Linda Connor, Patsy Asch, and Timothy Asch, *Jero Tapakan, Balinese Healer: An Ethnographic Film Monograph* (Cambridge: Cambridge University Press, 1986), 21–37, 177–181.

7. Quoted in Wikan, *Managing Turbulent Hearts*, 231.

8. Margaret Wiener; Connor, *et al.*, *Jero Tapakan*, 260.

9. Warren, *Adat and Dinas*, 46–48; Wikan, *Managing Turbulent Hearts*, 147.

10. Quoted by *ibid.*, 147.

11. Warren, *Adat and Dinas*, 46–48.

12. Covarrubias, *Island of Bali*, 360–370.

13. *Ibid.*, 366.

14. Warren, *Adat and Dinas*, 155–157, 162–163. Quotation is on 89.

15. *Ibid.*, 55; Connor, *et al.*, *Jero Tapakan*, 29. In addition to the above citations, I have relied upon Hildred Geertz and Clifford Geertz, *Kinship in Bali* (Chicago: University of Chicago Press, 1975), 14, 40, 195. For a helpful discussion of individual identity in Polynesia, see Michael D. Lieber, "Cutting Your Losses: Death and Grieving in a Polynesian Community," in *Coping with the Final Tragedy: Cultural Variation in Dying and Grieving*, ed. David R. Counts and Dorothy A. Counts (Amityville, N.Y.: Baywood Publishing Co., 1991), 166–189.

16. I've constructed this account from three sources: a partial transcript in *New York Times*, November 13, 1994, IV, 7:1, a hostile article by Herbert Hendin, "Selling Death and Dignity," *Hastings Center Report*, 25 (May–June 1995), 19–20, and a sympathetic review in *New York Times*, December 8, 1994, C18:1. For an almost identical story, see *New York Times*, February 9, 1993, A1:2. See also the sympathetic interviews with Dutch patients, families, and doctors in a two-hour documentary, "Choosing Death," "Frontline," 1993.

17. Paul J. van der Maas, Loes Pijnenborg, and Johannes J. M. van Delden, "Changes in Dutch Opinion on Active Euthanasia, 1966 Through 1991," *JAMA*, 273 (May 10, 1995), 1412; *New York Times*, February 9, 1993, A9:2.

18. Henk A. M. J. ten Have and Jos V. M. Welie, "Euthanasia: Normal Medical Practice?" *Hastings Center Report*, 22 (March–April 1992), 34–36; *New York Times*, September 11, 1991, C12:4; Timothy Quill, *Death and Dignity: Making Choices and Taking Charge* (New York: W. W. Norton, 1993), 148–150.

19. See Maurice A. M. de Wachter, "Euthanasia in the Netherlands," *Hastings Center Report*, 22 (March–April 1992), 23–24; ten Have and Welie, "Euthanasia," 35.

20. See Hendin, "Selling Death and Dignity," 19–20, for this interpretation. More generally, see Carlos F. Gomez, *Regulating Death: Euthanasia and the Case of the Netherlands* (New York: Free Press, 1991).

21. *Ibid.*, 35; Herbert Hendin, *Suicide in America*, rev. ed. (New York: W. W. Norton, 1995), 252–253; Margaret Pabst Battin, *The Least Worst Death: Essays in Bioethics on the End of Life* (New York: Oxford University Press, 1994), 136–137. For a hostile critique of the data, see John Keown, "Euthanasia in the Netherlands," in *Euthanasia Examined: Ethical, Clinical and Legal Perspectives* (Cambridge: Cambridge University Press, 1995), 261–282.

22. *New York Times*, September 11, 1995, A3:1.

23. Robert H. Cox, *Development of the Dutch Welfare State: From Workers' Insurance to Universal Entitlement* (Pittsburgh: University of Pittsburgh Press, 1993), esp. 60–65, 103–111, 133, 155–156, 166–167, and Appendix One; Robert C. Tash, *Dutch Pluralism: A Model in Tolerance for Developing Democracies* (New York: Peter Lang, 1991), 81–83, 87–103, 118–119. On religion, see *New York Times*, March 10, 1997, A6:1. On opinion toward euthanasia, see van der Maas, *et al.*, "Changes in Dutch Opinion," 1412.

24. Johannes J. M. van Delden, "Euthanasia in the Netherlands: The Medical Scene," in *Euthanasia in the Netherlands: A Model for Canada?*, ed. Barney Sneiderman and Joseph M. Kaufert (Winnipeg: Legal Research Institute of the University of Manitoba, 1994), 23.

25. Derek Humphry and Ann Wickett, *The Right to Die: Understanding Euthanasia* (London: Bodley Head, 1986), 177–181.

26. Gomez, *Regulating Death*, 28–36; Marvin E. Newman, "Active Euthanasia in the Netherlands," in *To Die or Not to Die? Cross-Disciplinary, Cultural, and Legal Perspectives on the Right to Choose Death*, ed. Arthur S. Berger and Joyce Berger (New York: Praeger, 1990), 119–125.

27. Van der Maas, "Changes in Dutch Opinion," 1412 and 1413, table 1. On bishops, *New York Times*, February 9, 1993, A9:3.

28. "Choosing Death," "Frontline," 1993.

29. Newman, "Active Euthanasia," 123–124; Battin, *Least Worst Death*, 132–133; *Washington Post*, October 29, 1993, A29:1.

30. Van Delden, "Euthanasia in the Netherlands," 23–24; "Choosing Death," "Frontline."

31. Caplan quoted in *New York Times*, August 14, 1996, C9:1. The study was by Kenneth E. Covinsky, *et al.*, "Is Economic Hardship on the Families of the Seriously Ill Associated with Patient and Surrogate Care Preferences?" *Archives of Internal Medicine* (August 12/26, 1996), 1737–1741.

32. Ten Have and Welie, "Euthanasia: Normal Medical Practice?" *Hastings Center Report*, 22 (March–April 1992), 34–36.

33. *Gallup Poll Monthly* (January 1991), 51–52.

34. Robert Blendon, Ulrike S. Szalay, and Richard A. Knox, "Should Physicians Aid Their Patients in Dying?" *JAMA*, 267 (May 20, 1992), 2660–2661.

35. Bruce Jennings, "Privacy vs. Autonomy: The Forgotten Legacy of Quinlan," in Princeton Conference, *Quinlan: A Twenty-Year Retrospective* (1996). Also Daniel Callahan, *Troubled Dream*, ch. 4, esp. 131, 146–147.

36. Leslie J. Blackhall, et al., "Ethnicity and Attitudes Toward Patient Autonomy," *JAMA*, 274 (September 13, 1995), 820–825.

37. Quoted in Barbara A. Koenig and Jan Gates-Williams, "Understanding Cultural Difference in Caring for Dying Patients," *Western Journal of Medicine*, 163 (September 1995), 244–245.

38. Carol B. Stack, "Different Voices, Different Visions: Gender, Culture, and Moral Reasoning," in *Uncertain Terms: Negotiating Gender in American Culture*, ed. Faye Ginsburg and Anna Lowehaupt Tsing (Boston: Beacon Press, 1990), 19–27; Bruce J. Neubauer and Carol Lee Hamilton, "Racial Differences in Attitudes Toward Hospice Care," *Hospice Journal*, 6, no. 1 (1990), 37–48; Linda M. Chatters, Robert Joseph Taylor, and Harold W. Neighbors, "Size of Informal Helper Network Mobilized During a Serious Personal Problem Among Black Americans," *Journal of Marriage and the Family*, 51 (August 1989), 66–76. Also, Joyce Aschenbrenner, *Lifelines: Black Families in Chicago* (New York: Holt, Rinehart and Winston, 1975); Marjorie H. Cantor, "The Informal Support System of New York's Inner City Elderly: Is Ethnicity a Factor?" in *Ethnicity and Aging: Theory, Research, and Policy*, ed. Donald E. Gelfand and Alfred J. Kutzik (New York: Springer, 1979), 153–174.

39. McPherson quoted in *New York Times*, December 18, 1996, B1:4. "Larky" years comes from Paul Monette, *Borrowed Time* (San Diego: Harcourt Brace Jovanovich, 1988), 141. Similarly, *New York Times*, January 17, 1983, B4:4, and Andrew Sullivan, "When Plagues End," *New York Times Magazine*, November 10, 1996, 60.

40. On inadequate medical care, see, e.g., Gerald H. Friedland, "Clinical Care in the AIDS Epidemic," in *Living with AIDS*, ed. Stephen Graubard (Cambridge: Massachusetts Institute of Technology Press, 1990), 141–144. On self-help, see National Research Council, *Social Impact of AIDS in the United States*, Jeff Stryker and Albert R. Jonsen (Washington, D.C.: National Academy Press, 1993), 160–165; Lewis Katoff and Susan Ince and the Staff of the GMHC Client Services Department, "Supporting People with AIDS: The

GMHC Model," in *The AIDS Reader: Social, Political and Ethical Issues*, ed. Nancy F. McKenzie (New York: Meridian, 1991), 551–553.

41. Katherine Boo, "What Mother Teresa Could Learn in a Leather Bar," *Washington Monthly*, 23 (June 1991), 34–40.

42. Interview with the Quinlans, May 29, 1996; E. Keerdja and P. Clausen, "Karen Ann Quinlan Still Lingers On," *Newsweek*, 95 (March 3, 1980), 14; Phyllis Battelle, "Karen Quinlan Ten Years Later," *Ladies' Home Journal*, 102 (April 1985), 178–179. On St. Christopher's as "mecca," see Cathy Siebold, *The Hospice Movement: Easing Death's Pains* (New York: Twayne, 1992), 92.

43. Sandol Stoddard, *The Hospice Movement: A Better Way of Caring for the Dying* (New York: Stein and Day, 1978), ch. 6; Parker Rossman, *Hospice: Creating New Models of Care for the Terminally Ill* (New York: Association Press, 1977), 86–88.

44. Quoted in Stoddard, *Hospice Movement*, 75.

45. President's Commission for the Study of Ethical Problems in Medicine and Biomedical and Behavioral Research, *Deciding to Forego Life-sustaining Treatment . . .* (Washington, D.C.: Government Printing Office, 1983), 112, n.59; Kenneth P. Cohen, *Hospice: Prescription for Terminal Care* (Germantown, Md.: Aspen Systems Corporation, 1979), 149.

46. "At Home with Death," *Newsweek*, 85 (January 6, 1975), 43. Also "Living with Dying," *ibid.*, 91 (May 1, 1978), 52–56; Joan Kron, "Designing a Better Place to Die," *New York*, 9 (March 1, 1976), 43–49; CBS Morning News, November 14, 1979; Marya Mannes, *Last Rights* (New York: William Morrow, 1974), 122–124; David Dempsey, *The Way We Die: An Investigation of Death and Dying in America Today* (New York: Macmillan, 1975), 233–240; Murray Klutch, "Hospices for Terminally Ill Patients: The California Experience," *Western Journal of Medicine*, 129 (July 1978), 82–84. On the influence of Kübler-Ross, see Stoddard, *Hospice Movement*, 45.

47. *New York Times*, November 24, 1982, C9:1; Jill Rhymes, "Hospice Care in America," *JAMA*, 264 (July 18, 1990), 369–372; Robert J. Miller, "Hospice Care as an Alternative to Euthanasia," *Law, Medicine & Health Care*, 20 (Spring–Summer 1992), 128.

48. Joan Teno and Joanne Lynn, "Voluntary Active Euthanasia: The Individual Case and Public Policy," *Journal of American Geriatrics Society*, 39 (August 1991), 828; Peter A. Singer and Mark Siegler, "Euthanasia—A Critique," *NEJM*, 322 (June 28, 1990), 1883–1886.

49. Mildred Z. Solomon, *et al.*, "Decisions Near the End of Life: Professional Views on Life-sustaining Treatments," *American Journal of Public Health*, 83 (January 1993), 14–25; Vincent Mor, David S. Greer, and Richard Goldbert, "The Medical and Social Service Interventions of Hospice and Nonhospice Patients," in *The Hospice Experiment*, ed. Vincent Mor, David S. Greer, and Robert Kastenbaum (Baltimore: Johns Hopkins Press, 1988),

90–104; Lonny Shavelson, *A Chosen Death: The Dying Confront Assisted Suicide* (New York: Simon and Schuster, 1995), 214–215; Quill, *Death and Dignity*, 79, 100. Some researchers claim, however, that hospice is no more successful in reducing pain than traditional programs: Siebold, *Hospice Movement*, 156.

50. Robert N. Butler, "The Dangers of Physician-Assisted Suicide," *Geriatrics*, 51 (July 1996), 15.

51. Arthur Frank at conference on "Telling Bodies: Medical Narratives and Narratives of Medicine," University of North Carolina at Chapel Hill, February 22, 1997.

52. Quill, *Death and Dignity*, 99–100.

53. Alice Lind, "Hospitals and Hospices: Feminist Decisions About Care for the Dying," in *Healing Technology: Feminist Perspectives*, ed. Kathryn Strother Ratcliff, *et al.* (Ann Arbor: University of Michigan Press, 1989), 272. On listening, see Mor, *et al.*, "Medical and Social Service Interventions," 90–104; Clive F. Seale, "What Happens in Hospices: A Review of Research Evidence," *Social Science and Medicine*, 28, no. 6 (1989), 551–559; *The Heart of the New Age Hospice*, UT-TV (University of Texas Health Science Center, 1987).

54. Sylvia Lack, *Terminal Cancer: The Hospice Approach to the Family* [a film] (New Haven: Hospice, Inc., 1978). For illustrative details, see this film and *Heart of the New Age Hospice*. For social scientific studies, see Seale, "What Happens in Hospices: A Review of Research Evidence," *Social Science and Medicine*, 28, no. 6 (1989), 551–559, and Mor, *et al.*, "Medical and Social Service Interventions," 90–104.

55. Quoted by Anne Munley, *The Hospice Alternative: A New Context for Death and Dying* (New York: Basic Books, 1983), 210, 213, 219.

56. Peter J. Greco, *et al.*, "The Patient Self-Determination Act and the Future of Advance Directives," *Annals of Internal Medicine*, 115 (October 15, 1991), 639.

57. Siebold, *Hospice Movement*, 154.

58. Nicholas Christakis and Jose J. Escarce, "Survival of Medicare Patients After Enrollment in Hospice Programs," *NEJM*, 335 (July 28, 1996), 172–174.

59. Miller, "Hospice Care," *Law, Medicine & Health Care*, 20 (Spring–Summer 1992), 128.

60. *Hillhaven Hospice Medical Newsletter* (Tucson, Ariz.: n.d.), quoted in Cohen, *Hospice*, 26.

61. National Research Council, *Social Impact of Aids*, ed. Stryker and Jonsen, 52–53. Some programs have made exceptions: Siebold, *Hospice Movement*, 173–178.

62. Quill, *Death and Dignity*, 102; Siebold, *Hospice Movement*, 134–143; Jill Rhymes, "Hospice Care in America," *JAMA*, 264 (July 18, 1990), 370–371.

63. Joanne Lynn, "Caring for Those Who Die in Old Age," in *Facing*

Death: Where Culture, Religion and Medicine Meet, ed. Howard M. Spiro, Margy G. McCrea Curnen, and Lee Palmer Wandel (New Haven: Yale University Press, 1996), 97.

64. *Ibid.,* 99.

Index

A NOTE ON THE AUTHOR

Peter G. Filene was born in New York City and studied at Swarthmore College and Harvard University. He has taught for thirty years at the University of North Carolina, Chapel Hill, where he is now professor of history. His other books include *Him/Her/Self*, a celebrated history of gender identities in America; *Home and Away*, a novel; *Men in the Middle*; and *Americans and the Soviet Experiment*. He is married with two children and lives in Chapel Hill.